Databases in Theory and Practice

Databases in Theory and Practice

J A Jones

TAB Professional and Reference Books

Division of TAB BOOKS Inc.
P.O. Box 40, Blue Ridge Summit, PA 17214

To Sylvia,
who helped in many ways

First published in 1987 by Kogan Page Ltd,
120 Pentonville Road, London N1 9JN

Published in the United States of America
by TAB BOOKS Inc

ISBN 0-8306-2600-X

Printed and bound in Great Britain

Contents

Preface

The term 'database' has become one of the most used and abused computing phrases of modern times. From its first coinage in 1963 to a few years ago the term was synonymous with 'a large collection of data, usually on a mainframe computer'. With the development of micros, however, the definition has changed subtly to include any collection of related data bound under a controlling piece of software. At the other extreme to the initial definition, certain TV programmes have referred to a *basic read* statement with an associated *data* statement as being a database.

This book is concerned with databases of the first definition, still very much in use in the business and industrial world, and still providing many of the benefits outlined within these pages. Moreover, it is not an archaic area of computing: much current work is being undertaken to develop new and more powerful database systems and many references are made here to the CODASYL committee who represent true pioneers in this field.

This book is in three sections:

(1) Part 1, in which the need for a database approach is looked at and the principal features of a database system are outlined.

(2) Part 2, in which the work of the database administration in creating and maintaining a database is looked at and, at the same time, the general database features are developed more fully (Chapters 7-11).

(3) Part 3, in which various existing database systems are looked at, their common elements identified and how each tackles the problems outlined in Chapter 1 described.

That the reader might see the relevance of much of the text in a practical sense, a case study is used throughout the book to highlight the principles and techniques. That the readers might try to use these techniques themselves, four more case studies are introduced here and revisited at the end of any relevant chapters; readers are invited to choose one and follow it through.

Case study I
The course administration system at your college, polytechnic or university is likely to use much data from different sources, e.g. course data, student data, courses' constituent module data, fees data, departmental data, staff data, etc. Try to obtain an enrollment form to gain perspective as to the variety of data requirements. What other data are kept?

Case study II
Student administration is also complex with much data similar to that just mentioned, but also includes student accommodation, class timetables, personal tutors, results etc. Such data are not likely to exist on a single form. Try to write out all the data you believe your college holds concerning yourself.

Case study III
The college (or town) library holds many books and access mechanisms exist to extract certain information. What are these mechanisms (for example, they might be microfiche or a card index system) and what items of data are needed to be maintained?

Case study IV
A mail-order company takes orders by mail or phone. How does it know whether the items are in stock? That the customer has ordered before? Who the suppliers are? Try to obtain a mail-order catalogue and investigate the data requirements from a business viewpoint. What data also needs to be stored relating to customers and suppliers?

At the end of this pre-book exercise, the student should have some notion of the data requirements of the chosen area, and should have grouped them together into a file or files identifying likely keys (which must be unique).

To be able to do this and to be able to follow a large proportion of this book, I have had to assume some knowledge of both basic data processing and, in particular, COBOL. For those who have a reasonable knowledge, go to Chapter 1. For the others, read on.

A *bit* is the smallest unit of data storage, being synonymous with binary digit and being able to store 1 or 0. A *byte* is defined as eight bits and, generally, is used as the storage requirement of a single character. 1 KB = 1024 bytes (though most people understand it to be 1000), 1 Mb = 1 million bytes; used extensively to describe the storage capacity of mainframe storage devices.

A computer *file* consists of a number of *records* each of which contain the same number of *data items*. For example, all customer data would form a file, the data pertaining to each individual customer would comprise a record, and each piece of data (e.g. name, address) would be a data item.

A *block* is a number of records grouped together on a physical device such that all can be read into memory with a single I/O, thus making sequential reading of files more efficient. On some machines, block is synonymous with *page*. Both are used in this book.

The difference between data and information is an important one. *Data* are raw numbers or characters, e.g. 68.42, which on their own have no meaning. They become *information* when we give them meaning. Thus, Mr Smith has £68.42 in his account is now information. For obvious reasons of storage efficiency, the computer only stores data. It is the task of the application software (or database management system here) to be able to interpret this data in a way relevant to the user's requirements (i.e. as information).

The knowledge of COBOL required revolves around the way in which COBOL defines a record. The reason for this is that many database systems use a language to define the database itself which has similar constructs.

Essentially, a record in COBOL is defined and given a name by using an 01 level. This is then the name of the whole record. It can then be broken down subsequently into constituent data items by using 03 levels. These themselves can be further broken down by using 05 levels and so on. Unless an item is to be broken down further it must be given a type and length via a PICTURE clause, here truncated to the usual PIC. For the purposes of this book, the item can either be alphanumeric (Xs) or numeric (9s). The length of the item is described by either repeating the Xs or 9s the required number of times or by a number in brackets. Thus 999 and 9(3) both describe a three-digit field. An example might clarify matters further:

```
01 INVESTMENT-RECORD.
   03 ACCOUNT-NUMBER          PIC 9(10).
   03 CUSTOMER-NUMBER         PIC 9(6).
   03 CUSTOMER-NAME           PIC X(20).
   03 CUSTOMER-ADDRESS.
      05 STREET               PIC X(30).
      05 TOWN                 PIC X(20).
      05 CODE                 PIC X(8).
```

Note that identifiers in COBOL can be composed of letters, digits and hyphens. The whole example describes the investment record which has been split into two numeric items and two alphanumeric items the second of which (CUSTOMER-ADDRESS) has been split into three further items.

Where the record sizes have been used to calculate storage requirements, my numbers may at first seem wrong. This is attributable (I hope) to the fact that where the record contains numeric data, I have allowed for the packing of data (a facility available on most machines whereby a numeric digit can be stored in half a byte instead of the usual one). Thus the storage requirement for the above example would total 86 bytes. In doing this I have deliberately not shown the items to be packed decimal in the record description because the manner of doing so varies from machine to machine (the items could be followed by COMP, COMP-1, COMP-2, etc.).

The database language definitions, where shown, similarly are lacking in punctuation. This is for similar reasons. (Even with CODASYL databases where the constructs are common, the punctuation varies from manufacturer to manufacturer.)

Part 1:
An Overview

CHAPTER 1

Traditional Approaches to Data Management

Introduction

It is both traditional and highly useful in books on databases to have some long running example to which the author can refer and emphasize points of interest. This book will be no exception.

In this book I have used the example of a medium-sized bank. The workings of such are both vast and complex and I hope I will not offend too many real-world banks by over simplification on occasion.

On the plus side it should be a business with which the reader readily can identify, being involved with money and people and, although the problems encountered in this chapter concerning the non-database approach are on a fairly large scale, they are exactly the same problems which would be encountered by any business using the traditional approach, though magnified somewhat. Moreover, the database approach dealt with throughout the rest of the book, can be shown to be just as strong no matter what the size of business.

Example

A rapidly growing bank has approximately
1 000 000 customers,
750 000 investment accounts,
100 000 mortgage accounts,
200 branches plus associated insurances, agents, etc.

A transaction occurs if a customer pays money into his/her account or draws money out (there are in fact many others but they need not concern us here). A customer averages 30 transactions on an investment account per year (by investment account I refer to all types of accounts, be they deposit, share, etc.), although individual values vary from two (both being half-yearly interest payments, which also count as transactions) to several hundred. A mortgage account averages slightly over 14 transactions per year (the norm is 12 monthly repayments plus one interest transaction plus one buildings insurance transaction, though some pay weekly). There are very few other variations so we shall take the maximum to be 54.

An investment account may be owned by up to four customers (though most are single or joint named) whereas a mortgage account is, generally, owned by two (husband and wife), but never more than two (in this book). In general, all mortgage-account holders are also investment-account holders (you try obtaining a mortgage from a bank if you do not save with them).

At year-end all transactions are wiped from the file (but are microfiched for historical information) when the accounts are capitalized (have interest added) and the new year sees mortgage and investment accounts with no transactions on file.

That brief description of the workings of our bank will suffice for the present. Now let us look at the problems.

The directors of the bank are very interested in introducing a branch network with all 200 branches connected to a single central mainframe which will replace the current obsolescent model. Also a 24-h cash-point service is felt to be highly desirable by some high quarters to be in direct competition to the larger banks. They wish a feasibility study to be carried out as to whether to go database or not. Whatever is to be decided on they want it to be implemented fully and working within 18 months and they also want the end product to be:

(1) fast
(2) efficient
(3) secure
(4) flexible
(5) expandable
(6) reliable.

During the feasibility stage the following points are likely to emerge before a recommendation can be made.

Inherent problems

As with many other large businesses, the bank's raw data

are decentralized because the business is decentralized. Customers perform their transactions at branches scattered around the country and, because the business revolves around the customer, most of the remaining business is performed also at the branch level. Now if every customer could be asked to transact only at one particular branch then the branches could become virtually autonomous, each looking after its own information. Unfortunately, this is not the case and for customers to be able to transact wherever they choose, the information relating to their accounts should, ideally, be available at all branches (because the alternative solution of bank cards as used at present is not suitable for various reasons). This implies a central storing of data and lines of communication (in whatever form) between this central store and the branches.

In most businesses the higher management, who are responsible ultimately for running the business, usually are sited at a head office. To be able to perform their functions properly they must have easy access to any piece of information that is relevant to their particular job. In the past this gathering of information took place either orally over the telephone network or through the post. Both are inefficient. The former is prone to error when communicating raw figures, the second is often too slow. Nowadays, when data communication is very fast and cost effective we tend not to give it a second thought but the whole process of how and where to store data to maximize communication throughput has to be considered at a very early phase of system development.

On a day-to-day basis the management often has to make snap decisions which will affect the success of the business directly. Those decisions are made on the basis of the information to hand. If they are wrong then the business will falter. Therefore, clearly, it is essential that all relevant information needed for the consideration of that decision is readily available. (This does not mean simply having data on a computer somewhere. There must also be software mechanisms available for someone to extract the information when and where it is wanted. This subject is dealt with specifically in Chapter 11.)

The two solutions to the above problems are clearly:

(1) To store all the data once centrally.
(2) To store all the data at every location.

The second option involves possible insuperable problems of data duplication and inconsistency (i.e. guaranteeing that all copies of the data are the same). Most businesses adopt the first approach with data being available to all users via:

(1) terminal networks
(2) circulation of reports (by whatever means).

Clearly, the first is faster but far more expensive so usually it is left to each business to decide on its cost effectiveness.

With the decision made that for a bank, where information needs to be available quickly to prevent fraud, the data needs to be stored centrally (in the absence of distributed databases which are beyond the scope of this book), then a branch network is highly desirable. It is now a matter of comparison of traditional data-storage techniques with database methodologies to look at which is best suited to support a branch network.

Large-record approach

Most business-orientated computers do not allow variable-length records on disk (and those that do will not allow variations on the number of item occurrences within a COBOL record, i.e. you cannot have a variable-length repeating group). This means that the COBOL record must cater for the maximum number of item occurrences possible within a given record. Since there is a business need to look at investment transactions and customer information at the same time as the investment details, a COBOL file description of an investment record to cater for this might appear as shown in Figure 1.1.

```
01 INVESTMENT-RECORD.
    03 INV-DETAILS            PIC 9(40).
    03 INV-CUST-DETAILS       PIC X(70) OCCURS 4.
    03 INV-TRANSACTIONS       PIC 9(20) OCCURS 300.
```

Figure 1.1 *An investment record catering for maximum occurrences*

Within this record the INV-DETAILS field contains the account number, balances, interest rates and all singularly occurring items relating to the account, INV-CUST-DETAILS contains the names and addresses of the four possible customers and INV-TRANSACTIONS contains details for each transaction against the account up to a maximum of 300.

It is apparent that we can locate and obtain all related data with the access of a single physical record which should make all relevant programs run quicker, but we have paid for it in disk storage requirements. The record is 3300 bytes long (see the Preface) which, if allocated to each of the 750 000 investment accounts, would require 2500 Mb of disk storage, an enormous amount. Moreover, it is space used poorly because most records will contain blank occurrences of most of the customer and transaction information. In fact the average account will only have a single named customer and 30 transactions at the maximum storage time (just before year end) representing an overall wastage of 2900 bytes per record (or 88 per cent).

We also have a problem of data duplication for if a customer owns more than one account then their name and address will appear on each. Can we guarantee that each occurrence of the logically same name and address will be identical? Clearly not without some piece of complicated cross-checking software.

Due to the large size of the file, taking security copies (backup) will take a long time, at current speeds about 5 h for a disk-to-tape dump and using 20 tapes. For that reason any form of recovery will be very slow (see the Backup and recovery section in this chapter). Memory requirements will be high because, even if a program is interested only in the account number and closing balance, the system will still have to read the entire 3300 bytes into memory (more if the file is blocked).

More problems arise when we look at the mortgage-file definition as shown in Figure 1.2.

The problems are similar to those of the investment record but to a lesser extent, because we have a maximum of only two customers and 54 transactions. However, the customers with a mortgage account will almost certainly own an investment account which means that 100 000

```
01 MORTGAGE-RECORD.
    03 MTG-DETAILS            PIC 9(40).
    03 MTG-CUST-DETAILS       PIC X(70) OCCURS 2.
    03 MTG-TRANSACTIONS       PIC 9(20) OCCURS 54.
```

Figure 1.2 *A mortgage record catering for maximum occurrences*

names and addresses will appear on both files. Again we have dangers of inconsistency and wastage of storage capacity.

There may be a business requirement to associate a mortgage account with the investment account(s) and, similarly, to associate all investment accounts owned by the same customer (bear in mind that they will all have different account numbers). This logical linking of records cannot be performed physically by most currently available non-database system software and, if required, would have to be supported by a user-written index system. An alternative might be to store on an investment account the account numbers of all investment records owned by the same customer, but how many should we cater for (bear in mind that a trustee could be a named customer on several hundred accounts)? Again, we would be introducing further wasted storage.

The normal flat file approach to data management usually finds it extremely difficult to represent the relationships between records and files which are meaningful to the business. If these cannot be represented then each record will have to be located independently and the efficiency of the system will suffer.

An easy solution to some of these problems of data access and data duplication might be to construct one large consolidated file containing both investment and mortgage data as shown in Figure 1.3.

Now the customer data are stored only once but what if the customer owns more than one investment account? And

```
01 ACCOUNT-RECORD.
   03 INV-DETAILS            PIC 9(40).
   03 INV-TRANSACTIONS       PIC 9(20) OCCURS 300.
   03 MTG-DETAILS            PIC 9(40).
   03 MTG-TRANSACTIONS       PIC 9(20) OCCURS 54.
   03 CUSTOMER-DETAILS       PIC X(70) OCCURS 4.
```

Figure 1.3 *A consolidated file*

what of the insurance records associated with the mortgage record? We could allow for these in a file structure as shown in Figure 1.4.

```
01 ACCOUNT-RECORD.
   03 INVESTMENT-RECORDS       OCCURS 10.
      05 INV-DETAILS           PIC 9(40).
      05 INV-TRANSACTIONS      PIC 9(20) OCCURS 300.
   03 MTG-DETAILS              PIC 9(40).
   03 MTG-TRANSACTIONS         PIC 9(20) OCCURS 54.
   03 INSURANCE-DETAILS        PIC X(70) OCCURS 3.
   03 CUSTOMER-DETAILS         PIC X(70) OCCURS 4.
```

Figure 1.4. *The consolidated file approach taken to extremes*

Already, the record size is getting out of hand (31 000 bytes) and if we extend the arguments to 'what of the related endowment policies (if there are any), deeds details, solicitors, etc?' then, clearly, the situation has become ridiculous. Also, what would be the key to this record? Most filing systems allow for a single key based on a unique identifier (i.e. the account number) plus a number of secondary keys (which need not be unique). This identifier cannot be a part of a repeating item (i.e. in an occurs clause) so which of a customer's accounts would we take the number of as the key? If we were to specify an investment account number as the primary key then we would have to maintain that number even if a mortgage account holder closes their investment account. Would that number still be meaningful to the business? or the customer?: not once their passbook had been thrown away. Alternatively, choosing the mortgage account number is, clearly, nonsensical because 650 000 investment account holders do not have mortgages.

Demonstrably, the large-record approach removes a few problems, but creates a lot more which cannot be overcome.

Small-record approach

A solution to many of the problems highlighted in the previous section might be to have several smaller files as shown in Figure 1.5. We now have five independent files. This view has reduced our storage requirements drastically because now we only need create a new investment transaction record (for example) when we need one instead of pre-allocating large amounts. In fact our maximum disk storage is down to around 225 Mb.

Unfortunately, we now need the investment account number on each transaction record plus a transaction number to identify each one uniquely (the transaction number was not needed before because the transactions could be kept in logical sequence within the occurs clause). Similarly, for the mortgage transactions.

However, there are still problems with the customer records. Unless we have separate customer records for investments and mortgages (with the problems of data duplication), we need both account numbers as keys. Even if our file management system does allow primary and secondary keys we still cannot cater for a customer having more than one investment account or an account being owned by more than one customer for reasons which are identical with those given in the previous section.

The only solution to this problem would be to invent a unique customer number for each customer. This number could be stored (in an occurs 4) on the investment file and (in an occurs 2) on the mortgage file facilitating access from those files to the customer information. It would not solve the problem if there was a business requirement to get to the account records from the customer file. Such a customer number would have no meaning to the business nor to the

```
01 INVESTMENT-RECORD.
   03 INV-NUMBER              PIC 9(10).
   03 INV-DETAILS             PIC 9(30).

01 INV-TRANSACTION.
   03 INV-NUMBER              PIC 9(10).
   03 INV-TRAN-NO             PIC 999.
   03 INV-TRAN-DETAILS        PIC 9(20).

01 MORTGAGE-RECORD.
   03 MTG-NUMBER              PIC 9(10).
   03 MTG-DETAILS             PIC 9(30).

01 MTG-TRANSACTION.
   03 MTG-NUMBER              PIC 9(10).
   03 MTG-TRAN-NO             PIC 99.
   03 MTG-TRAN-DETAILS        PIC 9(20).

01 CUSTOMER-RECORD.
   03 INV-NUMBER              PIC 9(10).
   03 MTG-NUMBER              PIC 9(10).
   03 CUST-DETAILS            PIC X(70).
```

Figure 1.5 *Example record layouts of the small file approach*

customer but it would be necessary in these circumstances. (Such a number also appears for similar reasons in the database approach, see Chapter 4.)

If such problems as mentioned can be lived with or overcome we are, nevertheless, left with a potentially very serious problem of disk accessing. In the single large-file approach, we may have used a lot of disk, but at least we could access all related data with a single I/O. In addition, by sorting the file into account-number order occasionally, sequential batch processing could be speeded up, particularly with intelligent usage of blocking factors (i.e. by reading enough records into memory to keep the processor busy while the next block is read).

With the multi-file situation, the transactions for both investments and mortgages will be stored on disk as and when they are created. Basically, this means that for a given account, its transactions will be scattered randomly across the storage media and, in general, if there are n of them, then n physical reads will be needed to read them all. Therefore to read all the related data for a single named investment account half way through the year will take an average of 17 physical I/Os (one for the investment, one for the customer and 15 for the transactions); indeed, this value will be increased if we have to read in indexes, etc., depending on the access mechanisms for our files.

This may be tolerable for on-line random access work (though it will not require many concurrent users before the situation becomes critical), but certainly it will not be acceptable for sequential processing.

Allowing an average of 20 ms per disk access, to read through the single large investment file sequentially will take a maximum of 4 h I/O (less if the file is presorted and blocked). With the separate file approach the records are placed too randomly for blocking to be beneficial, although sorting would still be of use. Without sorting the comparable I/O time is 70 h (far too long for most business requirements) and even with sorting we could still be talking of very many hours (including the time for sorting). Thus run-of-the-mill statistical jobs will become major problems and the managers who require statistics for their decision making will suffer.

In this way the small-file approach is not wholly suitable either. There is a trade-off between disk storage and access times. Moreover, a compromising half-way solution will still contain both problems to a certain degree plus various amounts of data duplication and related inconsistencies.

Backup and recovery

Whatever the system, whatever the hardware, it will not maintain its viability for long unless security (backup) copies are taken regularly.

Here again, there are problems with the large-file approach simply because of the length of time needed to dump the file to tape (or tape back to disk in the event of recovery) will discourage frequent copying.

What are the prospects in the event of some sort of failure (be it hardware, systems software or applications software)? With most machines the options are simple: reload the last backup copy of the file and rerun all subsequent programs up to the time of the failure. If, for whatever reasons, this fails, we must go back to the dump before that. In general, if 12 h work has been performed since the dump then 12 h work need repeating. Therefore frequent dumps are advisable. Unfortunately, while a file is being dumped, it cannot be in the process of being updated (otherwise the system would never know which updates have been copied to tape and which have not; therefore in the event of reloading we could have inconsistencies). The result of this is that it is impractical to dump files during the day when they are in constant use and so, in practice, they are dumped every 24 h, at night.

It is a further problem that programs seldom access a single file. If they did and file F was corrupted it would be a simple matter to reload F and rerun programs 1, 2 and 5 which have since updated it. In practice the situation usually is far less clear and any form of recovery involves the reloading of many files and the rerunning of many programs, due to the interrelations between them. This itself gives scope for a multitude of possible errors; for example, reloading one file too few or rerunning the wrong programs or the right ones but in the wrong order. Such errors are relatively easy to make and will probably not be detected for some time, by which time any corrupt data will have corrupted other data in exponential fashion. In the meantime the integrity of the system will have been lost (and if the error is not detected in the next three generations of backup it may not be recoverable at all!).

Concurrency

If a system exists in which only one user ever updates a file at a time, there would be none of the following problems, but the situation might not be very convenient in a large organization to only ever have a single on-line user updating a file. However, if the system allowed more than one user then the following could occur:

ACCOUNT	ACCOUNT
12345	12345
BALANCE	BALANCE
25.00	25.00
In the system buffer	In program A's user work area

Program A requires account record X. This is read into the system buffer and from there into the program's user work area. Program B also requires record X and, since it is in memory already, acquires its own copy.

Program A now updates the record by processing a receipt of £15.00 and changes the balance to £40.00, which gets written back to disk:

ACCOUNT
12345
BALANCE
40.00

Program B now processes its own copy with a withdrawal for £10.00 and changing its copy of the balance to £15.00. This is then written back to disk overwriting the original transaction.

Clearly, the balance is now wrong and the integrity of the system lost: the amount stored on the computer is not equal to the real-world amount that the customer possesses. And yet the system would never detect such an error!

To prevent this occurring, most file management systems will only allow access to one update program at a time (although as many read-only programs as required).

Such a situation can cause genuine problems to the business if, for example, both the investment and mortgage departments share the customer information (which is how we want it), but both want the facility to perform on-line updating. The only two sensible solutions for such a problem would be:

(1) For all user updates to be performed by a single program (with obviously no multiple copies allowed). This will cause severe problems of data privacy (see the Privacy section in this chapter) if several departments use the same program.
(2) One department to have on-line updating and the other to log all of its updates during the day and then to batch process them at night, or have half a day on-line each, but both these options rather negate the advantages of having an on-line system.

How can we arrange a branch network system with 200 concurrent users in such a situation?

Ability to change

Certainly, it would be most unusual if an organization's data requirements remained rigid and unchanging. In particular, markets are bound to change and hence volumes of data, new products will be developed, government legislation may affect financial matters and so our computerized system must also change. The problem is the ease with which it can be changed.

The general mode of changing the structure or content of existing files is to:

(1) write a special program to dump all of the existing file to tape (not usually a simple copy-to-tape option, but a logical record dump in some predefined order)
(2) create a new version of the file on disk
(3) load the new file from the tape dump record by record using another specially written program
(4) change and recompile all affected programs.

Both the dump and the load programs must be tested very thoroughly beforehand because the whole process is likely to be very time consuming for the larger files and any run-time errors could quite easily cause the whole task to be aborted (unless very careful restart mechanisms have been incorporated).

The process of changing affected programs can be very inefficient because programs will need, at the least, to be recompiled even if they simply declare the file without using any of the affected data items (for example, if the program uses only the account number and closing balance and the change is to add an extra digit to the account type field). The reason simply is that in the conventional file situation the program has to declare the whole of the application file on an all-or-nothing basis.

Let us suppose that we are adding an extra digit to the account type field. How do we know which programs actually use this field? For that matter how do we know which programs use the affected file?

In non-database systems the answers usually lie in manual forms of documentation. Whoever is responsible for the file change must search through both the system and then the program documentation to find out which programs will be affected. To discover which programs actually use the account type they may well have to hunt through each cross-reference listing. This whole process is both slow and error prone. Are there any guarantees that the documentation is complete? Up to date? In many cases it will be neither. What are the consequences of an error being made and a program missed? If the program is read only then the chances are that someone will notice errors on the printouts and little damage will be done. However, if the program is update then we could easily have the situation as shown in Figure 1.6.

```
01 INV-RECORD.
 03 INV-NUMBER              PIC 9(10).
 03 INV-ACC-TYPE            PIC 999.
 03 INV-BALANCE             PIC 9(6)V99.
 03 INV-CUST-NO             PIC 9(6).
```

True definition of the investment file

```
01 INV-RECORD.
 03 INV-NUMBER              PIC 9(10).
 03 INV-ACC-TYPE            PIC 99.
 03 INV-BALANCE             PIC 9(6)V99.
 03 INV-CUST-NO             PIC 9(6).
```

Program's wrong view of the data

Figure 1.6 *Incorrect file view of an unchanged program following a file structure change*

If the program is now run and updates the balance then because the fields after the account type are offset from the real file layout by one digit, the file will become corrupted quickly. Moreover, if the error is more subtle and is not detected quickly then a ripple effect may cause corruptions on other files and the whole system is in danger. Without strict manual checking this danger could become a real possibility; there is no system software to help the process.

Privacy

The normal quantity of information that an organization needs to contain will almost certainly contain various data items/files to which access should be restricted. Whether this concerns wages, personnel details or financial information useful to competitors is immaterial; there will be a few people within the organization who should be allowed to see the data and, at the same time, many who must be denied access. Whatever the situation, once a privacy decision has been made it should be enforceable whether the data are to be stored on a computer or in a filing cabinet.

In the early days of computers the problem was a relatively simple one. All work carried out on the computer was performed by input and output in the computer room itself. Thus if you restricted access (physically) to the computer room then you only needed to worry about who actually saw the various reports which came out of the computer room. Today, with data passing along many lines (both private and public) external to the computer room, the problem is far harder to handle.

In general terms, a conventional computer system requires a potential user to have or have knowledge of a particular user code (area-id) and its related password before they can gain access to the machine. However, most systems have all related files in a single user area with a single password. Thus if the password gets into the wrong hands the security of the entire system disappears (this is sometimes modified to having a read-only password and another for updating the files). Especially sensitive data, such as personnel or wages, normally are kept separate but again usually are protected only by a single password.

A partial solution might be to have a different password for each file within a system such that an unauthorized user would be afforded only a restricted view of the total sum of data, but since many programs access many files the system will be cumbersome for the valid user in trying to pass through the various privacy controls. This solution does not solve all problems either. In the bank example it may be permissible for cashiers to access account information for those accounts belonging to external customers, but it might be felt that they should not be allowed to see accounts owned by other members of staff. Similarly, staff working in the wages department may be allowed to see salary details for employees up to a certain level of management but no further.

The only practical solution to this problem (and the one most readily found in practice) is to hive off the sensitive records, put them in a separate file and give them a separate password. Such an action is inefficient and hardly satisfactory because both files are, essentially, the same in content and will be processed in identical fashion. Thus the system overall is degraded because it cannot cope with privacy decisions at the record level.

This situation is made considerably worse if we had data items within records requiring differing security levels. For example, in the personnel system, the general data relating to an employee may be available to any member of the personnel department, but certain items relating to an employee's promotion prospects or work standards should be available only to the personnel manager or other members of higher management. Again the conventional file system cannot cope with privacy decisions at the item level and so offending items are often split off again forming separate files.

These are the reasons why many organizations still run two payroll systems (one for management and one for everyone else) and, also, why many deny access to the whole system to users who might otherwise benefit from its usage purely because they are not allowed to see a single data item. The net result of this all-or-nothing approach is illustrated in the next section.

Application views

If there is a single common fault with many computerized systems within organizations it is that they tend to be a hotch-potch of many subsystems which have each been developed independently and implemented at different times, rather than a single integrated system supplying the data needs for all. The reason for this is that, initially, only a part of the business was computerized at one time. If that was seen to be successful then another part was computerized and so on. Perhaps, along the way, a package (such as a payroll system) was bought to speed things up although, obviously, it would not fit in with existing in-house systems.

The result of this, and with the privacy restrictions from the last section borne in mind, was that (by using the example) the mortgage department was computerized first, creating a mortgage file and customer file among others.

Next came the computerization of the investment department. Could they share the same customer file? Often the answer would be no because, for example, there would be a 'bad debts' item on the mortgage-customer information which they would not wish the investment department to see (and it cannot go on the mortgage file itself because it only relates to one customer). The outcome is that the investment department has to create their own customer file.

The overall results of this piecewise development methodology are clear: the fact that the system itself is split into many subsystems often means that each become independent and, too often, mutually exclusive. The outcome is data duplication, almost certain inconsistency and an overall loss of efficiency to the organization.

Summary

In this chapter the problems facing an organization adopting the conventional file-management approach have been looked at. Many existing installations still do employ these systems and most suffer from the problems outlined here to a greater or lesser extent.

With a smaller organization than a bank, the problems will be reduced proportionally in most cases, but they will still be there. In particular the problems of recovery, privacy and inconsistency are, generally, very much in evidence.

The major problem areas identified have been the following.

LARGE FILES VS SLOW ACCESS

There is a choice between large files with:

(1) large storage requirements
(2) difficulty in coping with deviations from the norm
(3) large backup overheads with correspondingly slow recovery times
(4) problems of restructuring files
(5) high memory overheads
(6) data duplication and inconsistency,
(7) relatively quick access times.

Alternatively, we can have smaller files with:

(1) many accesses required to obtain all related data
(2) extra items required to identify each record uniquely

(3) difficulty in linking related records
(4) data duplication and inconsistency.

SLOW RECOVERY
The only practical method for recovery available for any type of failure is to reload and reprocess, which is both time consuming and error prone.

POOR BACKUP FACILITIES
Backup is both slow and costly in as much as it must be performed off line when no programs are active.

POOR RESTRUCTURING FACILITIES
Changing of files is again very slow and error prone because of its dependence on often incomplete and out-of-date manual documentation. In general, many programs will need changing and/or recompiling for even the smallest of changes because of the all-or-nothing aspect to access.

NO CONCURRENCY
Because only one program is allowed to update a file at one time, many advantages of an on-line interactive updating system are lost.

PRIVACY
Access to files is on an all-or-nothing basis which means that privacy decisions only can be enforced at the file level resulting in the splitting of related data into separate files with data duplication and loss of efficiency.

APPLICATION VIEWS
Largely because of the way in which businesses are computerized, application by application, and also because of the organization's privacy requirements, the system is a mass of unrelated-but-should-be-related duplicated application orientated files and programs providing an overall increase in workloads and a decrease in efficiency.

It would be rather blasé (and, indeed, not always true) to state that database systems solve all of these problems. Database systems vary enormously in their effectiveness. The better ones will solve (or avoid) most of the problems as described, whereas the lesser ones will remove some and at least reduce others.

Case studies

The student should attempt to take the individual data items from their chosen case-study area and try to coalesce them into a conventional file approach, grouping related data into the same file. There will be, in general, many possible solutions. Try to equate your solution to the problems outlined in this chapter. Adjust your solution accordingly (e.g. by merging files or splitting into separate files). Have all the problems gone away? Have new ones materialized? Readjust again to see if an optimum solution can be found. How would that solution act in a 'live' situation if speed was all important? If storage costs were to be a minimum?

For the particular case studies see following.

(I) Your solution for the course administration will probably comprise of many files. If not then you must have a very large 'occurs' on the course record for every student on that course, every module of that course etc. So can you pick out all students on the astronomy course who pay their own fees, without long involved searches? Or all students taking a particular optional module on a course? Such answers would be very useful to the course administration department. You can make up your own questions about the information required and see whether your solution facilitates its production.

(II) Your solution to the student administration is likely to be similar with various files instead of one large one. Could you pick out easily all students who live in the same accommodation? Or all those who have the same personal tutor? Again the answer is likely to be that searching is the only solution. Compare your results with those of a colleague who has opted for the course administration. Despite the commonality of data, could the two systems be merged as one? Your solution would have the student number as its 'prime' key, their's the course code. Could both departments access their information easily on a common system? What of the privacy aspects? A student may be allowed to see much of his/her own information (particularly in the wake of the Data Protection Act), would they also be allowed access to all course information? How could privacy locks be applied in practice?

(III) As opposed to the above case studies, the library solution might, at first draft, be a single file of book data with associated authors, publishers, etc., all on a single record. Would this suffice for a library system? Could you find all books by the same author easily (particularly those of a joint authorship nature)? Or list out all the books currently on loan to another library? Doesn't the system need to keep track of who current borrowers are? To be able to flag all books which are overdue? Can your system cope with the volume of data? Is there a vast amount of data duplication (e.g. publisher's names)?

(IV) For the mail-order business you are likely to have at least three files: stock, customers and suppliers. Could an on-line telephone system determine quickly whether an item is in stock? Whether an out-of-stock item is available from more than one supplier? Whether a customer's credit is good? Could a customer enquiring about a particular type of product be given a comprehensive list of all similar items which are in stock? Would such searching be fast enough for an on-line system?

For each of these case studies the student hopefully will be able to determine that a conventional file approach is likely to be inadequate for an on-line system situation. It is left to the student to construct a database system which will provide true support to the user by removing duplication, data redundancy, privacy problems and all other constraints highlighted within this chapter. The basis for derivation of such a system is followed through in the next five chapters.

CHAPTER 2

General Concepts

Introduction

Having determined the need for solutions to the problems posed in the first chapter, we now need to define broad outlines as to an ideal database model, i.e. what will it consist of in terms of recognized existing hardware and software constructs? How will it interface with the operating system? How can it be used by our application programmers (or, indeed, by any other users)?

CODASYL: historical background

Much of the credit for rationalization of early views and concepts concerning databases must be given to the CODASYL (Conference On DAta SYstems Language) committee who, when founded in 1959, were responsible for the introduction of COBOL which, for all its reported disadvantages, is still the world's premier business language.

In 1965 CODASYL formed a List Processing Task Force which soon became the Data Base Task Group (the actual phrase 'database' was first used by the USA military in 1963 during a symposium titled *Development and Management of a Computer-centred Data Base*. Incidentally, this symposium also coined the first definition of a database which was:

(1) a database is a set of files
(2) a file is an ordered collection of entries
(3) an entry consists of a key or keys and data
(and perhaps no better definition exists today!).

The Database Task Group produced two reports: one in 1969 and a more major one in 1971. By the end of that year they had become a committee in their own right, the Data Description Language Committee, producing its own

Journal of Development (one being published in 1973 and another in 1978).

Since then many other CODASYL committees have been formed, each producing their own journals and reports. However, the aims of all have been the same: to collect together ideas via representatives from computer manufacturers, software houses, users, academics, etc. and then to standardize these ideas into unified reports to act as guidelines for any current/future database development.

How this has been achieved with regard to CODASYL database products is described more fully in Chapter 13. It has been mentioned here merely to show that much thought and discussion has been put into database development, the result being that many database architectures have very common roots and principles.

General definitions of an ideal architecture

In the example of the bank most of the data relevant to the business could be kept permanently on a database (it may be decided to split the data across several, but such matters are considered in later chapters).

The software that will allow one (or more) users to access the data will hereafter be referred to as the database management system (DBMS). In this role, the DBMS acts as an interpreter for the application program, translating raw data as stored on the computer into the users business-minded view (i.e. as information). This should, in effect, mean that the physical attributes of the computer's data, in other words where they are stored and how they are accessed, are invisible to the user or application programmer. Thus in its simplest terms we have the situation as shown in Figure 2.1.

Alternatively, because the physical storage is in binary digits and because the user wants an abstracted view of that data, we require the DBMS to translate the data into the required information, in other words 00011001000001111 0000110 becomes a six-digit date 190786 which the user possibly sees as 19th July 1986. In this way the users view (or *conceptual view*) is derived from the physical storage by the DBMS (Figure 2.2).

This idea is very important because the corollary, that the physical database is an implementation of the conceptual database model, is the keystone for the database analysis and design stages (Part 2 of this book).

The conceptual database must, by necessity, contain items and concepts which are meaningful to the user and, indeed, to the business as a whole. Thus the conceptual database of our example will contain different logical areas of information (e.g. investments, mortgages, customers, etc.), each of which will in itself contain items of data (e.g. account numbers, names, addresses, etc.) plus information

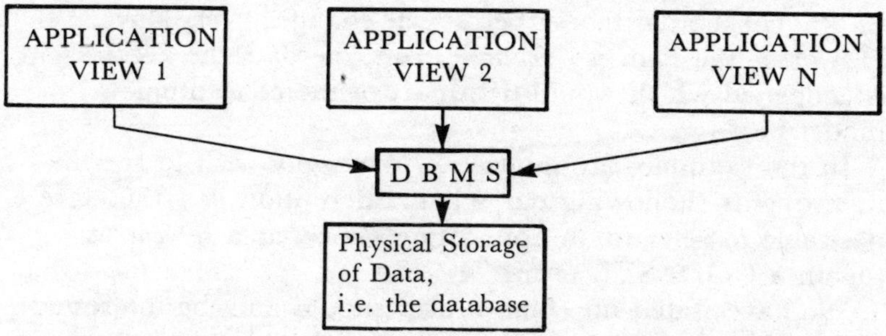

Figure 2.1 *Application views of the stored data*

describing the real-world interrelations between items (e.g. that a customer has an investment account, that an investment account will have associated transactions). This global view of the organization's data needs is referred to as

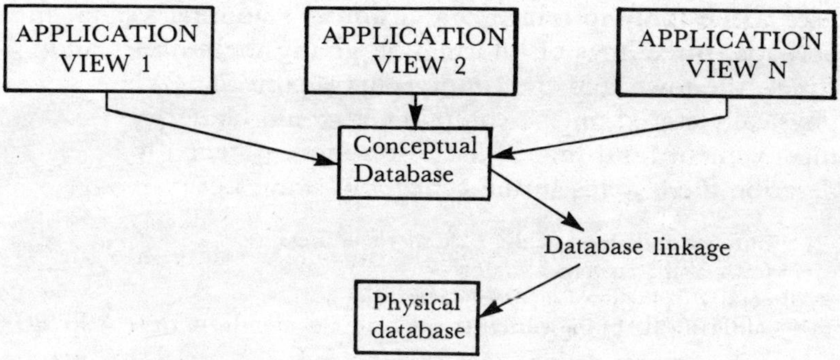

Figure 2.2 *Conceptual view of the stored data*

the *scheme* or, to use the more correct CODASYL name, the *schema* (it is the latter which will be used throughout this book).

An application's view of the data will probably form a subset of the whole. (*Note*: though not necessarily because the application's view may be derivable from the whole but not contained within it. For example, the investment department will wish to know how long a particular account has been open, for purposes of calculating interest accrued, but it is unlikely that this piece of information will be kept in any conceptual model because it changes every day. However, the item is derivable from the date the account was opened which would be a part of the conceptual model.)

In the example, an application may only wish to see the investments. Following our schema definition it is therefore desirable to refer to an application's view as a *subschema* (again a CODASYL term).

We have stated now that a user should only be interested in his own abstracted information but that the data are stored physically in binary digits. We now need to look for an interface between the two. First, the conceptual database is rationalized and defined by using its own language:the *data definition language* or DDL in CODASYL terminology. We have also stated that the user is interested only in the conceptual database. Need this necessarily be the same as the one implemented? The answer is no. For example, the user wishes only to relate to a customer's address as, perhaps, three lines of information giving the number and street, the town and the county plus a postcode. When physically stored on the computer it would be very inconvenient (and indeed illegal on most systems) to describe these items in the conceptual way, i.e:

(1) number and street of the customer's address
(2) town of the customer's address
(3) county of the customer's address
(4) address code of the customer.

(Note that the customer's address part is necessary to distinguish it from a mortgage address or an insurance company's address, etc.)

It is far more likely that this item would be implemented in a similar manner to:

```
03 CUST-ADD-1          PIC X(30)
03 CUST-ADD-2          PIC X(30)
03 CUST-ADD-3          PIC X(20)
03 CUST-POST-CODE      PIC X(8)
```

(Note also that our implementation of the conceptual view, in most systems, will also force us to define items as having a certain type and length; again this is radically different to the conceptual view where we wouldn't really mind how long the address was or whether, indeed, it took four lines instead of three.)

We therefore need to differentiate between the real-world conceptual model and the implemented conceptual model. The latter will therefore be referred to as the *logical model*.

Database architecture

To understand the workings of a computer fully, the student must study its architecture. In similar fashion, to comprehend the function of a database system, we must look at its architecture.

Again it must be stated that much of that which appears in this section is as a result of the CODASYL committees. Also, it must be underlined firmly that the architecture specified here is the practical goal aimed at by the CODASYL committees but that, to date, it is still very much a theoretical goal and that, at present, no existing database system is a full implementation of this architecture.

The ideal architecture is one of four distinct views or models, each of which is defined in terms of its own language and each of which is disjoint from the others except inasmuch as they are all bound together by the DBMS. For this reason the conceptual model (as defined previously) does not form a part of the architecture (although it appears very prominently in the data-analysis sections) purely because it does not form a part of the implemented database system. With this in mind we can define the four existing parts which are the:

(1) *device model*, where the data actually resides in terms of which disks, tapes, blocks, pages, etc.
(2) *storage model*, how the data are stored on the data device model in terms of access mechanisms
(3) *logical model*, implementation of the entire conceptual (global)

model in terms of what the data mean, how they are structured, how they relate to other data items, etc.

(4) *logical submodel*, the subset of the logical model relating to a particular application's viewpoint.

In general terms, each of the four components will be described in its own language. The device model will need to interface with the operating system since in all cases it is this which deals with the allocation and usage of system hardware resources. On the other hand, the logical submodel clearly will need to interface with an application program, generally written in a high-level language such as COBOL. This latter interface must also be able to cater for the possibility of more than one high-level language being used.

The overall system then, appears diagrammatically as in Figure 2.3.

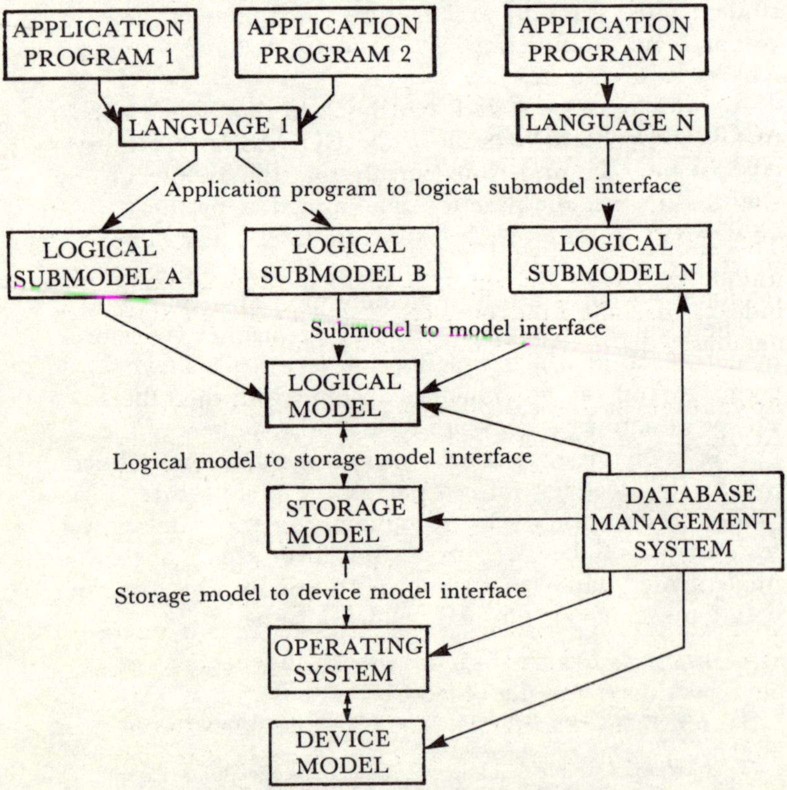

Figure 2.3 *A generalized database architecture*

From the diagram the importance of the DBMS in binding the whole thing together is shown. As the actual interfacing between components is carried out by a piece of software, in future this process will be referred to as a *mapping*.

The device and storage models are often referred to jointly as the *physical database* and the logical model and submodel are referred to as the *logical database*. The difference between the two is important: for a single item of data there will only be one logical representation (i.e. customer name = Williams). However, the physical representation of this item of data will be machine/device dependent (i.e. whether it is stored in EBCDIC, ASCII or whether it is stored in eight bytes, two four-byte words, two six-byte words, etc.).

Similarly, if we were to say that the investment record can be identified uniquely by the account number, i.e.

```
01 INVESTMENT RECORD KEY IS
ACCOUNT-NUMBER
   03 ACCOUNT-NUMBER              PIC 9(12).
   etc.
```

This shows the logical representation of the record and its unique key. How the key is implemented in terms of indexes, hashing functions, etc. is left to the physical database; the user does not want to know.

Advantages of logical/physical database separation

At the end of the last section it was stated that how the key is implemented should be a part of the physical database. With this distinction it can be seen that if the decision were to be taken to change the access mechanism, say from an index to a hashing algorithm, then the logical database will not be affected, i.e. will not need changing, and hence thc application program will not be affected. This is referred to as *physical data independence*; the user is independent of any physical changes to the database.

To return to machine dependence, although the device model is clearly machine dependent because it is controlled by the operating system, which is in itself machine dependent, the same cannot be said for the storage model. We should be able to refer to how a record is stored without having to look at what sort of machine is available.

Another advantage to the separation of the logical and physical database is that the the database can be tuned more readily (i.e. made more efficient) without affecting the logical database and hence programs. (See Chapter 10 on tuning the database.)

Advantages of logical model/submodel separation

The logical submodel represents an application's view of the full logical model. To that end it must be derivable from the full model. In general, therefore, to derive a submodel from the logical model we can:

(1) omit unwanted application areas
(2) omit unwanted files
(3) omit unwanted records
(4) omit unwanted data items
(5) change the ordering of items within a record
(6) change data types
(7) derive data items not in the full model from those which are.

The importance of this is that *logical data independence* can be achieved because a program can be protected from any changes to data items or records or files, other than those which it uses, simply because it does not see them and will therefore not be affected if they change. In other words if program A uses a subschema containing

```
01 INVESTMENTS-RECORD
 03 INV-ACC-NO                    PIC 9(10)
 03 INV-OPEN-BALANCE              PIC 9(5)V99
 03 INV-CLOSE-BALANCE             PIC 9(5)V99
```

if any fields within the investment record other than the three defined above need amending then program A will not be affected (note the difference between this and the situation as shown in Chapter 1).

As a corollary, whereas the logical data model will be described by using its own language, in a program-independent way, the logical data submodels will be, by necessity, program dependent. This implies that they will be defined by using a high-level programming language and this is indeed the case (hence the similarity between the submodel definition above and COBOL). Thus for every high-level language supported by the database system, therc will be one for defining associated data sub-models. At present this, generally, involves support for COBOL and FORTRAN in particular, though others such as PL/1 are supported by some systems. It must be stressed that the logical data sub-models are not themselves written in the languages that they support, but rather in similar languages with similar constructs.

Data manipulation languages

Having defined a logical data submodel for a particular application's viewpoint, we must now define a set of constructs by which our application programmer can access that submodel.

A moment's thought will show that there are two distinct possibilities here.

(a) The first is to write a whole new language, specifically for interfacing with the database, perhaps with similar attributes to an existing language; such a language would take years to develop, but would have the advantage of being highly efficient.
(b) The second would be to enhance existing languages, such as COBOL, by adding extra verbs and constructs with the sole purpose of providing an interface with the submodel; such an approach would be less efficient, but would be available in a much shorter time.

It is now history that most manufacturers adopted the second approach, now referred to as the *host language* approach, though mention must be made here of the special 'fourth-generation' languages developed for the sole purpose of database interrogation (Query languages; Chapter 11) or for the complete task of data manipulation with relational databases (see Chapter 16). Indeed, query languages are very end-user orientated inasmuch as they, to a large extent, bridge the gap between conceptual and logical databases by allowing the non-programming skilled user to access the database using very English-like words and sentences.

The extent of the additions to the host language has varied. With respect to the CODASYL approach COBOL has been enhanced considerably but FORTRAN, with the

CODASYL approach, has not been touched because all interfacing is performed via CALL procedures.

Mappings

As defined in the Database architecture section in this chapter each of the four models is independent but the database management system binds them all together by using mappings between subsequent pairs. The term mapping may seem a strange one to non-mathematicians but it simply means, in this context, a piece of software acting as a bridge between two models. How this is achieved actually is of no importance at this juncture.

Logical model to submodel mapping

The mappings between the logical model and the various submodels define how flexible the database is in terms of logical data independence. In general, the more complex they are the more flexible the database. The problem remains as to how complex we want them to be. To illustrate this, consider the three tables of data with reference to the bank example as shown in Figure 2.4.

Consider a database system that only allows the inclusion of whole records from the data model into the submodel for an investment application which requires investment records and their associated customer records. This would be a straightforward mapping of two files into one submodel. However, there is little logical data independence. If either the investment or the customer records change in any way at all, the submodel must also be changed and hence any programs which use them.

Now consider what happens in a database system which allows the investment application to access a submodel containing only the investment account number, the investment closing balance, the customer's name plus the mortgage account number if the paid-off flag equals one. Clearly, this is a fairly complex mapping since it involves selection, testing and comparison of items. Nevertheless, the degree of logical data independence is maximized; the application program will only see what it wants to see and hence only needs changing if one of the four items is changed.

I-ACC-NO	I-CUST-NO	I-OPEN-BAL	I-CLOSE-BAL
1038624	2938	29.42	55.61
2843691	12311	287.61	93.28
2738614	29943	407.94	409.23
2026643	13887	239.42	21.68

INVESTMENT RECORDS

M-ACC-NO	M-CUST-NO	M-BAL	M-ARRS	M-PD-OFF
8294163	1274	15428.63	0.00	0
8382199	2389	23914.21	–38.62	0
8394467	10368	6423.13	26.31	0
8776298	12311	0.00	0.00	1

MORTGAGE RECORDS

CUST-NO	CUST-NAME	CUST-ADDRESS
1274	F.FOWLER	73,LONDON ROAD,BOLTON
2389	S.BROWN	2,CROWTHER ST.,RUGBY
2938	G.PARKER	19,LEWES RD.,HASTINGS
12311	P.FORDE	142,GLEN VIEW,GLASGOW
13887	S.JACKSON	9,TOWER CRESCENT,DEAL
29943	B.WALMSLEY	13,DAVID ST.,CARDIFF

ASSOCIATED CUSTOMER RECORDS

Figure 2.4 *Sets of data relating to the bank example*

Clearly, what we gain in simplicity of run-time operation we lose whenever the database changes. The trade-off between the two is one of the more important aspects of creation of a database system.

Whatever the nature of the mapping, it must be described to, and be available for use by, the DBMS. Thus, whenever an application requests a particular set of data, the DBMS can look to the associated mapping and execute the relevant piece of code.

When and where this *binding* of the DBMS to the access code occurs is a further point to consider.

(1) It is made at application-program run time (in other words, the access code is a part of the DBMS which the application program uses whenever it is run). This approach is expensive in terms of software (the DMBS becomes large through having many embedded access routines which must always be present),

but does allow a good degree of logical data independence because, if the logical data model is changed and affects the submodel, then only the access routines need changing and not the program itself.

(2) The access routines are bound into the application program at compilation time. This means that the access routines and any associated look-up tables need only be present at compilation time, thus saving processor time at program execution time, but any changes to the logical data model now require recompilation of the programs.

The second of these alternatives is the one found in use most commonly.

Logical model to physical model mapping

Again this mapping could be very simple, e.g. putting the whole database on disk A starting at cylinder 4. Alternatively, the mapping could be far more complex.

Consider our investment transactions. They must be readily accessible throughout the current year, but after a year end they are no longer regarded as current data because the account will have been balanced up, capitalized and audited at year end. However, they may be required for reference purposes or for the odd statistical job. There may therefore be a business need to split investment transactions into 'live' and 'historical' data, the former being stored on a fast device for instant access and the latter could be on a much slower device. Likewise, it may be desirable to split the investment record itself into frequently accessed and infrequently accessed portions.

A similar consideration might be that the investment record and its associated current transactions are accessed together so frequently that it may be highly advantageous to store them together on the same area of disk. Note that this is different to the concept in Chapter 1 of storing them together as a single record, but would have the same advantage as being accessible through a single physical I/O.

Clearly, then, the mapping can be quite complex and the degree of complexity will govern both the efficiency of the database and the amount of physical data independence. Again, whatever the nature of the logical model to physical model mapping, it will need to be defined, and be available, to the DBMS. The choice remains as to whether this binding is performed at run time or at compilation time with similar considerations to those outlined in the previous section.

Summary

In this chapter we have defined a general desirable database architecture in terms of its four separate components and have also looked at some of the major functions that we would wish a DBMS to perform. In short these are:

(1) to control and manage the database generally
(2) to be able to comprehend the four languages of its four component parts

- (a) the storage data model definition language (SDDL)
- (b) the logical data model definition language (DDL)
- (c) the logical data submodel definition language(s) [of similar structure to the high-level programming language(s) that it supports]
- (d) the special language (Query) or additions to existing (host) languages (DML)

(3) the ability to interface between the languages outlined above by means of mappings.

Overall, the system will perform in a fashion as shown in Figure 2.5.

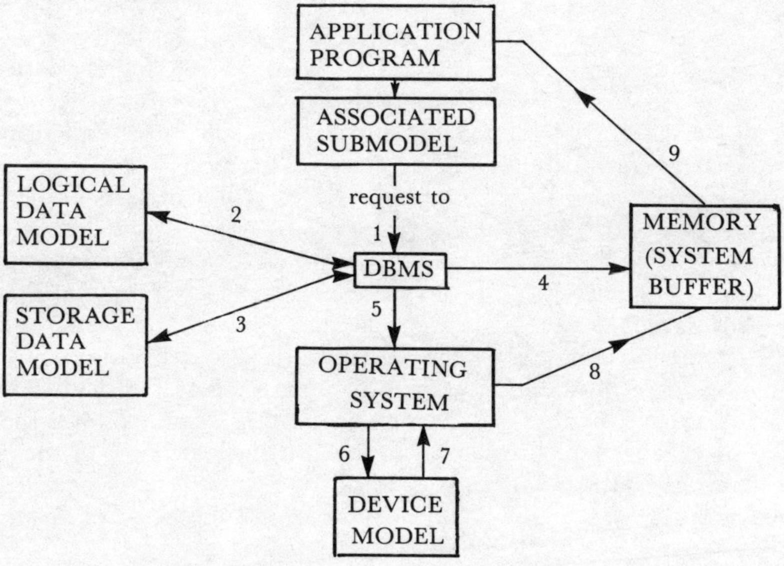

Figure 2.5 *Generalized operation of a database management system*

(1) the application program requests data as described within its own logical data submodel via its DML
(2) the DBMS picks up this request and maps it on to the logical data model
(3) the DBMS checks the mapping between logical data model and storage data model to see how the data are to be accessed
(4) the DBMS can now check whether the required data are extant in the system buffers in main memory. (If they are then we can proceed to 9)
(5) the DBMS passes a request to the operating system for a physical access to the required device on the device model
(6) the operating system goes to the relevant piece of hardware
(7) the data are returned and
(8) are placed in the system buffers in main memory
(9) the data are copied into the application program's work area and become usable by that program.

If, of course, any errors occur at any time along this path then it is another function of the DBMS to report suitable error messages back to the application program.

Having declared what we would like, the actual construction and implementation of a database with as many of the desired features as possible, and the trade-offs that usually occur, are discussed in Part 2 of this book.

Part 2:
Database Administration

CHAPTER 3

Conceptual View: Theory

Introduction

In the last chapter we distinguished the conceptual database (that seen by the user) from the logical database (implementation of the conceptual model). In this chapter and the next we shall look at how the conceptual model is derived. Chapters 5 and 6 describe how it is used to implement a logical and then a physical database.

At the moment it suffices to state that, within an organization, this forms an essential part of the work carried out by *database administration* and it will be left until Chapter 12 before we look at who they are and an overview of their complete functional role.

Database analysis vs systems analysis

It is essential to note that whereas systems analysis traditionally deals with a particular functional area of a business (e.g. investments or mortgages) database analysis must involve the study of the global requirements of the organization covering all applications but from a non-application's viewpoint. This is simply because any areas or items omitted (either accidentally or deliberately) at this early stage will, in general, be difficult to include later. For this reason alone the database-analysis stage forms the most important part of the creation of a database. A simple analogy would be the construction of a pyramid. If every brick is not put in place carefully at the ground level then there is a danger of the entire structure crumbling later. Thus, of the total time available between the decision to have a database and the running of a live version, some 70-80 per cent should be spent on the analysis stage (and most of the rest on testing). The theory here is identical with that of the writing of a program: if little thought is given to the planning out and analysis of a problem, a far greater time is needed to implement and maintain the finished product.

Traditional systems analysis

In the normal situation the systems analyst will go to the relevant users and extract as much information as possible from them on their requirements for:

(1) data
(2) access types
(3) frequency of access
(4) security
(5) output (reports, etc.)
(6) data sources.

From this information the analyst can produce eventually a systems definition: a report with the system overview gathered together and summarized. If this is acceptable to the user, and is feasible as a cost-effective system, then the files can be designed and the various program specifications produced, the programs written and tested, and, finally, the systems tested (Figure 3.1).

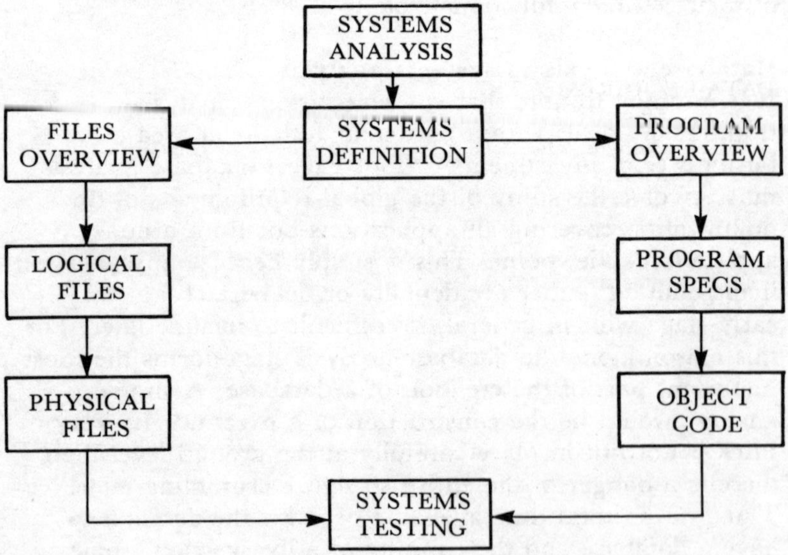

Figure 3.1 *Work involved with systems analysis*

Here the systems definition can be broken down into the following four areas.

INPUTS TO THE SYSTEM

(1) Origin of the inputs (e.g. counter, personnel office).
(2) Layout of the items on the input document/screen.
(3) Contents of each input in terms of the size, type and length of the individual data items.
(4) Relationship between an input and any other input or set of inputs, e.g. whether it is the first part of a multistage input: an 'open a new account' input would be related to a 'transaction for that account' input.
(5) Timing of the input. When does it occur? When is it most likely to occur? Are there peak periods?
(6) Volume of the input. How many per given time period?

OUTPUTS FROM THE SYSTEM

(1) Destination of the outputs. Who wants to see the output?
(2) Security. Who is allowed to see the output?
(3) Layout of the items on the print-out/screen.
(4) Contents of each output in terms of the size, type and length of the individual data items included in it.
(5) Timing of the response. When is the printout required? Is it regular or a one-off report? What are critical response times for screened outputs?
(6) Are any other outputs related? (e.g. the payslips and the wage analysis, etc.).

DATA REQUIREMENTS

(1) Combination of the input data and output data with any intermediate items (which are perhaps only input once or occasionally such as interest rates); in other words, the total sum of data items needed for processing.
(2) Natural groupings of these items; these will often come directly from the system inputs, although sometimes several inputs will be required to make up a single grouping.
(3) Key data items within these groupings that can be used to identify the grouping uniquely (e.g. account number or customer name and address).
(4) Type, size, length, range, origin and units for each data item.

PROCESS REQUIREMENTS

(1) Inputs, outputs and data items required by each process.
(2) Timing of the process. Must they be run within certain timescales? Are they instigated by other processes? How are they related to other processes?
(3) What does the process set out to do?

The work of the systems analyst has been detailed because also it is an integral part of the function of the database analyst. However, again it must be stressed that this involves covering the four areas just mentioned not simply for a particular application, but for the organization as a whole.

The outcome of this seemingly herculean task should be:

(1) a set of all the processes carried out by the organization and their frequency
(2) a set of *conceptual records* (or groupings of data of the same type)
(3) a set of data items making up each conceptual record with any associated key items
(4) a set of relationships between various conceptual records.

These together will form some kind of primitive conceptual database model.

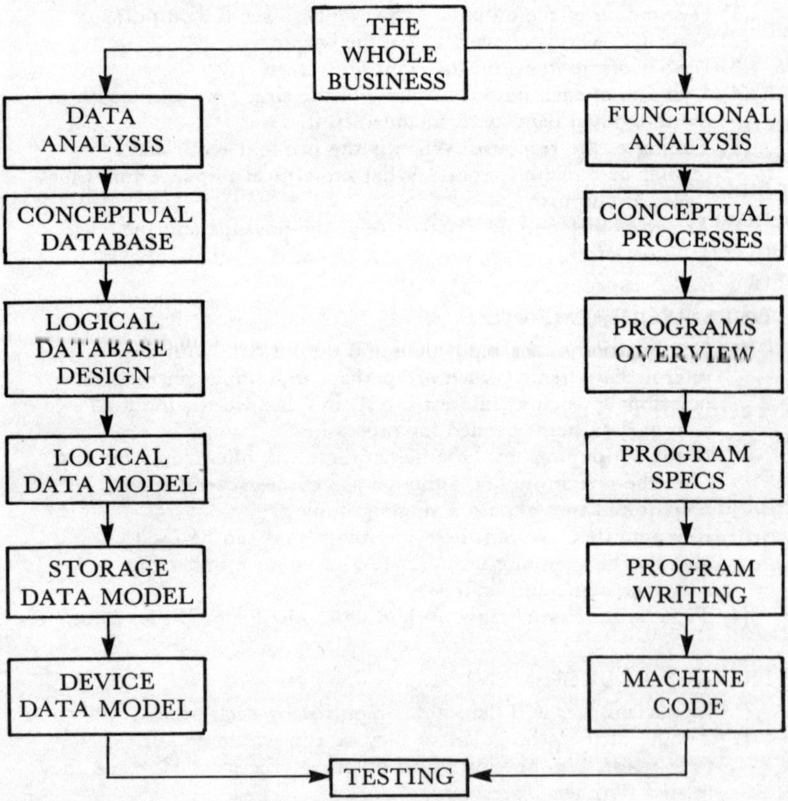

Figure 3.2 *Steps in the creation of a database*

Also, we can give now a preliminary diagrammatic representation of the construction of a database (Figure 3.2). Some of the terms have not been defined yet but it is of interest to compare it with the diagram shown in Figure 3.1. *Note*: *testing* in the diagram is only equivalent to the system testing of Figure 3.1 if we define the whole thing, i.e. the database plus application programs to be the system.

The natural groupings arrived at in our conceptual model will be used eventually to create conceptual files and records. As will be seen later some of the processes may fall also into natural groupings and these eventually will form the basis of a *conceptual process model* from which should emerge a programs' overview and individual program specifications.

Thus, as with the traditional systems analysis model, we have two distinct paths in the overall design being developed in parallel. Eventually, when we arrive on both paths at the physical machine implementation, the two will merge to form one complete system. This is certainly not to say that the two arms of the diagram (Figure 3.2) are completely distinct; throughout the development there must be a very close linkage between the two to ensure convergence rather than divergence and, in particular, between the logical database design and the program overview stages (i.e. at the assignment of logical data submodels to the various applications).

Creation of the conceptual model

As stated previously, the conceptual model is the end product of the data analysis and consists of an implementation free global view of the organization's data requirements. The term implementation free implies that the data analysis can be performed before the computer is chosen and purchased in theory. Such a view should be jargon free and understandable to any non-computer-specialist member of the organization.

To perform data analysis correctly all areas of the organization should be studied even if they will obviously never be computerized, the reason being that only after such a study can the analyst be sure that all complexities of interdepartmental data and function relationships have been considered.

By the conclusion then there will be three clear options for each piece of data:

(1) to keep it as part of a (possibly already existing) manual system
(2) to implement it as part of a conventional file (as often happens with workfiles and other transient data which are not suitable for inclusion in a database)
(3) to implement it as part of a database system.

The most commonly accepted method of constructing a conceptual model lies in the use of *entities*, *attributes* and *relationships*, each of which is defined and explained here separately.

An entity

An entity is an object or concept that is meaningful in itself to the organization and about which there is a need to record information, e.g. investment, mortgage, insurance, branch. Diagrammatically, these can be represented in a variety of ways, the usual being a box:

MORTGAGE

When the data-analysis stage is complete, there should exist a list of all possible entities. Each should be documented with regard to:

(1) an organization-orientated description of what the entity actually is
(2) any pseudonyms for the entity, e.g. CUSTOMER = ACCOUNT OWNER
(3) names of the data items (or *attributes* as defined below) which make up the entity
(4) any attributes which identify the entity uniquely (which will act as keys)
(5) approximate number of occurrences of the entity, e.g. 100 000 mortgages
(6) growth rate of the number of occurrences, i.e. is it constant? is it varying by a constant percentage? exponentially? does the number fluctuate widely over a given period of time?
(7) people within the organization who are concerned with the entity; who is allowed to read it, update, create or delete it?

It is usual for the database analyst to have a purpose-designed form for documentation. One for entities might appear as shown in Figure 3.3.

ENTITY NAME – Insurance PSEUDONYMS – None
OCCURRENCES – 175 000

READ ACCESS RIGHTS – Insurance and mortgage personnel
UPDATE ACCESS RIGHTS – Insurance personnel
CREATE ACCESS RIGHTS – Insurance manager
DELETE ACCESS RIGHTS – Ditto

KEY ATTRIBUTES – mortgage account number + insurance type
OTHER ATTRIBUTES – Insurance company code, company name and address, amount of cover, monthly repayment, etc.

Figure 3.3 *Example form for maintenance of entity information*

An attribute

An attribute is a subset of an entity which is meaningful to an organization in its own right and about which there is a need to store information.
[*Note*: at this stage it is sufficient to show the customer's address as a single attribute rather than line 1, line 2 and line 3. However, it may be of significance to the organization to maintain the address code as a separate attribute (for postal rebates). Only at design stage will the address itself be broken down into constituent parts and, similarly, only then will it be assigned a computerized data name (e.g. CUST-ADD). Until then it will be the customer's address.]

The information that needs to be recorded for each attribute is:

(1) an organization-orientated description of the attribute
(2) pseudonyms by which the attribute is otherwise known (to the business) e.g. investment customer number = mortgage customer number
(3) entities in which the attribute lies (we are not restricted to one entity per attribute at this stage; indeed, it would be most unlikely for all attributes to be associated with a single entity uniquely)
(4) source of the attribute, e.g. where within the organization is the customer number generated?
(5) format of the attribute, i.e. its size, type and length
(6) any range of values and units for the attribute
(7) people within the organization who are allowed to access the attribute subdivided into those who can read, update, create or delete it.

Again a special form is useful for the documentation of this information. That shown in Figure 3.4 is an example.

ATTRIBUTE – Insurance type PSEUDONYMS – None
ENTITIES – Insurance, mortgage

READ ACCESS RIGHTS – Insurance and mortgage personnel
UPDATE ACCESS RIGHTS – Never updated once created
CREATE ACCESS RIGHTS – Insurance personnel
DELETE ACCESS RIGHTS – Insurance personnel

SOURCE – Customer requesting buildings, contents or all risks cover
ALPHA/NUMERIC – Numeric LENGTH – 1
RANGE OF VALUES – 1, 2 or 3 UNITS – None

Figure 3.4 *Example form for maintenance of attribute information*

(*Note*: many of the names on this form have been shortened because of the width of the page. This is not the norm in practice; all names and identifiers should be understandable to anyone not involved in the data-analysis process.)

As can be imagined, for large organizations there might, easily, be upwards of a thousand separate attributes discovered in the data-analysis exercise. This represents quite a lot of paper! Sometimes it is desirable therefore to combine the forms for entity and attribute documentation, giving something similar to that shown in Figure 3.5.

ENTITY NAME – Insurance PSEUDONYMS – None
OCCURRENCES – 175 000
KEYS – Mortgage account number + insurance type

ATTRIBUTE	LENGTH	RANGE	ACCESS RIGHTS			
PSEUDONYMS	TYPE	UNITS	READ	UPDATE	CREATE	DELETE
Acc. number	10	–				
none	num.	–	I&M	–	M	M
Ins.type	1	1 2 3				
none	num.	–	I&M	–	I	I
Co. code	4	–				
none	num.	–	I	–	I	I

Figure 3.5 *Single form for entities and attributes*

If this approach is used then two important points must be noted:

(1) There is now no single list of all the entities to which an attribute belongs. This would have to be created, if required, by searching through each entity chart manually. This in itself may cause problems at the design stage.
(2) This approach assumes that the access rights for the entity is the sum of the access rights to all of the constituent attributes. This may be the case, but exceptions are possible, such as a cashier in a branch finds that the customer's account on the computer does not match up with their passbook. Suppose that there exists an entity of outstanding transactions (i.e. those which have not been processed yet against the accounts for one reason or another). All the cashier wants to know is whether the customer has an outstanding transaction to account for the discrepancy. They therefore need access rights for the existence of the entity outstanding transaction without needing to look at its constituent attributes. Such an access right would not show up on the above form.

A relationship

A relationship is an association between entities that is meaningful to the organization and about which there is a need to maintain information, e.g. an investment account has many transactions. Before defining what information needs recording about relationships, we really need to look at all the various possible types and show how they are diagrammatically represented normally.

ONE TO ONE
Entities are related one to one if a single occurrence of one is associated with a single occurrence of the other, e.g.

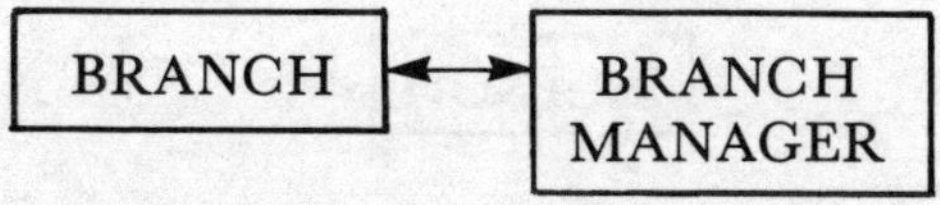

One branch has a single branch manager and each branch manager is manager of a single branch.

ONE TO MANY
An example should suffice:

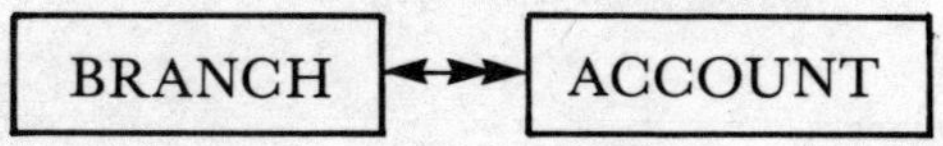

One branch has many associated accounts (hence the double arrow at the account end of the connecting line), whereas each account is associated solely with a single branch.

(*Note*: *account* is singular, the plurality being shown by the double arrow.)

MANY TO ONE
The reverse of the above. The accounts are related to the branch at a many-to-one level:

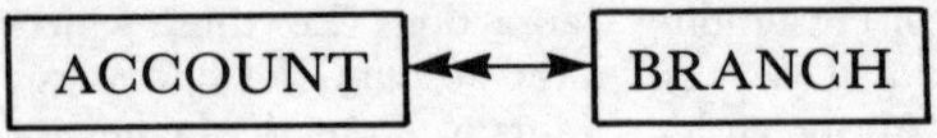

MANY TO MANY

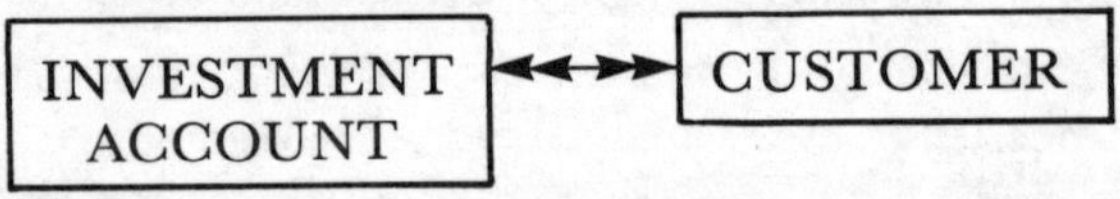

An investment account can be owned by many (up to four in our example) customers. Each customer can own many accounts.

Notes:

(1) The relationships may not necessarily be between distinct entities. For example, an area branch office might itself be a branch which supervises other branches in the area, but each sub-branch would only be supervised by a single area branch office.

Note that for clarification it is always permissible to write the name of the relationship along the connecting line.

(2) Many of the relationships at the data analysis stage are generalizations to avoid confusion. For example, it might be that one particular branch manager manages two branches because the other manager has just left/is on a course, etc. In most cases such temporary relationships, if they occur frequently, can be shown by the methods described overleaf.

EXISTENCE

A relationship may be mandatory, contingent or optional. The difference between them is shown below.

MANDATORY

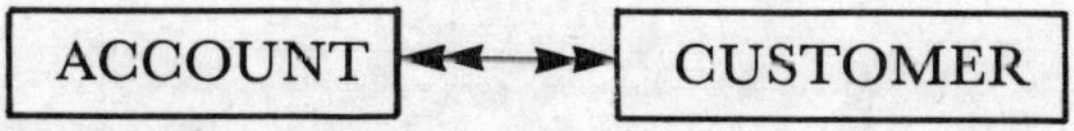

An account must be owned by at least one customer. A customer must own an account (be it mortgage or investment), otherwise he/she would not be a customer!

CONTINGENT

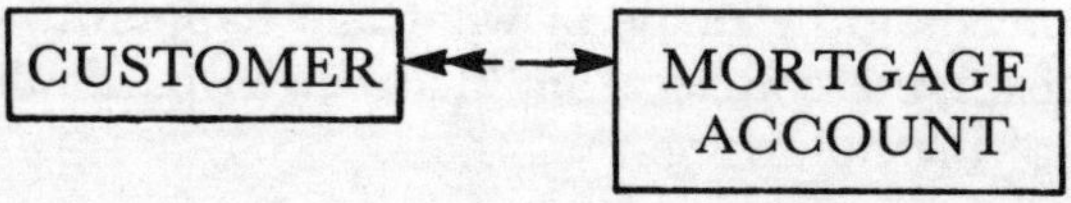

The mortgage account must be owned by a customer, but a customer need not necessarily have a mortgage account.

OPTIONAL

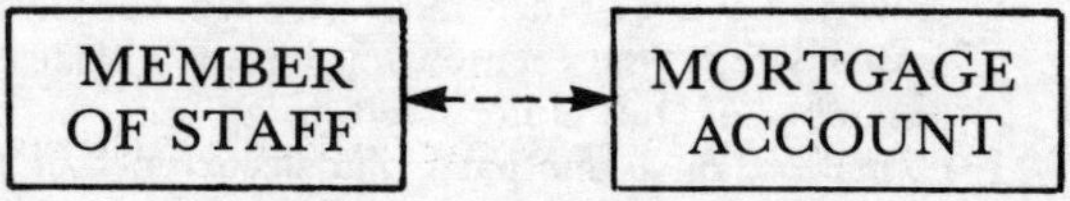

A member of staff may have a mortgage account and a mortgage account may be owned by a member of staff.

EXCLUSIVITY

One type of relationship may exclude another:

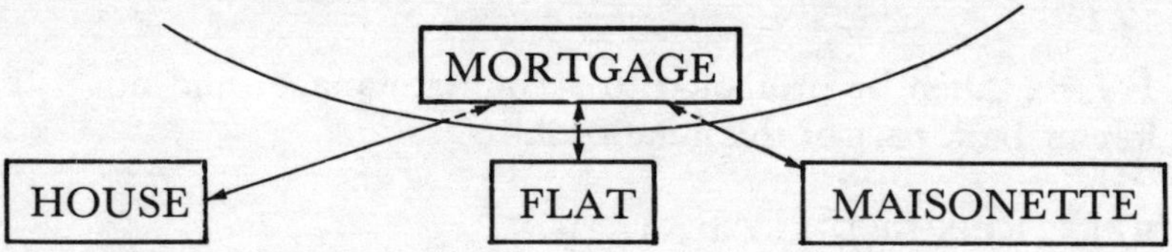

i.e. the mortgage will relate to a house, flat or maisonette, but only one of the three.

INCLUSIVITY

One relationship may imply another:

You cannot obtain a mortgage without also obtaining a buildings insurance policy.

PERMANENCE

This defines how long a relationship might last, though it is not, generally, shown diagrammatically. Also consideration needs to be made of what can happen to the relationship over the course of its lifetime. In particular it may be one of the following:

(1) *Fixed*: once created it is a permanent relationship, e.g. between an account and its transactions.
(2) *Transferable*: once the relationship is created then an occurrence of that relationship must always exist between the entities, but not necessarily the original relationship, e.g. a branch should always have a branch manager, but not always the same one. In other words, the relationship between branch and a particular member of staff is not fixed.
(3) *Transient*: once one particular occurrence of the relationship has been created then one (or both) of the entities can be removed from all occurrences of the relationship permanently, e.g. a member of staff may be a branch manager.

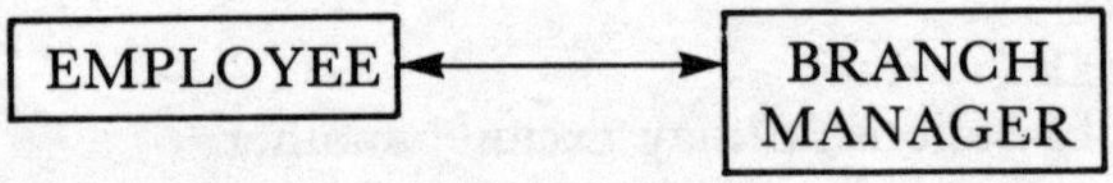

He may then be promoted to accounts manager and no longer be a part of this relationship.

RELATIONSHIP DOCUMENTATION

The various types of relationship defined, we can now look at the documentation requirements.

(1) An organization-orientated description of the relationship.
(2) Entities joined by the relationship.
(3) Type of relationship as defined above.
(4) People within the organization who are allowed to access the relationship subdivided into those who can read, update, create

and delete it. There is an important point to note here. Often less importance is given to privacy on relationships at the design stage in the false belief that the securing of the entities at each end of the relationship is sufficient. However, consider the following:

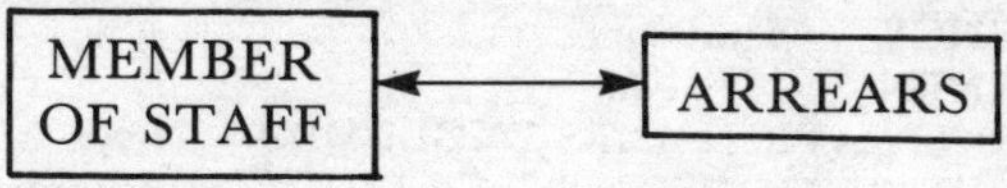

Access to the arrears entity might be fairly commonplace and everyone will know the members of staff, but knowledge of a relationship between them (i.e. that a member of staff is in arrears) may well be a very restricted piece of information.

(5) Number of occurrences of a relationship. Rather than just saying one-to-many, an actual or predicted value may be useful.

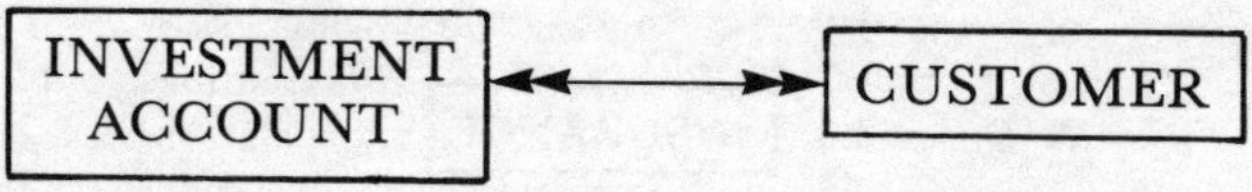

An investment account may be owned by a maximum of four customers. The number of accounts that a customer may have is more indeterminate.

As before a special form on which to record this information is desirable. An example might be as that shown in Figure 3.6.

Data model diagrams

These reams of paper concerning the entities, attributes and relationships written out, it would be useful to be able to show on a diagram all the interconnections. To show all attribute connections would make the diagram very complex indeed, but it is quite normal to show all entities and relationships using a *Bachman diagram* (named after C.W.Bachman who was a leading person in the CODASYL developments). Such a diagram is especially useful because it gives a global picture of the organization (i.e. the conceptual model) revealing all the interrelations between people and departments and functions.

A very simplified Bachman diagram for our bank might appear similar to that as shown in Figure 3.7. (A truer representation would fill many pages.)

DESCRIPTION OF RELATIONSHIP – a mortgage owns transactions
NO. OF OCCURRENCES – 100 000 (every account has transactions)

ENTITIES JOINED – Mortgage and mortgage transaction
DEGREE – One to many (1 – 14 on average)
EXISTENCE – Mandatory
PERMANENCE – Fixed
OTHER RELATIONSHIPS EXCLUDED – None
OTHER RELATIONSHIPS IMPLIED – An insurance record (one of the transactions will be a buildings insurance payment).

READ ACCESS RIGHTS – Mortgage and insurance personnel
UPDATE ACCESS RIGHTS – Mortgage and insurance personnel
CREATE ACCESS RIGHTS – Mortgage and insurance personnel
DELETE ACCESS RIGHTS – Mortgage manager

Figure 3.6 *Example form for maintenance of relationship information*

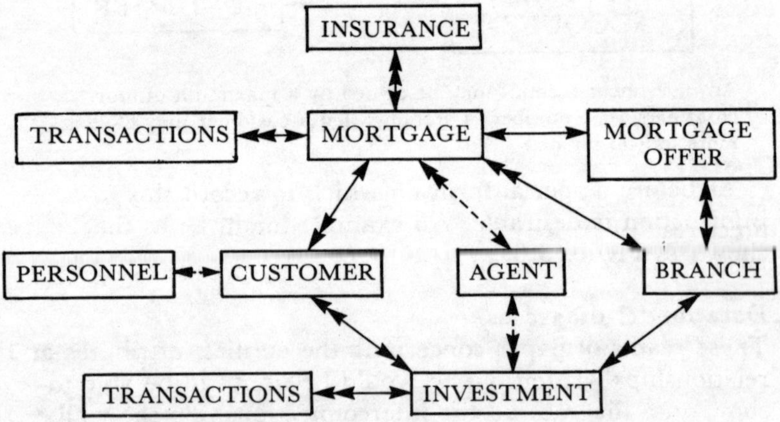

Figure 3.7 *Entity/relationship (Bachman) diagram*

The points of note to be mentioned here are that a data model diagram will nearly always end up as highly debatable. For example, in Figure 3.7 should the customer be connected to the insurance record? The agent? The branch? Should the mortgage-offer entity be shown as it cannot exist at the same time as the mortgage record?

Suffice it to say that the data model diagram is not the ultimate goal of data analysis; it is merely a diagrammatic representation that can show the relations between entities and which may be useful as a tool at the design stage. However, they can show useful features at the global level. For example, in Figure 3.7 the personnel entity is barely related to the rest of the model (and only by the fact that some customers will be members of staff). It looks therefore a reasonable candidate for being implemented as a separate database.

Functional analysis

We have now looked at the tools needed to perform the data-analysis side of the model shown in Figure 3.2, but what of the other side which is equally as important?

Functional analysis is the study of how a particular area of an organization performs or functions. To do this the organization is split into obvious functional areas, e.g. investment department, mortgage department, personnel, etc., and then each is analysed in terms of what functions it performs. First, again, we must define appropriate tools for the job.

Operations and events

An operation is defined as a task that is performed as a direct result of an event. An event is defined as that which triggers off an operation. If this does not sound altogether clear then a few examples should clarify matters.

(1) *Event*: a customer comes in to open an account.
Operation: process of opening an account is initiated.
(2) *Event*: message is received by the computer from a terminal.
Operation: message is processed.

In fact we can take the definitions further by declaring:

(1) operations can cause events
(2) operations can often be broken down into simpler operations
(3) operations can imply other operations.

As with the data-analysis methodology, when the functional analysis is performed, documentation needs to be maintained for both events:

(1) what causes the event to happen? (though it may be totally random)

(2) when does the event happen?
(3) what operations follow the event?
(4) which people are involved with the events? (security is again involved here because only certain people may be allowed to cause events, such as the request of a payroll analysis).

And operations:

(1) which event(s) causes the operation to happen?
(2) what does the operation actually achieve?
(3) what data are involved? (an important tie with the data analysis)
(4) are any other operations triggered off by the operation?
(5) can the operation be broken down into suboperations meaningfully?
(6) which people are involved with the operation?

By taking the opening of an investment account as an example, here are some possible answers to the aforementioned questions.

EVENTS

(1) Customer wishes to invest some money.
(2) Any time during opening hours.
(3) Operation initiated is the 'opening of an account'.
(4) Customer and a cashier on a till usually (though many other possibilities exist and all should be listed, e.g. an agency, a letter and a cheque, etc.).

OPERATIONS

(1) Customer asking for an account to be opened.
(2) Placing of a new account on the investment file. The posting of a first transaction to that account.
(3) Branch name, account number, opening data, initial receipt, customer name and address, account type, single or joint account, interest rate, etc.
(4) No, but see (6) following.
(5) No.
(6) The operation might be split down into the following:
 (a) a receipt form is filled out
 (b) a new account number is obtained/generated
 (c) investment department of the new account is informed
 (d) possibly a new customer record is generated if the customer is new to the bank
 (e) a new passbook is issued.
(7) People involved might be:
 (a) the cashier

(b) whoever issues the passbooks/account numbers
(c) investment department
(d) customer in as much as he/she will supply the necessary information.

Further examples of this process are given in Chapter 4.

Summary

Work of the data analyst has been likened in this chapter to that of the systems analyst, except that it is on a grander scale. Rather than a single area of the business being studied, all areas must be looked at: any omissions causing serious difficulties if they require insertion at a later stage.

From this global interpretation of the business, the data analyst will fill a set of forms relating to the constituent entities, attributes and relationships of the organization, from which he/she will hope to derive a conceptual data model including a data model diagram. From these, in turn, they will pass on to the database design stages and the eventual implementation of the database. In theory, the data analysis has seemed a relatively straightforward if somewhat long-winded exercise, but the next chapter will show that this assumption is correct only on the second point and that the process of data analysis is far from straightforward and must, ultimately be a 'patched together' analysis of all the business areas, rather than a true global overview.

CHAPTER 4

Conceptual View: Practice

Introduction

In the last chapter the theory of both data and functional analysis was looked at. In this chapter we see whether or not the theory can be put into practice.

Problems with data analysis

In Chapter 3 it was stated that data analysis should be performed at the global or organizational level, which implies a huge one-off exercise. Indeed, it should be a one-off exercise which does not have to be repeated even if a conventional file approach is later changed to become a database system, or any other major upheaval, and certainly not for minor changes such as updating the database level from, say, CODASYL 73 to CODASYL 78. The reasons for this are as stated previously: that the global conceptual model is implementation free (a change to the computer environment should not change the way that the business is run).

Unfortunately, it is difficult to see where such a global view of the organization might come from. In practice, all the data analyst can ever hope to do is visit all the user departments, extract all the information he needs and then consolidate the sum into a single global view. In other words, it is difficult to arrive at an implementation-free non-application-orientated view when it must itself be composed of a number of implemented application-orientated views.

Secondly, it was stated in the last chapter that the decision as to whether to implement as manual files, conventional files or database files should be taken at the design stage. However, the decision to perform a data-analysis exercise is taken normally before a database system is implemented, and therefore there will exist a certain bias toward database systems, even if they are not appropriate wholly. In short, it is unlikely that a company will undertake n man-months of data-analysis study, unless it is committed at least partially to a database system to begin with.

A solution

It has been shown that the processes of data and functional analysis are related closely. We cannot define data items sensibly without noting in what processes they will be used. Similarly, we cannot define operations and processes without remarking on which items of data are involved.

Bearing this in mind, we can work on a compromise with respect to the data analysis by collecting the data as we perform the functional analysis (i.e. on a department-to-department basis), thus creating a set of subconceptual models which we can piece together at the end of the exercise (see the Creation of a consolidated conceptual model section in this chapter).

It must be borne in mind, however, that these submodels may not form simple subsets of the full conceptual model that we require. In short:

(1) entities in the full model may only be attributes in the submodel; for example, in the customer system, the entities of investment and mortgage may only be represented by their respective account numbers
(2) relationships in the full model may be entities in a submodel; for example, a relationship in the full model, that a set of customers own an investment account (shown as a many-to-many relationship), might be shown in the investment department as an entity containing 'the set of owners'
(3) the degree and nature of any relationships in the full model might be different in a submodel, for example, in the global data model a mortgage might be shown as having a one-to-many relationship with insurances (i.e. a mortgage might have a buildings insurance, a contents insurance, an all-risks insurance, etc.), but to a buildings insurance department the relationship would be one to one because they would not be interested in the other types
(4) attributes of entities in the full model may be described as attributes of different entities in the submodels; for example, to the mortgage department, the customer name and address might well be included in the mortgage entity, but in the global model

it would be more advantageous to have them in a separate customer entity accessible by all departments.

This process of performing data analysis at a functional level, though not theoretically correct, is helpful especially at the design stage because the resulting data submodels will, eventually, become our logical database submodels.

Sources for analysis

Before looking to the practical side of performing data and functional analysis, we can define some general areas from which information can be gleaned in the general exercise:

(1) existing input documents, e.g. receipt slips, withdrawal slips, etc.
(2) existing output documents, e.g. reports, balance sheets, etc.
(3) existing computer files (if there are any)
(4) existing manual files
(5) existing computer programs (very useful for process definitions)
(6) job descriptions (who does what, where and when)
(7) by talking to all relevant members of staff in the functional areas and not just the management.

Normalization

So far the process of data analysis might seem a fairly arduous but straightforward process of visiting user departments one by one and extracting all useful information from the sources listed in the previous section. Unfortunately, as it stands we have no way of knowing whether the entities arranged intuitively by natural grouping are good entities in as much as they will map nicely into compact, efficient data structures which display none of the problems outlined in Chapter 1 (e.g. data duplication, redundancy, etc.).

Once the database has been designed and is being implemented it will become progressively harder for any changes to be made at the root level. The data analyst needs some sort of tool for measuring the quality of his conceptual model before proceeding further. Such a tool is *normalization*, a process that owes much to the work of E.F.Codd on relational databases, but which is suitable for most other database system types also.

The following definitions of the various normal forms may seem meaningless if stated simply, therefore a worked example has been included for clarity.

Supposing that we have a group of attributes grouped together intuitively to form a mortgage entity, these attributes being:

Account number
Customer name
Customer address
Amount borrowed
Amount outstanding
Supervising branch code
Supervising branch name
Account type (monthly repayment, weekly, etc.)
Type of mortgage (repayment, endowment, etc.)
Interest rate
Insurance type 1 (buildings, contents, all risks)
Insurance company code 1
Insurance company details 1
Insurance details 1
Insurance type 2 (as above)
Insurance company code 2
Insurance company details 2
Insurance details 2

This may be a full list of all attributes which the mortgage department wants with regard to a mortgage. It would seem natural enough to group it all in a single entity, but problems of data duplication may not be obvious until the database is implemented, and that may be too late. (Note that this simplified single-application view is reminiscent of many existing conventional file approaches.)

Unique identifier

The first rule of normalization is that the entity should have an attribute or set of attributes which identify an occurrence of the entity uniquely, such that no attribute can be removed from the key without the key losing its uniqueness. In other words, the key should be the minimum set of attributes which identifies an occurrence of the entity uniquely.

This is not such a strange idea because all non-computerized files and records will have such a key. In the mortgage example both the account number and a combination of customer's name and address would form unique identifiers for a mortgage record so we have two possibilities. What this rule says is that there should be at least one and that it is not worth having a composite key of all three because it would not contain the minimum number of attributes.

Functional dependence

An attribute of an entity is functionally dependent on a second attribute if and only if each occurrence of the first attribute has associated with it exactly one occurrence of the second.

First normal form

An entity is in first normal form if and only if the attributes which are not a part of the key are functionally dependent on the key. What this means is that there must be no repeating groups within the entity, because that would contradict functional dependence. Hence in our example, insurance details should not belong in the mortgage entity because they repeat, and should therefore be removed to form a separate entity. To do this we must bear in mind that the new entity must also have a unique identifying key (Figure 4.1).

Here we must note that both the insurance type and company code are needed to identify uniquely the insurance entity because each insurance company will, no doubt, offer several types of insurance. Also, it is apparent that the insurance company details are not functionally dependent on the whole of the insurance key, only on the company code. This leads to the second set of definitions.

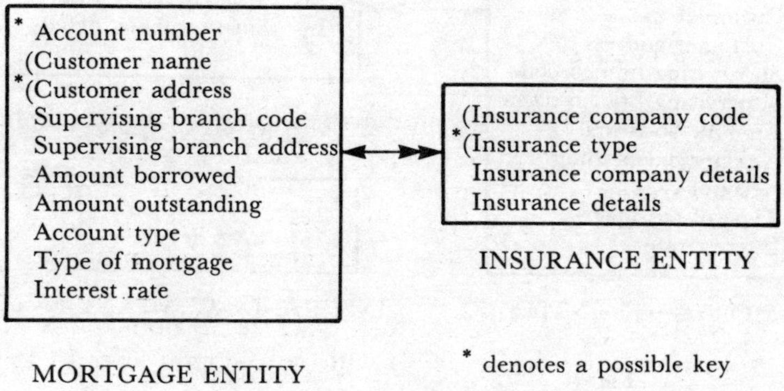

Figure 4.1 *Mortgage data in first normal form*

Full functional dependence

An attribute is fully functionally dependent on a second attribute if and only if it is functionally dependent on the second attribute but not on any subset of the second attribute.

Second normal form

An entity is in second normal form if, and only if, it is in first normal form and every non-key attribute is fully functionally dependent on the identifying key. Clearly, this is not the case with the insurance entity which therefore needs to be separated further (Figure 4.2).

Note the possible key item of customer name and address has been removed from this diagram. This is because, for the sake of clarity, it is easier to represent only a single key at the moment and, in addition, the account number key is shorter and more meaningful to the business. However, other 'candidate' keys will not be forgotten but will be looked at later.

We have now removed some of the data-duplication problems by having only the insurance company details held once. Inspection of the mortgage entity, however, reveals that the customer name and address may well be stored elsewhere (if they own an investment account) and the supervising branch name certainly will be. Such problems are removed by our third set of definitions.

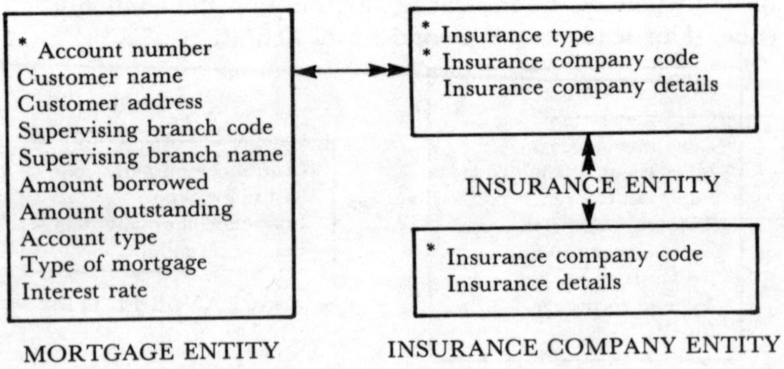

Figure 4.2 *Mortgage data in second normal form*

Transitive dependence

For three distinct attributes, if attribute 3 is functionally dependent on attribute 2 and attribute 2 is functionally dependent on attribute 1, then attribute 3 is transitively dependent on attribute 1 if, and only if, attribute 1 is neither functionally dependent on attribute 2 nor on attribute 3.

This may sound very confusing even after a couple of reads but relating it to the example it means that the branch name is functionally dependent on the branch code, the branch code is functionally dependent on the account number but that the account number is not functionally dependent on the branch code or the name; similarly, the customer name and address.

Third normal form

An entity is in third normal form if it is in second normal form and every attribute that is not a part of the key is non-transitively dependent on the identifying key. Since an entity in third normal form must, by definition, also be in first and second normal forms, we can define a third normal form in terms of the conditions that the entity must have:

(1) a unique identifying key
(2) no repeating attributes
(3) no attributes that do not require the whole of the identifying key
(4) attributes that are mutually independent.

Returning to our example, we now have the situation as shown in Figure 4.3.

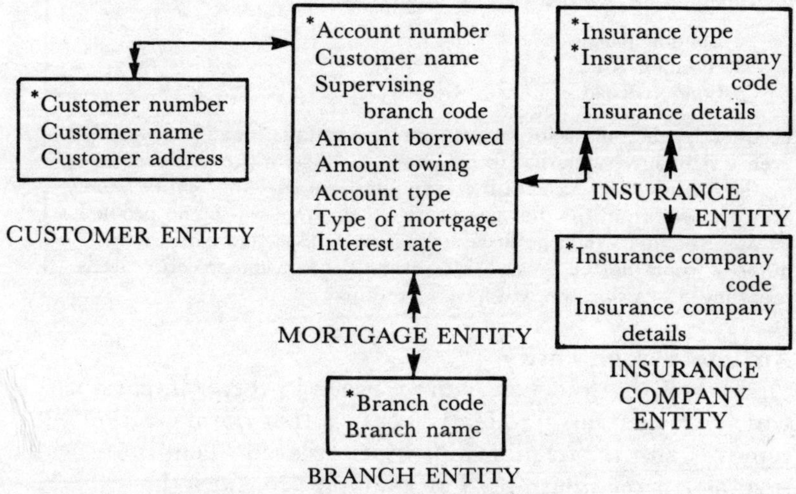

Figure 4.3 *Mortgage data in third normal form*

Notes:

(1) We now have data duplication with the supervising branch code, but it is a controlled redundancy because the item is never likely to change in value and cause problems. Note that there is no provision for storing repeating key links (such as customer number) on the mortgage entity. This is done in the knowledge that the database system will provide the necessary links implicitly. However, the 'bulkier' items such as the customer name and address, branch name, insurance details and insurance company details are now only in one place instead of on every account so certainly we have reduced our storage capacity needs in comparison with the initial entity before normalization.

(2) At this final stage we have had to invent a customer number. Unless there is already in existence a customer number unfortunately this will be meaningless to the business and the customer, but short of concatenating the name and address it is the only way of identifying a customer uniquely (in fact even the name and address combined may not be unique if there is a father and son of the same forename living in the same house and both with accounts).

This problem of unique identifiers is common on any computer-based system. People's names are not guaranteed unique even in a small business. In general, any long alphanumeric items will not make good keys simply because when entered, the keying in must be exact. For example, if the address is the key and is stored as

5, London Road

then none of the following will find the record:

5 London Road
5, London Rd
5,London Road.

Frequently, the only solution is to create a unique identifying number even if it is purely internal to the computer system (i.e. is never used by the business as such). In the example if the customer entity is only ever accessed from the mortgage entity then there will be no problems because the link would be provided by the DBMS and a customer number would not be needed. However, if the customer entity needs accessing direct then we will have to rethink.

An intersection entity

One result that did not actually occur in the example but which, in general, frequently does, is that normalization removes all m:n relationships by translating them into several 1:n relationships. For example, consider the investment system. If we normalized this in a similar fashion we would end up with the following scheme as shown in Figure 4.4 (in basic form).

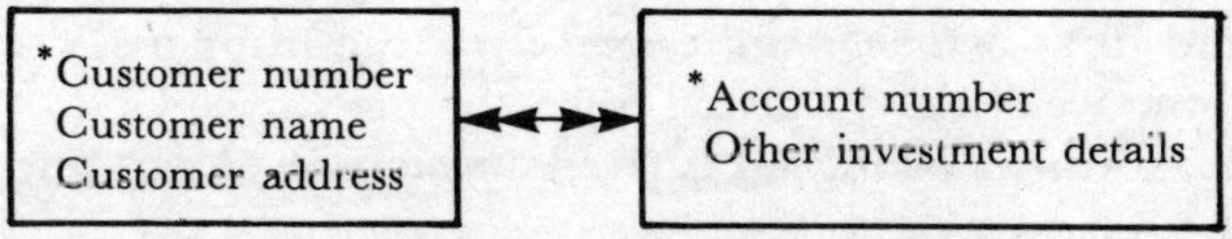

Figure 4.4 *m:n relationship after normalization*

Clearly, an investment account can have more than one customer, and a customer can have more than one investment account so we have an m:n relationship.

In this situation we must use what is known as an *intersection entity*. This is, in practice, a bridging entity placed between two existing entities to circumvent the m:n relationship.

In the above example we can define an entity called an Account Owners containing the account number plus a customer number plus a number to say whether that customer was the first named on that account (or second or third or fourth: such a numbering does have a business meaning because, in general, only the first named is sent the statement). One account would have up to four associated AO entities but each AO would only relate to a one account. Therefore we have a 1:n relationship. Similarly, a customer can be first named on many accounts (i.e. have many associated AO occurrences), but each AO will relate only to one customer occurrence (Figure 4.5).

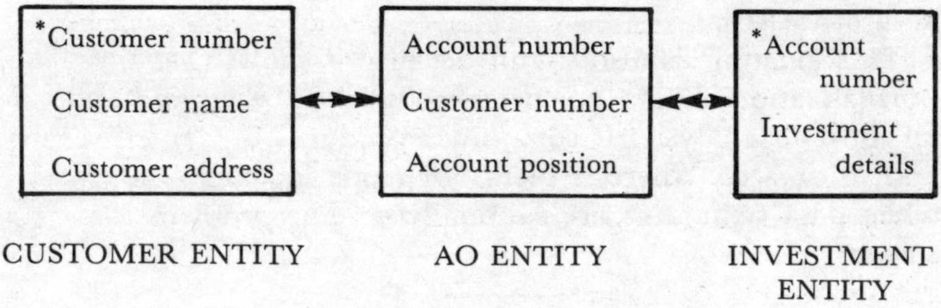

Figure 4.5 *Intersection entity*

A determinant

A determinant is an attribute or set of attributes on which

some other attribute is fully functionally dependent. We can now study another third normal-form definition which does not involve first and second normal forms. It is sometimes referred to as a *strong third normal form* (the prior definition being the weak third normal form) or the Boyce-Codd normal form following an early definition by Boyce and Codd.

A strong third normal form

An entity is in strong third normal form if every determinant is a candidate key. An example should show this to be the case. Suppose now we look at the normalization of the branch entity.

A branch might include:

Branch code
Branch name
Branch address
Manager's name
Regional code
Area branch code
Sub-branch codes
Telephone number
Monthly statistics

Here the region code is a numeric field denoting which region of the country the branch lies in. The area branch code is that of the area office (which is a branch in its own right), and the sub-branch codes are those of any branches controlled by the branch in question (i.e. if it is itself an area office).

This example is also useful because it shows that normalization should not be taken as the 'be all and end all' of data analysis. It sometimes produces unwanted results and, ultimately, there is plenty of scope for common sense when data structures are rationalized. The problem is shown as:

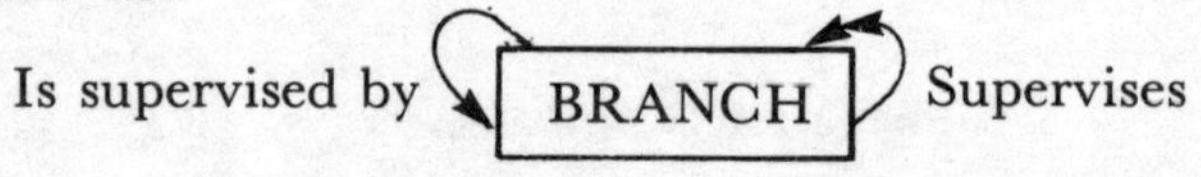

The entity branch has a relationship with itself because the area offices supervise other branches (a 1:n relationship) whereas sub-branches are supervised by an area office (a n:1 relationship). If we had regional offices that supervised area offices then the situation would be even more complex. Unfortunately, this linking of an occurrence of an entity to other occurrences of the same entity is quite common in the real world.

According to our definition of first normal form, the fields sub-branch codes are a repeating group which should not be a part of the branch entity. However, common sense tells us that from a business viewpoint it makes little sense to create a new entity called *sub-branch*, which contains only the branch code, which in turn links back to the branch entity for the sub-branch details. (However, with certain DBMS formats, the above would be a useful structure to implement as it would provide an index file to the branches. This is not possible with all DBMS implementations so it will not be pursued here.) Here, we can gloss over the problem by declaring the sub-branch codes as sub-branch 1, sub-branch 2 etc. Now they are disjoint attributes and no longer a repeating group.

Disregarding this problem we now try normalization techniques. First, with our definition of a strong third normal form in mind we look for possible keys. These would appear to be:

(1) branch code
(2) branch name
(3) manager's name
(4) telephone number.

Are these the only determinants? To begin with we apply the definition of the first normal form (Figure 4.6).

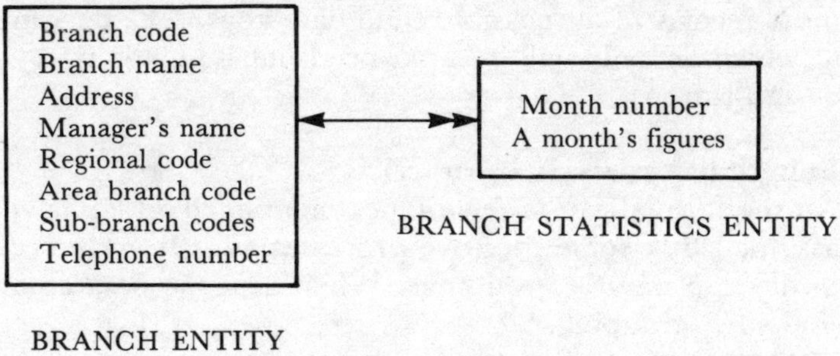

Figure 4.6 *Branch data in first normal form*

There is no need to look to second normal forms because we have no split key. Consider the weak third normal form definition. Is the branch address transitively dependent on the branch code? The answer is no because, although the address is functionally dependent on the name, the code is both functionally dependent on the name and the address (on the assumption that the branch name is unique), there being a 1:1 relationship between each pair.

There is a slightly harder task with the manager's name. Although managers can change branches, at one instant the manager's name will be functionally dependent on the branch code and also the code will be functionally dependent on the manager's name. In other words, given a manager's name we can identify the correct branch. (Clearly, this assumes the manager's name to be unique. If this cannot be guaranteed then it can no longer be considered as a candidate key because it will not identify a single branch uniquely. Again common sense would rule this to be the case coupled with the fact that over a period of time the manager is likely to change, and therefore his name would not make a suitable key.)

Looking at the branch entity therefore we have three determinants: the code, name and phone number. A cursory glance will reveal there to be no further determinants and therefore the branch entity is in strong third normal form. (The case for branch statistics entity being in strong third normal form is trivial.)

One lesson to be learned from this is that in the real world we would not dream of having either the manager's name or the telephone number as the keys to the branch, but if we are to undertake data analysis rigorously then we must recognize all possible candidate keys. The decision as to which actually will be used need not be made until design time.

Functional analysis in practice

All the normalization techniques mentioned so far have assumed that some intuitive processes already have occurred to develop natural groupings. Where can the data analyst find such groupings?

The answer can be found when existing reports and documents are looked at. In these the main nouns will usually be entities and the verbs will be the relationships between them. For example:

A customer owns accounts
A mortgage may be covered by an endowment policy.

As stated previously, functional analysis involves the study of each functional area of the organization and documentation of all the processes that it performs. The processes can be split into events and operations and, by defining the input needs and output needs for each operation, we can derive the data needs for the operation and, by extension over all operations, the data needs of the whole functional area.

An example of this process might be: a customer enters a branch to see the manager about a mortgage application. This is a process that can be split into an event (i.e. the customer coming into the branch) and an operation (i.e. the manager checking through the details with the customer).

The application form is an input document which should provide the data analyst with a wealth of data items (Figure 4.7).

Customer name
Customer address
Customer telephone number
Property address
Type of property (detached, semi, terraced, flat, etc.)
Type of construction (brick, concrete, wood, etc.)
Loan required
Type of mortgage required (repayment, endowment, etc.)
Repayment term
Investment account number
Solicitor's name and address
Estate agent
Vendor's solicitor's name and address
Husband's income
Husband's employers
Wife's income
Wife's employers
Valuation
Valuer's name

Figure 4.7 *Mortgage-offer data*

A fine mass of information! The operation here simply would be to check that the customer has filled in details correctly or to fill them in with the customer's guidance.

Will any other operations and events be initiated by this process once the customer has gone? The following are some likely possibilities.

(1) The manager checks his monthly quota to see if his branch has money to lend to the customer. This involves looking at some entity containing mortgage monthly quota statistics, presumably identified by the month number.

Month number
Monthly quota

(2) He must check the customer's investment record to see if they are regular savers and have enough for the deposit.

Investment account number
Investment current balance

Transaction date
Transaction amounts

(3) He must contact the husband's and/or wife's employers for references and check on their salaries

Employer's name
Employer's address

(4) If all is well he must contact the bank's surveyors and/or valuers to ask them to survey and value the property.

Valuer's name
Date of valuation
Valuation

(5) He will, presumably wish to check some details with the vendor's solicitor (and possibly the customer's also).

Solicitor's name
Solicitor's address
Solicitor's telephone number

(6) Only if all has gone okay can he make a mortgage offer to the customer which if accepted will, eventually, become a mortgage account with its own account number.

Customer's name
Customer's telephone
Mortgage offer number
Mortgage account number

This is a gross simplification but it does show how relatively simple events and operations can initiate others (each with their own data requirements) but, by following the chain of events through, the data analyst can build up a complete picture of the 'mortgage offer' function. By merely analysing the application form the analyst would only see half a picture. All the other detail could only come by a personal interview with a branch/mortgage manager as it is unlikely to be documented.

If the above six processes were complete then we would have a full set of the data requirements for the mortgage offer function. Normalizing this data we should obtain the results of Figure 4.8.

Notes:

(1) It is highly likely that the customer is already known to the business (through an investment account number) and hence the customer number (that unique identifier of the customer entity) can be assigned to the mortgage offer.

(2) Although in practice the mortgage offer will not exist at the same time as the resulting mortgage, it is nevertheless correct and meaningful at the data-analysis stage to associate the mortgage account number with the offer in case the information is later stored for historical purposes.

(3) Again normalization has given us unwelcome results in terms of what we would expect in real life. Because we cannot assume the solicitor's name to be unique and because our third normal-form definition insists that a solicitor's entity be split off because of transitive dependence, we have had to invent a solicitor's ID. The same applies to the husband's/wife's employers.

It may well be the practice of the business to keep a register of all qualified solicitors in the country in which

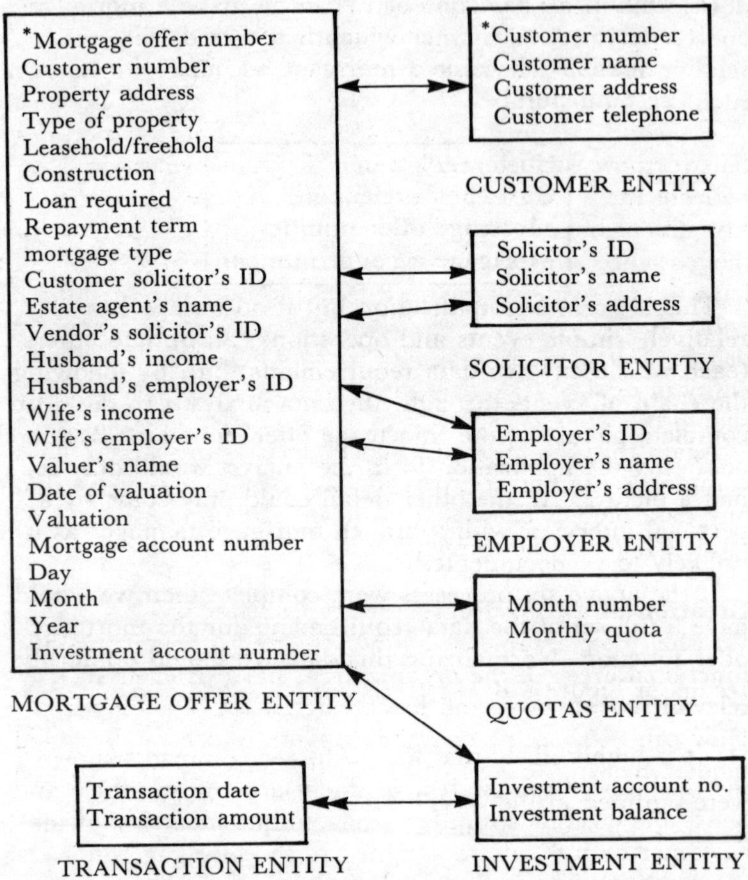

Figure 4.8 *Mortgage-offer data in third normal form*

case assigning them a special identifier may be a meaningful exercise. Alternatively, it may be more meaningful actually to implement the solicitor's name and address as a part of the mortgage offer entity. It would, certainly, be more sensible to store the employer's information on the mortgage offer record; one of the advantages of normalization is that we end up with one fact in one place. However, unless most people living near a particular branch all work for the same employers, there is little to be gained by having the employer details as a separate entity with its corresponding increase in access times.

The moral of this is that these are implementation

decisions which need not concern us here. The role of data analysis primarily is to highlight potential entities and relationships, which may or may not be implemented as such.

A second problem of normalization is that it sometimes fails to show entities at all. If, in the above example, we had not included the process of checking the customer's investment balance, perhaps changing it to merely checking the existence of an investment record, then as we would only have the investment account number in the mortgate offer entity and no repeating groups or transitive dependencies, no degree of normalization will ever show investments to be an entity in its own right even though, intuitively, we know it should be.

Again this demonstrates that there is always room for common sense and intuition during data analysis and that any data models derived from it are not necessarily the data models that will be implemented.

Creation of a consolidated conceptual model

We shall now assume that the data analyst has visited all functional areas of the organization, has extracted all relevant information and has created a set of submodels. How can he/she now consolidate these into a single global model? Bearing in mind the possible inconsistencies which were outlined in the A solution section in this chapter he/she may have problems.

The additive approach

Perhaps the most logical approach would be to take one of the submodels (arbitrarily) as the main model and then to add the other models to it one by one until the global picture is complete (Figure 4.9).

This is not a good approach. If submodel N is being added to the global model and contains an attribute A which conflicts with an attribute A, already extant in the global model, then which takes precedence? It is very unlikely that the submodels are all disjoint and so, whichever order they are processed in, there will almost certainly be problems of conflicting entity, attribute and relationship types.

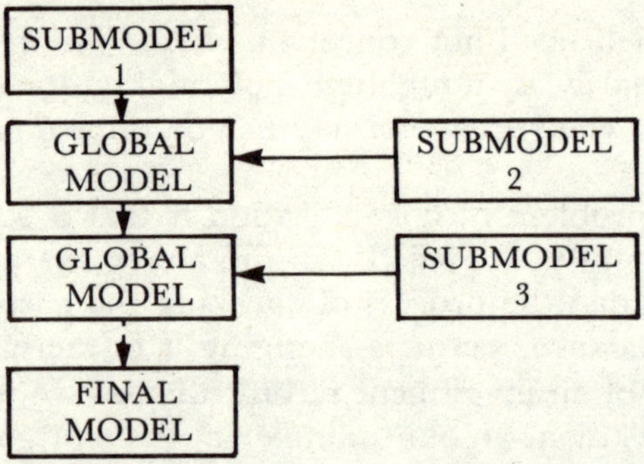

Figure 4.9 *Additive approach to creation of a conceptual model*

The incremental approach

An alternative to the above approach might be for someone with a sound knowledge of the business to construct an intuitive first model based on a global view of the organization. Such a model may not be too complex, but it can be refined by the addition of the submodels one at a time. This is sometimes referred to as *stepwise refinement*. For example, a basic model for our bank might appear as in the diagram shown in Figure 4.10.

Such a model would probably, at best, show the functional areas of the organization plus a few ambiguities (m:n relationships) but these should be removed by the stepwise refinement process.

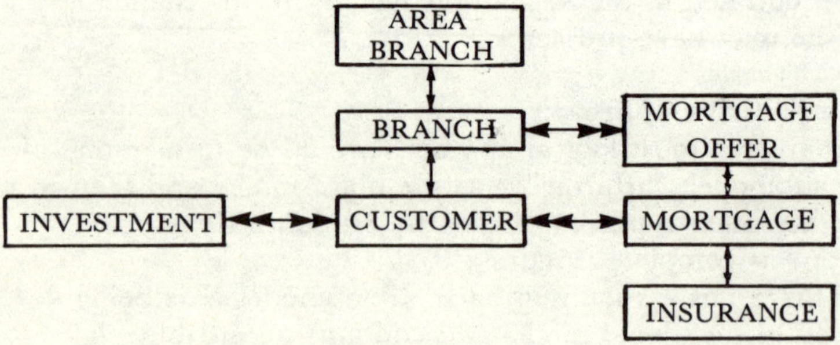

Figure 4.10 *Incremental approach to creation of a conceptual model*

Problems with consolidation

During the process of consolidation the data analyst must be aware of certain potential problems that must be eliminated before the design stage is started.

(1) *Synonyms*. By bearing in mind that the pseudonyms described on the entity/attribute form are likely to refer only to synonyms

within the particular area of study, in the global model the data analyst must determine whether or not two attributes with differing names are logically the same. For example: Is the property address on the mortgage entity necessarily the same as the customer address on the customer entity? Is the date on the investment entity (for the opening of the account) necessarily the same as the date on the first transaction entity.

(2) *Homonyms* (i.e. words or phrases which look the same but actually refer to different things). Does the account type in the mortgage entity (referring to whether the account is repayment, endowment or whatever) relate to the account type on the investment entity (here referring to whether the account is deposit, special shares, etc.). Clearly not, in this case, but the data analyst must be aware that they should not be implemented, in general, with the same name.

It might be thought debatable whether or not to give the attributes longer and more meaningful names to begin with and check whether two attributes are the same, as opposed to them being given shorter names and checked to see if they are different, but in the long run it is far better to start off with meaningful (and different) names, particularly if consideration is given to data dictionary systems (Chapter 11).

(3) *Subentities*. These consist of occurrences of subsets of the full entity. For example, if our business has a buildings insurance department and a separate contents insurance department, then the insurance entity generated from the building department will be a subset of the global entity insurance.

Recognition of subentities is important when we come to the implementation stage because they might show the need for different storage mechanisms for the differing subtypes (e.g. the buildings records may be required at different times/access speeds/frequency to the contents records).

It is also important when different conceptual views are highlighted. For example, overall we may have modelled a single investment transactions entity covering all transactions relating to an account. One particular department within the business, however, might only be interested in the transactions from the current financial year, whereas another might need all of them over the past 5 years. Normalization will not show the differing views, but there may yet be a need to split the transaction entity into a current and an historic, storing each in different ways on different devices.

Summary

In the last two chapters we have looked at the process of data analysis; if it appears to be a long, arduous process then that is because it is necessarily so. Database design can be carried out after poor data analysis, but a poor database will result. In particular, any corrections or additions necessary at a later stage generally will be very difficult to implement. It is therefore far better to perform data analysis meticulously, paying many visits to the user departments and cross-checking all results, to ensure that the final model is as free from ambiguities as it can be practicably.

Case studies

Following the discussions and examples of this and the previous chapter, it should be possible for the student to conduct his/her own data analysis on their chosen case study. If the latter is familiar to the student then the functional analysis may seem superfluous. However, to interview a relevant member of staff may, certainly, be worthwhile and may turn up events and operations not considered by the student initially.

Probably, it would be advantageous to obtain data with respect to entities, attributes and relationships from this functional analysis as described and to transcribe it on to forms of similar design to those outlined in the An entity, An attribute and A relationship sections in Chapter 3.

The next phase is to group the data intuitively (if this has not been done already) and perform the process of normalization until strong third normal forms are reached. Has this produced unwanted results? If so, leave them for the moment until we have followed through the stages of database design.

Once normalization is complete, a Bachman diagram can be drawn and judged as to whether or not it represents a reasonable overview of the area of study.

There will be no right or wrong answers at this stage though some solutions will be better than others. The proof of the pudding will be in the implementation of this conceptual model and in its usage thereafter.

Note that because each of the case studies is an autonomous area in itself (with the possible exception of the first two) there should be no problems of consolidating a global model. With respect to the first two, although the course and student-administration areas are counted as being different, it would be an interesting exercise to try to consolidate the two models into one and observe whether the end product would be applicable to both departments.

CHAPTER 5

Logical Database Design

Introduction

I make no apologies for repetition when I restate how important it is that database design is not initiated before the data analysis stage has been finished completely.

In practice, the processes of data and functional analysis rarely are performed except when a database is to be implemented. This is certainly to the detriment of many businesses who do not want a database system and therefore do not gain this overall picture of the efficiency of the organization. For example, in large businesses it is not too rare to find two different departments spending n man-hours in producing independently exactly the same set of statistics, each for their own personal use. Data and functional analysis would highlight such wastage and eliminate the inefficiency in this autonomous environment.

With a database approach the theory shows that such inefficiency would be removed because all data would be shared and one fact will only be stored in one place. Such autonomy as is desired, particularly with respect to privacy, can be maintained adequately as is shown in Chapter 7.

However, this is not to say that all data should be thrown into a single database as a cure for all evils. By considering the results of the data analysis exercise, the database administrator should have some ideas about how to implement each of his conceptual structures.

The design stage is therefore split into two distinct parts:

(1) mapping of the conceptual model into the logical data model
(2) mapping of the logical data model into the physical data model.

Manual vs conventional database files

The decisions as to how to implement the conceptual model

should be reasonably intuitive; a brief set of rules as a guideline would be:

(1) little used data (e.g. historical transactions)
unstructured data (e.g. free format correspondence to/from customers)
static data (e.g. the name of the business, public holidays)
temporary data (e.g. daily work files).
(these structures would be implemented best as either manual or conventional files)
(2) frequently used files in which the data are highly structured and updated during processing often are implemented ideally as database structures.

For those structures which will, eventually, become database files it is also worth considering whether they all belong to the same database. Here the data model diagram is particularly useful as it shows which structures are unrelated to the bulk of the data. In Figure 3.7 it is clear that the personnel structure is only tenuously linked to the accounts data by the employees who happen to own accounts. It may be decided that such a link does not involve enough processing to justify inclusion of personnel in the main database, especially in view of the fact that the privacy aspects will be different.

In general, such splits will be intuitive because of the natural splits in the functions of different departments within the organization. As a further example, if we were to include a management expenses structure or a payroll structure into the data analysis, we would not expect it to form a part of the accounts database (though there might be strong reasons for incorporating them in the personnel database).

Some care has to be taken, however, because no existing database system allows relationships to be defined between databases. On the other hand, it may not be desirable to have one huge unwieldy database containing everything in which, perhaps, the payroll system cannot be run because of errors on the mortgage file. Thus, in general, we have the situation as shown in Figure 5.1.

As this book is concerned primarily with databases we shall now consider only those structures that are to be implemented as part of a database.

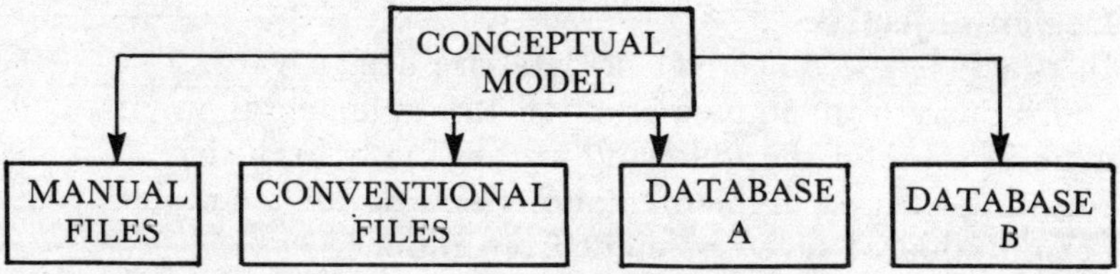

Figure 5.1 *Implementation of the conceptual model*

Problems with architecture

In Chapter 2 we stated that we would like the following

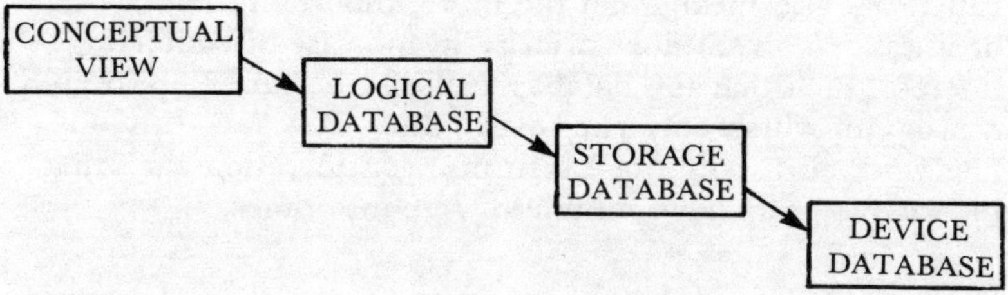

and gave the advantages of logical and physical data independence as reasons for wanting this.

At this juncture it must be stated that, at present, there are no commercial database systems able to supply an overall model similar to that above. In many cases the manufacturer's implementation has been machine orientated and the storage database has been merged in with the logical database and thus has been defined by using the latter's own language: the DDL. Clearly, this has meant a loss of physical data independence with the result that, if how or where a record is stored changes, the logical database and hence the application programs also need changing.

Progress is being made to rectify this deficiency, in particular in the CODASYL 78 report which shows a distinct storage model, but manufacturers are some way off from actually producing a marketable product.

The end result of this is that the 'how and where' decisions of database implementation, in practice, have to be taken at the logical database implementation stage, although in this book such issues have been left until Chapter 6.

Design objectives

In practice, the objectives of database design vary enormously from implementation to implementation. In general some of the following are mutually exclusive resulting in most implementations aiming for a suitable permutation of seven or eight from nine.

EFFICIENCY

Efficiency is generally considered to be the most important. Given a piece of hardware on which the database will run and a piece of software (DBMS) to run it, the design should make full and efficient use of the facilities provided. Efficiency also means that the more important areas of the business are given more priority in the case of conflicting interests such that the database will not be tuned up around a program which only runs every third Tuesday. Any on-line work also should be taken into consideration such that interactive users have minimum response times.

INTEGRITY

The database should be as accurate a reflection as possible of the business that it serves. Such considerations might seem obvious, but their importance can vary from business to business. For example, a financial institution maintaining a balance of £1058 for an account instead of the true £1059 is more likely to be 'found out' than a stock control system which shows the quantity of part A in stock as being 1058 when it is in reality 1059.

PRIVACY

The database should not allow unauthorized access to files, data items and relationships (both at the read only and update levels) which would not be allowed in the 'real world'. Again this requirement might vary from a business where the data held is public knowledge to one which maintains state secrets.

SECURITY

The database, once loaded, should be safe from physical corruption: whether from hardware or software failure or from unauthorized access. This is a general requirement of most databases.

IMPLEMENTABILITY
The conceptual model should not be so complicated that it cannot be implemented as a logical database. Also it must not be implemented in such a way that it is very difficult for application programs to find their way through (navigate) complex structures and paths. This is another very desirable aim.

FLEXIBILITY
The database should not be implemented in a rigid way that assumes the business will remain constant forever. Changes will occur and the database must be capable of responding readily to such change. Many existing databases fall down on this point: they are very difficult to change.

MAINTAINABILITY
The database must be implemented in such a way as to be comprehensible to any subsequent database administrators, as well as the existing one.

COMPATIBILITY
Initially, the business data may be implemented as several disjoint databases. These should be compatible such that any future merging of data is possible. This is perhaps the least important of the objectives (unless we are considering distributed databases).

PORTABILITY
The database should be implementable on a variety of hardware and software. This is not such an important objective as it should be in theory. Given the previous comments about the current DBMSs being written for particular machines, the database is nearly always designed with a piece of hardware in mind. Despite this the data analysis should still be carried out in an implementation-free way. However, in practice the database should be portable across different releases of software (e.g. from CODASYL 73 to CODASYL 78).

The exclusivity of these nine is probably strongest between efficiency and portability because a given database will have been 'tuned' (Chapter 10) for the chosen environment and will not perform as efficiently elsewhere.

Other differences in pairings are mentioned in subsequent sections.

It must be borne in mind that, whatever the objectives, data analysis may have thrown out items which are not implementable on the chosen database. For example, m:n relationships (if they have not been removed by normalization) and variable-length data items (it would always be desirable to implement names and addresses as variable-length fields but, unfortunately, not all database systems support them).

Efficiency vs privacy

Following the problems concerning privacy as outlined in Chapter 1, it would be highly desirable if privacy control could be implemented at all levels, i.e. at database, structure, record and data-item levels, and, indeed, many systems allow this. However, processor overheads may be too high (i.e if every time a record is accessed several checks have to be performed to verify the validity of the user with respect to that record and, possibly, also to some embedded data items) and the efficiency will suffer.

The alternative is to arrange the records so that the data items in each have the same level of privacy. Unfortunately, this is rather reminiscent of the conventional file approach where items had to be hived off into separate files, which itself was inefficient.

Efficiency vs logical data independence

As outlined in Chapter 3, one of the advantages of the database approach is that submodels can be defined allowing the user to see only that which the user wants/is allowed to see in an application-orientated way, thus providing effective logical data independence. This mapping from logical model to submodel can be quite complex and, in general, the more complex it is, the higher the processor cost. For that reason, it happens quite frequently that, whereas a given DBMS can support a more complex mapping, in practice the logical records are designed so that the submodel is a simple subset of the logical model resulting in a much simpler mapping and hence lower processor overheads. With this approach there is a danger of data duplication creeping in to 'save time'.

Problems with the operating system
As outlined in Chapter 2, most DBMSs leave the actual storing and retrieving of records to the operating system because, in general, this has been tailor made for a particular machine and is therefore likely to be efficient. A problem here is that, to the operating system, the DBMS appears as a single user as shown in Figure 5.2.

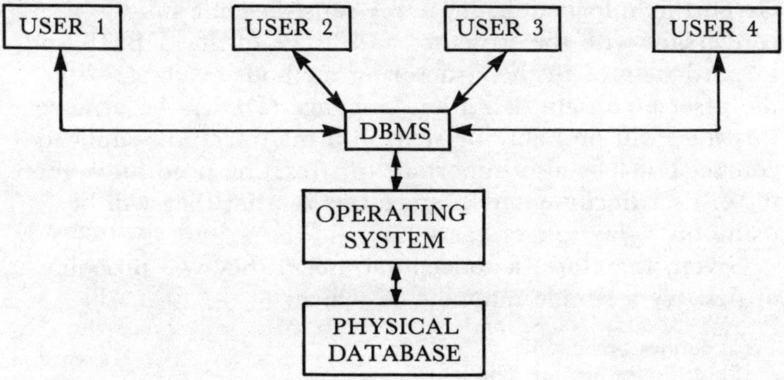

Figure 5.2 *Influence of the operating system on data access*

This means that the DBMS must route all data plus any error messages back to the correct user. This is a processor overhead in order to do something which is normally done very efficiently by the operating system.

A further problem is that the operating system might not allow the fine placement control required for maximum efficiency. For example, if data analysis has shown a need to store the investment record, its transaction records and the associated customer record close together because of frequent access, it would be ideal to store them on the same page. Such a convenience would be possible if we had separate storage and device data models. However, this is not the case and the operating system might not be equipped to follow such a request unless it has been written with the DBMS in mind. The end result is that the logical data model is often designed to combine logical records to ensure that all the related data are on the same page.

Database design methodology

Having looked at some of the pitfalls and limitations of current database-design techniques, we can now consider how the database administration (DBA) actually go about their task.

First, we must assume that the relevant computer has been decided on, and that its limitations have been taken into account, and, similarly, that a DBMS is available. Given this information the DBA must become fully conversant with the structure and usage of that DBMS and, in particular, with the structuring methods available with the associated data definition language (DDL). To achieve this they will probably be sent on a manufacturer-supplied course, but it is also important to stress the need for a good set of user documentation since this is what they will be using on a day-to-day basis.

Given, therefore, a conceptual model they will probably at first try a simple mapping in which:

(1) entities become files
(2) attributes become data items
(3) relationships become sets (CODASYL notation).

Note: it is very difficult to generalize about database design without lapsing into the terminology of a particular database system. For that reason, much of what follows in both this chapter and the next will use CODASYL phraseology (Chapter 13). The corresponding terminology for other approaches will be given in Part 3 of this book.

Following this initial translation, the DBA must then decide whether the constraints described previously in this chapter are still present or at least balanced correctly. For example:

(1) will the privacy afforded by the DBMS facilitate items of differing privacy levels being stored in the same record?
(2) will the DBMS allow related records to be stored physically on the same page?

Clearly, the question asked in (2) should in theory be included in the physical database design, but following the assertions made in the Problems with architecture section in this chapter all such considerations must be evaluated together.

If the result of the initial mapping is satisfactory in terms of constraints then the first model will become the final logical data model. However, if constraints are still extant then the initial model must be subjected to a process known as collapse and fragmentation.

Collapse and fragmentation
This is the general process whereby entities are combined together (collapsed) or split (fragmented) to form new entities, for the purpose of removing unwanted constraints from the database design. A single example of each should be enough to outline their usage.

(1) Suppose that as a part of our branch records we keep quarterly totals relating to data such as totals for receipts, withdrawals, new accounts, moneys received through agencies etc. At the end of the year the four quarterly sets of statistics are totalled for the year and analysed to show the business progression of each branch. As most of the year only the current quarterly values are needed, and despite the format of the file remaining constant, the data analysis revealed the need to store the individual quarterly statistics separately (i.e. normalization found them to be a repeating group) as shown in Figure 5.3.

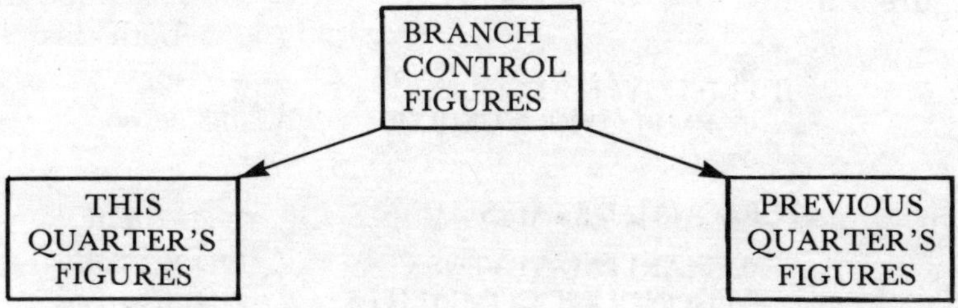

Figure 5.3 *Fragmentation of the branch control file*

However, sometimes one of the managers in the finance department wishes to run a statistical program which involves comparisons between statistics over the past four quarters. To prevent a high number of I/Os it would be convenient if the four sets of data could be stored together on the same page, such that all the statistics for branch 56 could be accessed with a single I/O, and so this is what is decided on at the data-analysis stage. However, at the design stage it is discovered that the DBMS will not afford such fine control. The decision must be made now as to whether to tolerate the high number of I/Os or to collapse the two files into one: thus guaranteeing that for one branch, one access.

There are no ground rules for such a decision, it is based purely on the importance of the 'offending' program.

It should be noted that if collapse is performed it will produce a result contrary to that necessitated by normalization. In other words, we have a repeating group as shown in Figure 5.4. Again this emphasizes that normalization is a tool and does not always produce the final desired product.

```
01 BRANCH-FIGURES.
   03 BRANCH-CODE           PIC 999.
   03 Q-FIGURES             OCCURS 4.
      05 etc... .
      05 etc... .
```

Figure 5.4 *Collapsed record as a COBOL file*

(2) Suppose now that the data-analysis stage produced a personnel entity composed of the attributes as shown in Figure 5.5.

```
01 EMPLOYEE-RECORD.
   03 EMPLOYEE-NUMBER              PIC 9(5).
   03 etc... .
PERSONAL DETAILS
   03 MARITAL-STATUS               PIC X(10).
   03 CONDUCT-COMMENTS             PIC X(30).
   03 CLOCK-NUMBER                 PIC 9(5).
   03 etc... .
SALARY DETAILS
```

Figure 5.5 *Personnel data*

As all the attributes were functionally dependent on the EMPLOYEE-NUMBER with no repeating groups or transitive dependencies, then normalization produced the above as a collection of related data. Suppose that the privacy rights for this record are as follows:

The whole record	Only top management
MARITAL-STATUS	Only senior members of personnel department (bear in mind that this may include information such as divorced, living together, etc.)
CONDUCT-COMMENTS	Only top management
SALARY-DETAILS	Only top management plus wages Department.

If this entity were to be implemented as a single file, then every time a record is accessed the system would have to check whether the user is:

(1) top management
(2) personnel department
(3) wages department
(4) any other valid user (such as the DBA?).

Such checking would be expensive in processor time, possibly too expensive, and the decision might be taken to fragment the personnel entity as shown in Figure 5.6.

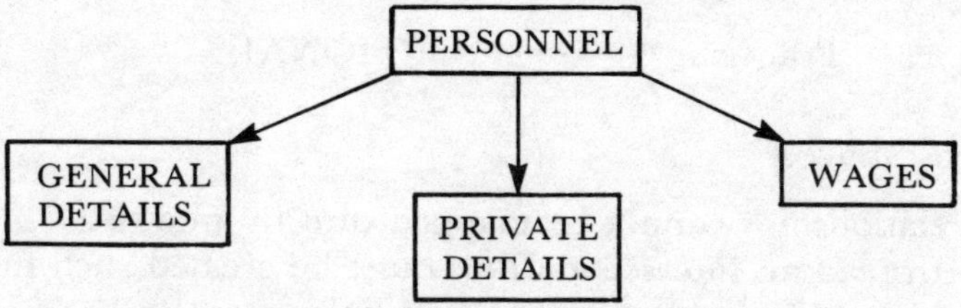

Figure 5.6 *Fragmentation of personnel data*

Clearly this decision must be taken in conjunction with the decision, as outlined in the Efficiency vs logical data independence section in this chapter, as to how complex the model/submodel mapping is to be. If it is considered reasonable to have a more complex mapping then there is no reason to fragment, the entity can be kept as it is and we can rely on the submodel design to provide any necessary privacy constraints (i.e. such that top management would have their own submodel as would the personnel department and wages, resulting in only a single privacy lock being needed for each).

CODASYL relationships

As mentioned in the Database design methodology section in this chapter, in the design of the CODASYL database, relationships in the conceptual model become *sets* in the logical model.

The rules concerning relationships as outlined in the A relationship section in Chapter 3 can be mapped simply into CODASYL form:

Mandatory → AUTOMATIC
Contingent } → MANUAL
Optional }

(Note that this only applies to existence rules for members in 1:n relationships.)

Fixed → FIXED
Transferable → MANDATORY
Transient → OPTIONAL

(Note as above.)

M:N relationships cannot be mapped directly into the DDL. Instead an intersection link must be created such that each entity relates to the intersection link on a 1:N basis, for example:

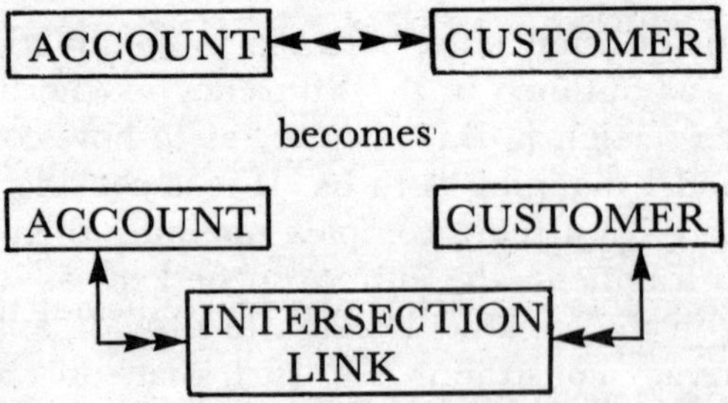

The involuted relationship with the branch entity can be broken down in the same way.

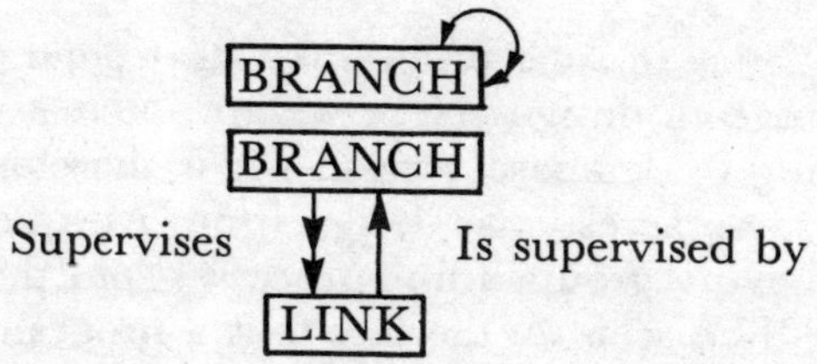

Program design
As shown in Figure 3.2, at the same time that the database design is being carried out, the database administration (probably in conjunction with a systems analyst), should also be formulating program-suite design. This will be as a result of functional analysis. Operations that involve the same data items and that take place at the same time will be grouped together intuitively to form conceptual programs. The problems of program design do not form a part of this book, but it is useful to state that the process can take place concurrently with database design, and the connections between data submodels and application programs should be clear at this point.

Efficiency
Having performed the mapping from conceptual model to logical model, and with any necessary collapsing or fragmenting having removed all hardware/software constraints, we now have a logical database. But how can we determine whether or not it will be efficient?

In practice, far too often a database is created, loaded and then monitored to see if it is efficient. If it is not then the database has to be reorganized or restructured (Chapter 9) to improve efficiency which is a time-consuming process in general. Instead, a little thought and effort at the design stage will save much work later (though this is not to say that the database should not be monitored continuously as outlined in Chapter 10).

At the design stage the DBA should look to the conceptual programs and determine how efficient they will all be with the database as it stands currently. (If there is no time to cover every process then at least the critical ones should be included, e.g. on-line programs or frequently used batch programs.)

The efficiency of such programs will depend on many facets of program design. Here we are interested only in those relating to database accesses. It is therefore useful to document these accesses at design time. An immediate benefit of having grouped like processes into the same program will be seen by the fact that a program performing both processes A and B on the same file (sequentially) should have half the access cost of two separate programs.

The task therefore is to list the major programs and the number of logical record accesses they will employ (the values used here obviously will have to be derived from an average run of the program in on-line terms though in batch mode the number of records accessed is, usually, more fixed).

For example, it may be found that a critical program A at our bank is run daily and accesses:

750 000 investment accounts
3 000 000 investment transactions (average at half year)
750 000 customer records.

If this program is essential to the running of the business (e.g. it balances the accounts) then its importance may be enough to convince the DBA to design the database around that one program. This situation is perhaps unlikely in a large-scale organization, but many small businesses revolve around having a single very efficient on-line program to supply immediate information, and in such cases the database could be constructed about that program.

Such decisions cannot be quantified, nor can they be a part of collapsing and fragmenting. They are based intuitively on what is important to the business in question. An example of the documentation which could be used to show access costs is shown in Figure 5.7.

Notes:

(1) The program contains two separate processes which have been combined because both involve reading through the entire investment file (looking for today's transactions or new accounts) and which are both run at the same time (daily).

(2) The estimate is the number of transactions daily and is available from business-supplied statistics.

(3) The relevant files and relationships can be shown diagrammatically by:

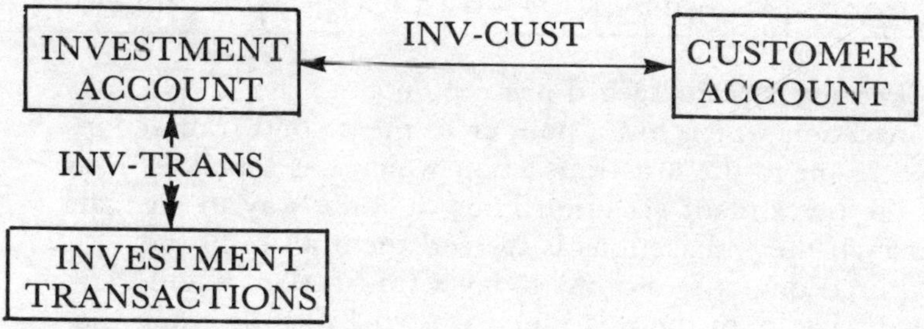

(Only first named customers are accessed.)

(4) All transactions need to be read, but only those bearing today's date actually are used.

Program description: to calculate any moneys received on accounts today and to print the names of any customers who have opened new accounts.

RECORD	SET	NUMBER ACCESSED	NUMBER USED
INVESTMENTS	DIRECT SEQUENTIAL	750 000	750 000
INV-TRANSACTIONS	INV-TRANS	3 000 000	30 000 *
CUSTOMERS	INV-CUST	2 500	2 500

* ESTIMATED

Figure 5.7 *Access costs of a sample program*

Conclusions:

The program will be inefficient because of the point made in (4) (i.e. three million reads for 30 000 records is not a good hit rate). This problem assumes that the set INV-TRANS has been implemented in the standard CODASYL manner, i.e.:

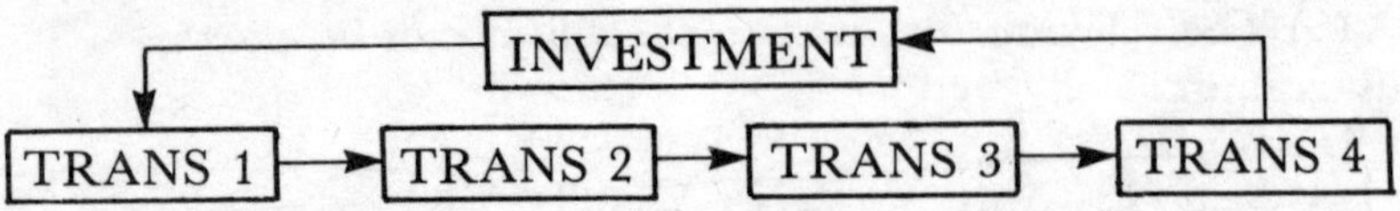

The investment record has a pointer to the first transaction which has a pointer to the second transaction and so on to the last transaction which has a pointer back to the investment account. Thus the only way to navigate through the transactions is to read them all until the required one is found. As today's transactions should always be the last ones there is much wasted I/O time when the first ones are read. It might therefore be decided that, if this program is important, the introduction of a second set of pointers is worthy:

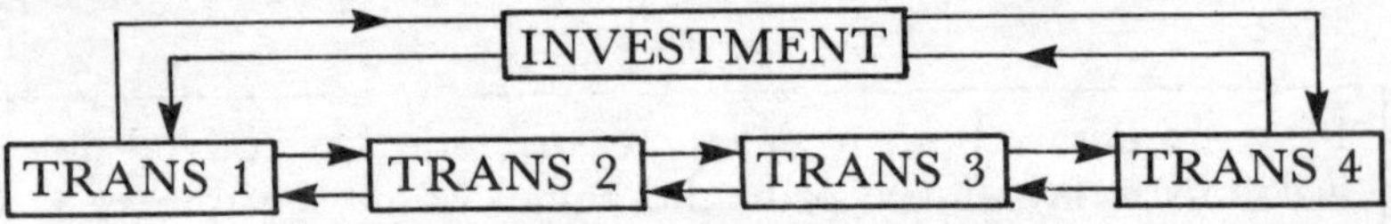

Now, by using these backward pointers, the program only has to access one or two transactions (until the date on them does not match today's date). This would have the effect of cutting down our transaction accesses to around 750 000 (since we must access at least one per account): this is a saving of over two million accesses!

An even more drastic solution would be to have a flag on the account itself denoting whether there was a transaction today. This would cut the number of transaction accesses to 30 000 but would have the disadvantage of two extra updates to the investment record per day (one to add the flag, one to clear it).

Such decisions would become possible only at design time because only then is the information available. Data analysis would almost certainly not show the possible need for a flag, as outlined above, on the investment record.

Summary

If a single piece of information is to be gleaned from this chapter, it is that there are no hard and fast rules for database design. As such it is the DBAs responsibility to ensure that the database:

(a) optimizes the usage of the available hardware and software

(b) provides the required balance of constraints as outlined in the Design objectives section in this chapter
(c) shows none of the hardware/software constraints as outlined in this chapter (i.e. features that cannot be implemented on a given DBMS)
(d) optimizes all aspects of efficiency for all programs, particularly for those which are critical to the business.

CHAPTER 6

Physical Database Design

Introduction

Perhaps before long this truly will be a chapter in its own right! At present, however, considerations described here must be taken at the same time as those of the previous chapter. Indeed the processes of collapsing and fragmenting are concerned with how records should be stored, so already we have encroached on aspects of the physical database.

Data-item implementation

In the previous chapter we have seen how a logical data model, free from constraints, can be derived and so now we can turn our attention to how the individual parts of that model can be implemented physically.

In the data-analysis process attributes were described largely by their functional relevance and there was little need to suggest how they might be implemented. For example, within the customer entity we might have had attributes described as:

SEX – MR, MRS, MISS, MS
MARITAL STATUS – SINGLE, MARRIED, DIVORCED, WIDOW, WIDOWER
ADDRESS – NUMBER, STREET, TOWN, COUNTY, CODE

We now have to decide how these items can be represented in our DDL. It would seem sensible and is, indeed, usual to translate multivalue alphabetic items such as SEX and MARITAL STATUS into multivalue numeric items such that we have

```
03 SEX            PIC 9.
```

and the application program can decipher its value as 1 for Mr, 2 for Mrs, etc.

Note that as in all forms of data storage it is advisable not to have zero representing any definite value, unless there is need for a default value, because most database systems make all numerics zero when creating records (although others tend to fill them with high values).

MARITAL-STATUS can be handled in a similar way, but there are many possible implementations of ADDRESS. It could be represented best as a free format variable-length field or set of fields if the DBMS supports such types, or as a free format fixed-length field of 70 characters or, indeed, one of the following:

```
03 ADDRESS.
   05 NUMBER          PIC 999.
   05 STREET          PIC X(20).
   05 TOWN            PIC X(20).
   05 COUNTY          PIC X(10).
   05 CODE            PIC X(8).
03 ADDRESS.
   05 ADD-LINE-1      PIC X(30).
   05 ADD-LINE-2      PIC X(30).
   05 CODE            PIC X(8).
```

Clearly, it will be stored in the way most suitable to the organization (e.g. if the address is used mostly for printing on letters then a letter format representation would be the most suitable).

Having decided that an item is to be numeric, the DBA must now look to its usage. If it is only to be used for display purposes then they may wish to store it as a character field. If the item is required for extensive arithmetical operations, it might be wiser to store it as a binary field (again only if the DBMS allows them the choice). As mentioned in the Preface, most database systems will store numeric data in packed decimal format by default, as this saves on storage space.

Checking functions

It is not only possible for the DBA to describe all data items in the DDL, but with most DBMSs it is possible within the DDL to describe formally any data checks which might be associated with a particular data item. Such methods allow data validation within the database code and lift the onus from application programs to perform such functions. Examples of this might be as follows.

(1) If a key item is described in DDL as being unique then the DBMS will not allow a new record to be stored with a duplicate key value.
(2) Range checking. In the example of the previous section, it could be stated that SEX has to have a value v where 0<=v<=4 (care must be taken to include all values: 0 might be acceptable if the customer is only known as J Smith with sex unknown).
(3) Value checking. If MARITAL-STATUS was implemented as a PIC X(8) field with possible values of married, single, divorced, etc., then the DBMS could be required to check for a valid value.
(4) Existence checks. If an item has to be given a non-zero value before the record can be stored, then this can be described in the DDL.
(5) More complicated checks. The above are fairly simple and standard checking functions, but what if we wished to ensure that the interest due on an account was equal to the sum of all the interest dues stored on each transaction? For this, the DBA could specify a procedure name against the record. When that record is stored the given procedure is executed and the check performed.

It must be stated that the more complicated the checking required, the higher the processor and/or I/O cost at run time. Perhaps such a cost will be too high.

Direct access methods

The definitions of file storage and access methods given in the following sections are similar to those of non-database files. For those unfamiliar with such definitions, a brief outline is given in Appendix B. Where there are variations in terminology it is the CODASYL definitions that are used here.

The CODASYL definition for *Direct* access is similar to the normal definition (i.e. that the user supplies an algorithm to translate the key (database or logical) into a physical address) but, in practice, most manufacturers of CODASYL products have implemented this such that the database key is the physical address (i.e. it contains the page number on which the record resides plus the position of that record on the page).

Direct provides a very fast access mechanism with a maximum of one physical I/O (none if the record is in memory already). However, there is one big disadvantage in that the record is physically dependent on that address. If a restructuring takes place (see Chapter 9), and the record is moved physically during that process, then the Direct key must also be changed and hence programs will need changing; this is contrary to the desired features of Chapter 2.

So when might direct access methods be used? Clearly, when:

(1) very fast access is essential
(2) the record structure is not likely to change (and cause the need for a restructuring)
(3) the file does not contain too many records (so that, if reorganizing or restructuring is necessary, the results will not be too traumatic).

Calc keys
This is also a direct access method which is more flexible than *Direct* and therefore in more common usage. An application program wishing to access a record provides a value for the key item (often more than one key is possible). Using this key value the DBMS can derive the physical address of the record in one of two ways: by hashing functions or by indexes.

Note: in CODASYL the two methods are described thus
LOCATION MODE IS CALC
LOCATION MODE IS INDEX SEQUENTIAL

HASHING FUNCTIONS
Hashing functions are similar to those described for random files. Given the input key the DBMS can perform a transformation on it to derive the physical address. As with the random files, there are problems inasmuch as the range of actual keys will probably not be random so that clustering of records on certain pages may occur, with possible overflow problems.

The advantages are that a given record can be accessed, usually, with a single physical I/O (only more if overflow exists) and thus it is as fast as Direct. The disadvantage (and it may be very significant) is that there is no provision for sequential processing, i.c. the file cannot be read in key sequence.

Note that in comparison with the Direct method the Calc key method may come out unfavourably if the hashing function is complicated and requires much processor time. However, as the physical addresses are not a part of the record, the application programs are physically independent of the storage position and will not require changing if the file is restructured or reorganized (though the hashing algorithm will need changing).

INDEXING

Indexing is similar to the indexing techniques of non-database files as described in Appendix B. The most common type within database systems is *index sequential* whereby only the highest key for each page is stored in the index. Even so the disadvantage is that almost certainly two physical I/Os are needed to access a record (one for the index and one for the record) and, if the number of records is high, we may need indexes to the indexes to reduce table searching, with a corresponding increase in the number of I/Os. The advantage over hashing techniques is, of course, that records can be processed sequentially and, if several different indexes are possible, then I/O time for many varied application programs can be minimized.

Other access methods

In general, there are no other direct access methods available with most database systems, but there is always use for a *serial* or *linear search* whereby the file is read in its physical ordering until the required record is found or until the end of the file if it is not found. This may seem to be an enormous overhead when Direct or Calc keys are available but in some cases where a file is accessed rarely, the overhead of maintaining an index may not seem worthwhile, in which case linear searching is the only solution. However, the process of searching can be improved if the DBMS offers some sort of placement control with records.

Consider the scheme shown in Figure 6.1 and the desire to find all the insurance transactions resident in the mortgage transactions file.

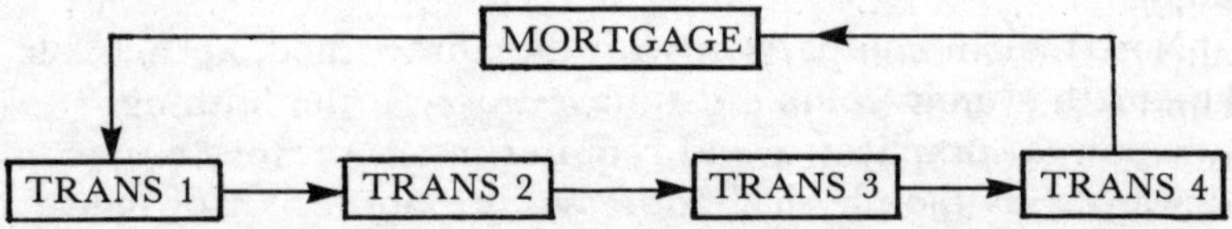

Figure 6.1 *A simple owner/member set implementation*

It is unlikely that we would wish to implement a direct access method for every transaction with the key as the transaction code (which we will take to be 03 for an insurance record) – the reasons being that the transaction file is too large and volatile for Direct entry, the hashing function method is likely to provide too high a processor overhead, and the index sequential method too high an I/O overhead.

As CODASYL is very good at representing owner/member relationships (as sets), it would be wise to use those facilities, particularly as they also often allow related data to be stored in physical proximity. This would mean that the physical I/Os needed to search through all transactions would be minimized. [Admittedly, the I/O time could be reduced yet further by grouping all transactions together, but this would rule out efficiency for the important and more frequently used relationship between a mortgage account record and its transactions, (another example of important processes being given priority at design time).]

Access-type decisions

Clearly, the decision as to the access type can only be made on a business-to-business basis, and in some cases the solution will be far from obvious. For example, the DBA will have to weigh up the different access patterns by each application program on each file and then prioritize them. The most difficult decisions concern files in which insertions and deletions are commonplace, particularly if fast access is also required. Insertions will lead to eventual overflow situations occurring for Direct entry and Calc keys and overflow in tables occurring in index sequential methods. Similarly, deletions could lead to holes in files in each storage type unless the DBMS is good enough to maintain available space tables. Unfortunately, through lack of any alternative methods, one of the storage methods must be chosen although problems can be relieved somewhat by the pre-allocation of storage space (i.e. creating blank records) if the DBMS allows it.

Thought also must be given to how the file is likely to expand (if at all) in the future. It is fairly pointless having a database which is very efficient for its initial data population, but which degrades badly if the number of records increases. This is especially noticeable when overflow situations occur.

Relationship implementations

Possibly the greatest advantage of most database systems is their ability to show relationships between records and files in a manner unobtainable generally with conventional file approaches. The three main ways in which this can be done are:

(1) linked lists
(2) indexes
(3) aggregates.

Though it is unlikely that all three would be available for one particular database system (for example CODASYL is concerned predominantly with linked lists), all three are described here.

Linked lists

These are constructed of an owner record (the 1 in a 1:n relationship) and a number of member records (the n), as shown in Figure 6.2.

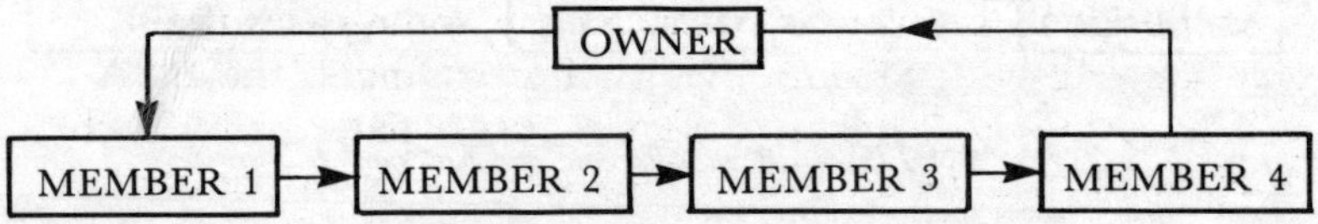

Figure 6.2 *Example of a linked list*

The owner contains, as part of its record contents, a physical address pointer to the first member, and that member contains a pointer to the second member and so on until the last member has a pointer back to the owner (in general), thus forming a closed chain. Such pointers are system maintained and are, in general, invisible to the user.

Insertion of a new member in this structure is simple if the preceding member has been accessed already (ORDER IS NEXT in CODASYL). The forward pointer of the existing record is changed to that of the new record, and the old forward pointer is copied into the new record, as shown in Figure 6.3 where member N + 1 is being inserted.

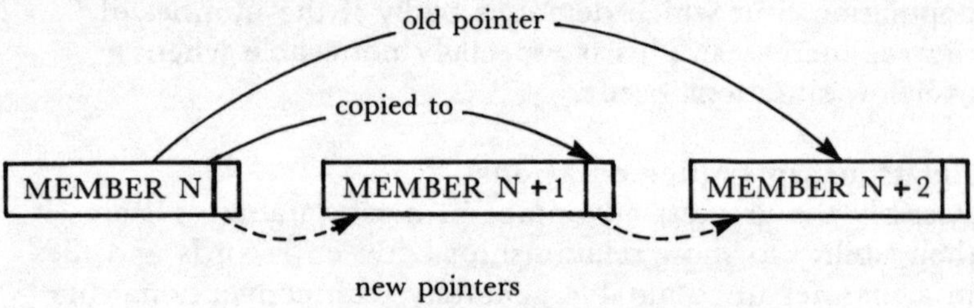

Figure 6.3 *Insertion of a new record within a linked list*

However, this simple linked list is inefficient if the members are stored chronologically because to insert a new member (i.e. at the end) involves chaining through all existing members to reach the previous last member. This can be avoided by declaring a second set of pointers, this time backwards as shown in Figure 6.4 (ORDER IS PRIOR in CODASYL).

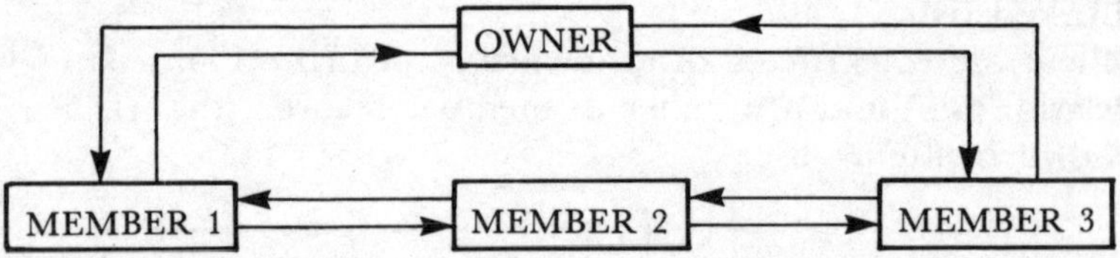

Figure 6.4 *Linked list with forward and backward pointers*

Thus given an owner record we can find the last member record immediately.

Note: in all these examples, if a member record is inserted it does not mean that the other members are moved physically to accommodate it. In other words, the physical storage may be similar to that shown in Figure 6.5.

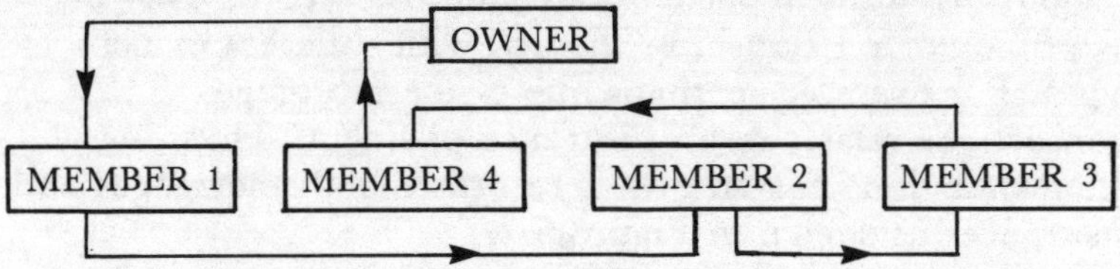

Figure 6.5 *Actual physical ordering of a linked list*

If the owner/members relationship involves much existence verification on the members then, clearly, all members would have to be read if the record does not exist and an average of n/2 reads if it does exist. To circumvent this problem it is possible to presort the members on a defined key (i.e. making them sequential rather than serial). Now n/2 reads are required on average to detect existence whether or not the record exists. The saving on this is dependent on the number of members per set, but against that is the increase in overheads in having to sort the members in the first place. In CODASYL there is an ORDER IS SORTED clause which achieves this aim, but care must be taken if the physical ordering is likely to be similar to that as shown in Figure 6.5 because with the existence of many members they are likely to be spread over many pages, and the number of I/Os needed to read through them could be high as shown in Figure 6.6.

	page 1	page 2	page 3
Members numbered	M1	M4	M2
in logical (i.e. sorted)	M5	M6	M3
sequence	M7	M9	M8

Figure 6.6 *Possible I/O difficulties with linked lists with member records spread over several pages*

To read through all members of this set could take eight physical I/Os.

Also, it must be borne in mind that if the members (as in the example of transactions) are created naturally in the required sequence (i.e. by date), then there would be a waste of processor time in having them sorted.

Consider what happens if our member records exist in two different relationships, in each with different owner types. For example, perhaps one of the mortgage transactions relates to an insurance payment. Thus one of the transactions has an owner record of both mortgages and insurances as shown in Figure 6.7.

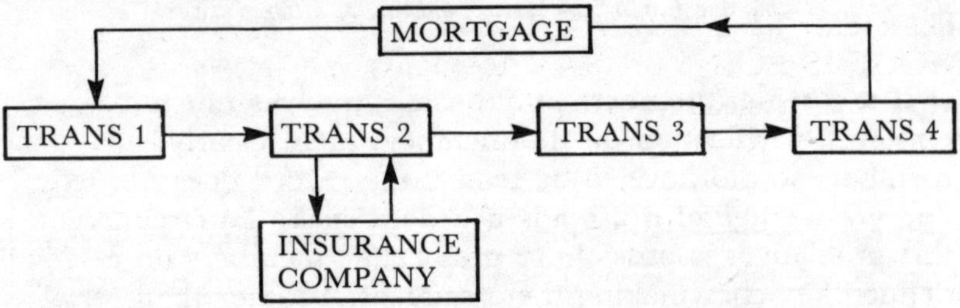

Figure 6.7 *A record participating within two distinct set types*

A certain process may involve reading through the insurance company records, using the linked list to access the insurance transaction. Also, it may be necessary to access the mortgage record itself to obtain details. From what we have defined so far, to reach the mortgage record from the insurance transaction involves chaining either forwards or backwards through the other transactions to arrive at the mortgage. Clearly, such a process is wasteful of processor and I/O time. If the process is an important one, then it might be deemed useful to be able to link each transaction to the owner record (LINKED TO OWNER in CODASYL), giving the situation as shown in Figure 6.8.

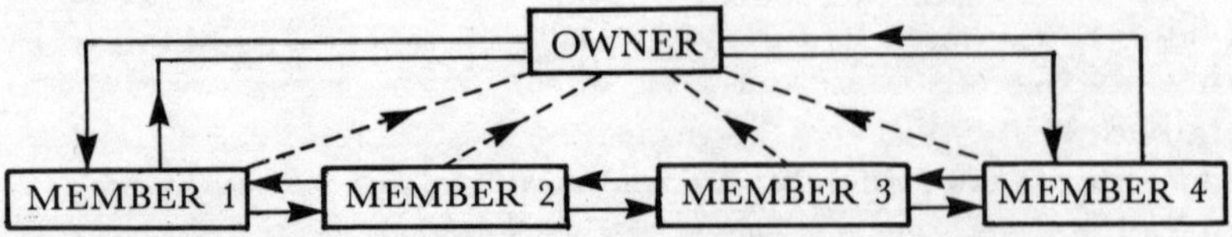

Figure 6.8 *A set in which each member contains a pointer to the owner*

Note that in this diagram each member contains three pointers (one forward, one backward and one to the owner). These pointers will probably take up a word of storage so that, if the member record is itself only a couple of words in length, we are adding a high percentage overhead in storage requirements in introducing all three pointers. In practice it is unlikely that all three will be needed in one relationship, but such considerations should be noted when it is decided whether or not to collapse small member records into their owners. Again it highlights the balance which must be found between high storage costs and efficiency.

Indexes

These date back mainly to early CODASYL systems. A MODE IS POINTER ARRAY clause was used to set up what was, basically, an index, in the form shown in Figure 6.9.

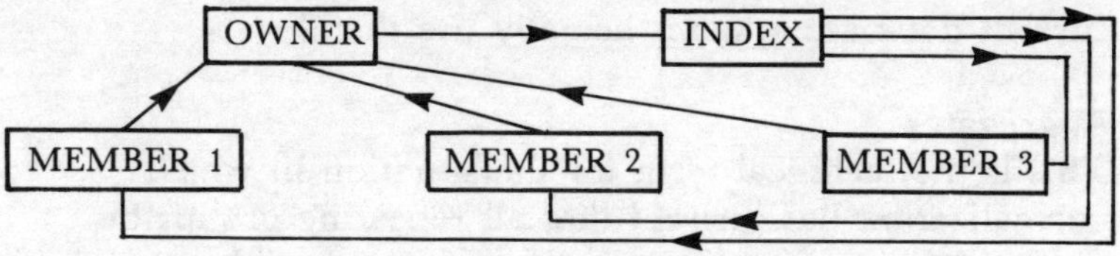

Figure 6.9 *Early CODASYL index implementation*

To access the members from the owner an index must be accessed (each owner/member set occurrence having its own index) and this contains a table of the addresses of each of the owners. The index can also maintain a set of key values against the addresses so that particular members can be chosen. This is a big advantage over linked lists but, because each member is only linked back to the owner, a disadvantage becomes apparent if we wish to chain through all member records. However, another advantage is that, because the storage addresses of the members are kept in one place (the index), if the members are physically moved (as they would be in a restructure or reorganize) then only the index needs changing and not all of the pointers on the individual member records. A third advantage lies in the fact that if we wished to access the members in some predefined sequence then that sequence can be maintained within the index.

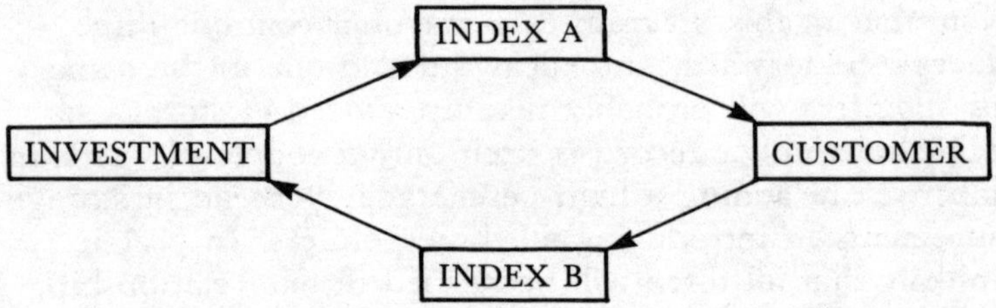

Figure 6.10 *Indexes used to maintain m:n relationships*

Indexes can be used also to maintain m:n relationships such as that shown in Figure 6.10 between customer and investment records. From the customer we can go via index B to access all the accounts owned by that customer. From the investment we can go via index A to access all the customers who own that account.

Although it has been said how wonderful indexes are when used in this way, it must be noted that very few current database systems actually use them!

Aggregates

This is the technical term for the situation in which normalization has insisted that all repeating groups be removed from an entity and then, for a possible variety of reasons, at the design stage we have decided to put them back.

This is of particular use when:

(1) the number of occurrences of the repeating group is fixed or at least variable within narrow confines, i.e. the single consolidated record can be given a fixed acceptable length without having the great wastage involved as described in Chapter 1
(2) it is advantageous to access all the related data with a single physical I/O.

Thus if we were concerned only with a mortgage record and its (probable) two associated customers, then normalization would have split the customers away to form a separate entity, but the design stage would have shown (by common sense not theory) that the customers might as well be stored as part of the mortgage record. (Such a system might be used in practice were it not for customers also owning investment accounts and so to prevent data duplication we must store customers separately.)

The last point emphasizes the main problem with aggregates. If the members in question have relationships with any other owner types, or are themselves owners in another relationship type, then aggregation is not appropriate becausc the other relationships would not be maintainable.

Device model

As has been mentioned previously, the theoretical database model gives independence to a device model which will place the database files on physical units of storage. In practice, this task is performed by the operating system which cannot in general offer the fine placement required by theory, thus forcing the device model to become embedded in the storage model which is in turn embedded in the logical data model.

By bearing in mind this dependence on the operating system it is odd that the terminology for physical storage, *areas* and *pages*, should have superseded the terminology for traditional storage methods, *files* and *blocks*.

The DBA should determine how big an area (file) is going to be (such statistics should be available from data analysis; see Figure 3.3), and then add on a suitable amount for future expansion, that percentage spare varying depending on the file in question.

Definition of the population of an area is particularly important with some DBMSs because the manufacturer-supplied hashing functions for Calc keys will often generate so many pages available for the file based on the proposed population. Too high and disk storage is wasted; too low and overflow problems may follow. Similar considerations are valid for table sizes with index sequential files.

Some systems allow for future expansion without the overheads of pre-allocation, for example:

```
AREA SIZE IS 1000 PAGES EXPANDABLE TO
                               2000 PAGES
```

in CODASYL.

Not many systems will allow the physical file attributes to be changed once a file has been created without the necessity to reorganize (Chapter 9): a high overhead as punishment for a lack of preplanning.

It should be noted that, with the above, most systems will have the extra available space at the end of the area, but it is often the case that physical grouping of records is desirable, and hence the need for spreading the available space across the area.

The DBA must specify also the required *page size* (the default is usually somewhere around 2000 bytes). Too low a value and it might not be possible to store associated data on the same page with a resulting increase in I/O. Too high a value and, for random access where only a single record is required, too much unwanted data is read into memory. (The fine balance between I/Os and memory usage is described more fully in Chapter 10.)

Physical placement

It has been stated that often it would be very useful to be able to store associated records physically close to each other, but no mention has been made to date as to how this can be achieved.

If there exists a distinct storage model implementation in a given database system (such as in CODASYL 78) then we might expect language clauses specifically for record placement. This is not to say that it cannot be done in existing database systems. For example, in CODASYL 73 there is a LOCATION MODE IS VIA SET clause which allows a certain degree of coarse placement. The DBMS will attempt to place the owner and members as physically close together as possible, and if there is no room on the same page an adjacent page will be used if possible, but the fine placement is out of the hands of the DBA.

Loading the database

Assuming that we have described the database fully using the DDL (examples of what such a definition might look like are given for each database type in Part 3 of this book), and have included the necessary storage and device mapping details, and have compiled the database with no errors, now we can look to how the data can be loaded physically on to the database.

First, the database areas must be created physically on disk. This is done as the last stage of compilation with some systems, with others it is a separate process which has to be initiated by the DBA.

The loading of data is an extremely important exercise because the whole integrity of the database will disappear if the initial data are wrong. To that end some sort of load strategy should be developed which may well involve the need to:

(1) write a program to load part of the data (perhaps mortgages and insurances)
(2) load the data from their existing source (if currently on conventional computer files, it could be dumped to tape in a suitable format for loading)
(3) check the data by using a file validation program
(4) if okay, run the database system (with its own versions of application programs) in parallel with the older system for a reasonable period of time (usually weeks rather than hours) and compare outputs
(5) while the parallel running is taking place, the next functional area can be going through phases a to c, and so on until all the data that should be on the database are loaded.

Note: many larger sites in practice have two mainframes for backup purposes. This means that, in general, one can be used for testing.

The above approach works well in some cases, but in others problems arise where a lot of the functional areas and their data are interrelated. It becomes difficult to load part of the data and test the system comprehensively without loading all the data.

In the example, could mortgages and insurances be loaded without also loading customers? Or branches? Many of the mortgage programs will require customer or branch information so any form of parallel running will be against only a part of the system. On the other hand, if we load the customer data, should we load all of it or just those customers who own mortgages? If we choose the latter, will there be difficulties in adding the investment customers later?

Probably, we could get away with splitting the conversion into two portions, investments and mortgages, but probably no more than two. Each part would involve many files and programs such that the testing and parallel running would take many months.

Conversion from non-database into database files can therefore be a long process even once the data analysis and design stages are complete. Conversion from manual into database files can take even longer. The following list highlights some of the problem areas.

(1) Many of the database users at this loading/testing stage will be using the software/hardware for the first time. Therefore errors of ignorance may occur.
(2) Any of the DBAs errors from the design stage (e.g. not allocating enough pages to an area) will come to light. Also the DBA may well actually be using the DBMS for the first time.
(3) The load programs are one-offs and as such may not be tested fully or as tuned up for efficiency as established programs would be. This is the opposite of what the load program should be: efficient and error free. Another factor is that record creation is generally the slowest database process because related pointers, table entries, etc., have to be set up.
(4) An extremely arduous problem to solve during (or before) the load process is that caused by data duplication. In Chapter 1 it was stated that data duplication often occurs on conventional files with resulting inconsistencies. Now that data are being loaded to (hopefully) a single destination, in the case of inconsistency, which is the correct piece of data (e.g. two different addresses for the same customer)? Load the wrong one and the integrity of the database disappears before we start. Often the solution is to load both as two separate customers and sort it out later. This, in turn, often means that:

    (a) the problem is put off indefinitely (there will always be more important things to do)
    (b) as mentioned, the integrity is lost
    (c) if one occurrence is found later to be wrong and deleted, holes will be left in the files impairing the efficiency.

There are several things that the DBA can do to alleviate the third problem above. The first is to make the load program restartable. This may involve the 'turning off' of rollback (Chapter 8) and the implementation of a simple record counter whose value can be determined in the case of failure as a restart point. Alternatively, it may be easier to keep rollback, but only load a certain percentage of the file in a single run (this way a run-time error is less disastrous).

A second solution is to write the load program to load the data in a specific and efficient way and not necessarily in the standard key ordering. Such a possibility is dealt with in the next section.

Load programs

It was mentioned in the Physical placement section in this

chapter that most DBMSs do not allow fine placement of records. This in turn puts the onus on the load program to achieve this aim. To aid this, files often are merged or sorted before the database load such that records which should be stored physically close are loaded consecutively. For example, in the existing conventional situation the mortgages and their transactions will probably exist on separate files. If these can be merged on to a tape file in the sequence

M1,T1,T2,T3,M2,T1,T2,T3,M3,T1,T2,...

then if the LOCATION MODE IS VIA SET is used in the DDL, we can be reasonably certain that the transactions, when loaded, will end up on the same page as the mortgage (their owner) record.

Sometimes, there will be clear advantages in the file being sorted into key sequence, particularly if index sequential database files are to be created, because the pages/tables can be filled sequentially with a minimum of I/Os. Similarly, if the hashing functions for Calc keys are known and their results predictable, then the input file can be presorted such that all database records being directed to the same page will be loaded consecutively.

Load versions of the database

The third method of optimization of load efficiency is for the DBA to create a special version of the database. Checking functions as described in the Checking functions section in this chapter are an extremely important part of ensuring database integrity. However, they do take up a large amount of processor time and so the load programs will be much slower if all input data have to be validated before the new records can be stored. Generally, it can be assumed that if the data already exist on computerized files then they will be valid. If this assumption cannot be made then the load program itself can do the validation (which will tend to be more efficient than the DBMS checking functions because the former will have the routines compiled into the machine code, whereas the latter will have the routines as separate code which will have to bound in at run time). Thus if we could turn the DBMS checking functions off, the load would be more efficient. Other functions of the DBMS may also be removable for the duration of the load. These might be:

(1) the UNIQUEness of a key can be determined by presorting the input file into key sequence
(2) DUPLICATES NOT ALLOWED clause can be removed for similar reasons
(3) range, value and existence checks can be performed by the load program
(4) the ORDER IS SORTED option can be removed from sets because the members can be loaded in the prescribed order
(5) any SET SELECTION clauses can be removed because the selection can always be CURRENT OF SET (see Chapter 13)
(6) all recovery statements can be omitted if it has been decided either to:
   (a) make the program restartable by conventional means
   (b) have the program non-restartable.

(This option will mean that there is no need to write to journal files with large subsequent savings in I/O and processor time.)

(7) all access controls can be removed in the assumption that the load program has the authority to create and access all data
(8) with some database systems it is possible to create index sequential files without actually creating the indexes, which can be generated later; this process can save on index building, which is one of the slower of the DBMS functions, particularly if there is more than one level of table (such a strategy is not needed if the file is loaded in key sequence, but the desire to do that may conflict with the desire for fine placement control).

Summary

The possible storage/access methods for the physical database are extremely varied across current database management systems. The DBA must determine which methods are:

(1) available
(2) most likely to produce an efficient database for their own application.

Many databases provide intricate storage mechanisms in terms of access mechanisms and/or placement control. Many of these will not be suitable for the database in hand. In other words, the DBA should not use every method merely because it is there.

They should also be aware of the fine balance between a well-analysed and a well-designed database. You cannot have the second without the first, but this does not mean that a nice-looking conceptual model should be mapped piecemeal into a logical model. Some collapse and fragmentation may well be necessary to optimize the efficiency of the database.

Case studies

That the student might pursue the case studies to some form of conclusion, a database system type must be chosen (be it CODASYL, relational or whatever). Ideally, a machine will also be available actually to compile and generate the database code. To this end the database design will be found to be almost totally machine dependent. For that reason, little help can be given here, except in the outlines of the various database methodologies given in Part 3 of this book.

Nevertheless, the principles of the access mechanisms (whichever are applicable) still stand, as do the considerations, outlined in the last two chapters, as to the implementation of data items and relationships.

Pick on a few important programs that you think might be important to your case study area. What would these processes involve? How many accesses? Is your database optimally efficient for those programs? If not then it may need some design alterations.

CHAPTER 7

Integrity, Security and Privacy

Introduction

The three terms integrity, security and privacy are often confused in database terminology: integrity sometimes being synonymous with security and security often being synonymous with privacy. This book uses the following interpretations (with respect to databases).

INTEGRITY

Once the database has been created and loaded, then each data item and relationship should be an accurate representation of their counterparts in the real world. Thus if Mr Smith has £10.25 in his account then the computer should maintain £10.25 and not accidentally round it to £10.26. Maintenance of integrity should therefore be a matter of prevention of invalid (as opposed to illegal) updates to the database.

As well as the obvious need for integrity on records and data items there are also relationships to be considered. The DBA should be responsible for setting up relevant relationships where there is a business need for them but thereafter those relationships should be maintained accurately. Thus if Mr Smith owns five investment accounts then he should be shown to have five accounts on the database, no more and no less.

SECURITY

Security in the database sense involves ensuring that the database is corrupted neither by hardware nor software error, nor indeed by illegal updating, and it is here that security overlaps with privacy. If it is corrupted then it loses integrity. Thus security revolves around recovery procedures, timestamping and related matters (see Chapter 8 and later in this chapter).

PRIVACY

Privacy is the prevention of unauthorized access of data. As mentioned previously, this usually revolves around letting the user see only what the user wants/is allowed to see, but there are different levels of privacy as discussed later.

Data redundancy and duplication

As a partial step toward guaranteeing integrity we should only allow one fact to be stored in one place on the database (since inconsistency automatically gives rise to a loss of integrity). To this end normalization is a useful tool because it guarantees one fact in one place barring key items which, clearly, can appear in several places (unless set structures and physical pointers are employed), but this would be a controlled redundancy and is unlikely to cause major headaches because any errors would be spotted quickly. However, as mentioned previously at the design stage, collapse and fragmentation may undo the normalization's guarantee (the Collapse and fragmentation section in Chapter 5) and an implemented database may no longer have one fact in one place. The problems here would have to be weighed up very carefully against the decision to collapse or fragment.

Integrity constraints

The integrity of the database is unlikely if errors are not trapped at the data-analysis and design stages such that the database no longer represents the business that it serves accurately. This is one of the reasons why these initial stages are so important. If, for example, there is no reason why the mortgage interest rate cannot be in eighths of a percentage (i.e. three decimal places), but the database was only implemented as having two decimal places (since the DBA did not know better at the time), then as soon as the real-world interest rate becomes an odd eighth, the database can no longer maintain its integrity and will have to be restructured (see Chapter 9).

Once created, the database must be loaded and, as outlined in the Checking functions section in Chapter 6, the load program should bear the brunt of any integrity constraints to ensure that the initial database is free from inconsistencies (bear in mind that the conventional or manual files from which the database is to be loaded are even less likely to be integral).

Throughout its lifetime, the integrity of the database can be checked regularly by either the applications software and/or the DBMS. The latter involves the application of constraints via the DDL as outlined in Chapter 5, such as range checking, uniqueness, etc. If such bound-in procedures involve too high a processor overhead then sometimes it is easier to perform the checking through those application programs which actually create or modify the data.

Concurrency

As shown in Chapter 1, if two programs were allowed to update a conventional file, concurrently, then there is no way that we could guarantee integrity. Database systems tackle this problem in one of two ways.

(1) Two update programs are running against the file F and program A accesses records 21, 17, 18, 3, 24, 5 ... while program B accesses records 4, 7, 9, 20, 18 as shown in Figure 7.1.

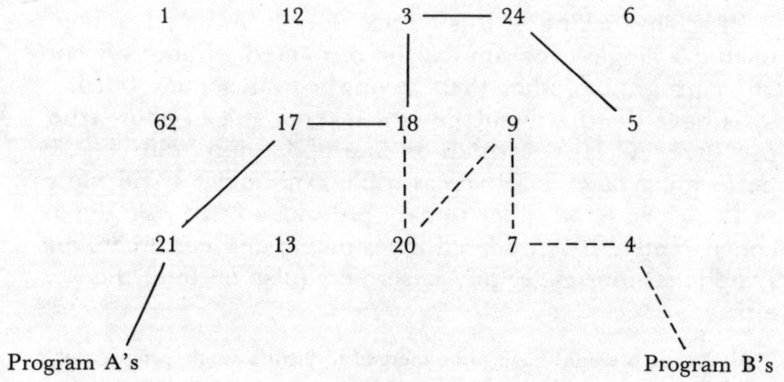

Figure 7.1 *Access paths of two concurrent programs*

While program A is running it *locks* each record before updating. The records updated by a program are only unlocked when that program terminates normally (i.e. does not terminate with an error condition). When program B reaches record 18 it finds it locked already and cannot therefore access it. Program B is therefore *rolled back* (see Chapter 8) to its beginning and all its records unlocked (rolling back will undo all of the updates which have been carried out by program B). If and when program A terminates successfully then program B will be allowed to run.

The reason why B cannot simply be suspended at its current point is that if, for example, program A later wants to access record 7, then it cannot because it was locked by B. Thus A would be waiting for B and B would be waiting for A (this situation is called a *deadlock* or *deadly embrace* and is a serious problem of concurrency which must be avoided).

Note: a common variation on the above, and that employed by most CODASYL installations is for a whole page to be locked rather than each individual record. Thus if each row of the scheme shown in Figure 7.1 represents a group of records on a single page, program B could not have started at all because A would have locked all three rows in its first four reads.

Program locking of this nature does have its advantages in that a single program can be recovered without affecting other programs (other than having to wait for it), but it does have the disadvantage that it tends not to allow true concurrency. If A were an on-line update program performing page locks across a file randomly, it will more or less exclude all other update programs from running concurrently. If A updated investments and customers and B updated mortgages and customers (also on-line) then either:

(a) A and B would have to be merged to form a single program or
(b) the customer file would have to be fragmented into two parts, one for investments and one for mortgages.

Either of these alternatives is likely to affect efficiency and/or privacy.

(2) Other database systems have a different locking

strategy. Program A locks a record while it updates it and then unlocks it immediately allowing other programs to access it. If program B wants that record while A is updating it then it only has to wait a few milliseconds. However, deadlocks can still occur. A group of related updates is called a *transaction*. Thus if a single event caused the updating of an investment, an investment transaction and a customer record this process generally would be carried out as a single transaction against the database. In this instance the investment record, then the transaction record and finally the customer record would be locked and, if that is completed successfully, then all three would be updated. (This prevents the unwanted situation wherein the investment record is updated and while that is taking place another program amends the transaction file possibly invalidating the investment update.) However, in this situation program A may have locked the investment and transaction and be trying to lock the customer, while program B (an entirely different application) has locked the same customer record first and is trying to lock the investment and/or transaction. Hence deadlock!

Usually, this is resolved by a system of priorities used by the DBMS. If A has the higher priority then B's locking would be undone (and any updates performed in that transaction rolled back). Program A can now lock the customer, complete its transaction and then unlock the records allowing access to B. This method therefore allows true concurrency but the disadvantage lies in the fact that if a file has been updated by more than one program then all programs will have to be rolled back in the event of failure.

Note: the process of locking need not be exclusive to update programs. A statistical program may be processing the file sequentially to derive certain totals. If that file is also being updated then the totals may not be correct. To counteract this problem CODASYL has a USAGE IS EXCLUSIVE clause in its data manipulation language which prevents any other program from accessing the file while the current program is still active.

Error handling

In conventional systems errors are detected and reported by the operating system. The messages given are often generalized and incomplete because the operating system is written for general usage and covers a wide range of applications. For example, a program might terminate with an

END OF FILE

message without distinguishing between

END OF FILE – ALL RECORDS PROCESSED

and

END OF FILE – NO RECORDS FOUND.

Such a difference might be important to the application programmer who is trying to decide whether the task is completed or whether the wrong file was loaded in the first place. Thus the differences are important if each type requires a different response from the user. Too often the programmer/operator is left in the dark as to why the program failed and how to correct that failure.

As mentioned previously, most database systems pass requests for physical accesses through the operating system which treats the DBMS as a single user. For this reason, any error messages passed from the operating system back to the DBMS have to be:

(1) interpreted by the DBMS
(2) acted on by the DBMS if necessary (i.e. go into automatic recovery)
(3) routed back to their originating program (if there is one).

Clearly, the DBMS must first decide what the error is and how it affects the integrity of the database. There are three levels of error as follows.

(1) If a disk has crashed or the DBMS itself has a software error, it is likely that all current programs will need to be suspended and

an appropriate error message displayed. It is then often up to the DBA/operator as to how to proceed unless recovery is automatic.

(2) If the error is serious, but has been caused by one particular program and no other programs are affected, the DBMS will terminate that program automatically and roll it back (see Chapter 8), undoing all of its updates and preserving the integrity of the database, at the same time displaying a suitable error message. Clearly, whether this option is possible depends on which of the two options as outlined in the previous section are available.

(3) If the error is minor (such as an end of file) the error is routed back to the originating program which, if designed correctly, will be able to handle that error and proceed accordingly. The error is usually returned as a four-digit code which the program must have defined within itself as (for example, in COBOL):

```
77 DBSTATUS                PIC 9(4).
```

The first two digits specify the error type as a broad category, e.g. OPEN ERROR, READ ERROR, STORE ERROR, etc, and the last two digits define the subcategory of that error. For example, if the error number was 0104 then the appropriate error might be

READ ERROR – NO MEMBER RECORD FOUND FOR CURRENT OWNER.

Knowing the exact error the program can detect that it is non-fatal and can proceed accordingly (perhaps by looking to the next owner). Thus by testing the value of the DBSTATUS after each DBMS command the programmer can trap any errors and decide whether to:

(a) proceed normally because the error is what they expected
(b) report the error and proceed
(c) terminate the program.

Note 1: full lists of error messages generally are given in the manufacturers' database manuals.

Note 2: some database systems zeroize the DBSTATUS field automatically at the start of each database command. With other systems the field must be cleared by the program before proceeding.

Physical data checking

In the previous section it was stated that most database systems are good at error interpretation allowing any problems to be corrected promptly. Most of these errors will have been detected initially by the operating system (for example, while trying to read a disk), but some database systems have their own physical data checking functions.

For example, the Burroughs DMS-II employs a *checksum* method by which all the on-bits within a block of data are counted and a checksum written at the end of that block (a similar idea to the parity bit on tapes, etc., but on a wider scale). If the block is read then the checksum can be rederived and tested quickly and any errors reported quickly. Processor overheads of such a system are high but, because every block is checksummed whenever the database is dumped, the DBA can be sure that:

(1) the dump is sound if no errors are detected
(2) disk errors will not be extant on the disk for days/weeks without being detected.

Dumps and journal files

As with the conventional files, the security of the database system is based on having a recent dump which can be reloaded in the case of hardware/software failure. Here the comparison ends because the database system can go one stage further in being able to recover right up to the time of the failure (or some conveniently close point) without having to rerun all programs subsequent to the dump. Such recovery is accomplished by use of journal files in a way described more fully in Chapter 8.

Database versions and timestamps

One of the easiest ways to corrupt a set of files is to accidentally run out-of-date programs (whose file format does not equal that of the current file) or reload the wrong version of files while trying to recover. Such errors are very difficult to either detect or avoid. Many database systems tackle this problem in the following way.

(1) The database is compiled initially. The exact time of the successful compilation is stored by the DBMS as a *database*

timestamp, each file (structure) in the database is given a *format timestamp* and the *update level* of the database is set to one.
(2) Programs are compiled against the database by passing them through a preprocessor which appends the update level of the database and the format timestamp for each structure used by that program to the object code.
(3) If at some time a database structure is reorganized or restructured (see Chapter 9), then the update level of the database would be set to two and the format timestamp of that structure would be changed to reflect the timing of that change.
(4) If the DBA now recompiles all programs affected by that change, but accidentally misses one, the DBMS would prevent that program from running against the database because its format timestamp for the file in question would no longer equal that of the actual file. Hence an old version of a program cannot corrupt the database. (Such a system works well, but its use depends on the physical data independence of the program. If submodels were used extensively then the format timestamp could be affixed to only those submodels which are affected by the change.)

It must be noted that those programs not affected and not recompiled will still contain a database update level of one. This is okay; it is permissible for a program to run against a database with a higher update level as long as no timestamps are infringed, but not against one with a lower update level. Such a situation can arise in one of two ways.

(1) If an old database dump is reloaded accidentally, and the live one has been restructured since, then the loaded database will have an update level less than any programs recompiled since that dump and the DBMS will highlight the error quickly.
(2) It is often the case that a test database is derived from the live version (see Chapter 12). If this has been done to plan out and test a proposed future change to the production model (i.e. the live model has been restructured to create a test model), then the programs compiled against the test database will have an update level greater than that of the live model, and will not therefore be allowed to run against it without recompiling (which is precisely what we would want).

There are other possible timestamps. All changes to the database are recorded on the journal files, but with some database systems there is a utility to initialize a file (i.e. create a blank one), which clearly would have the effect of deleting all existing records on that file. Generally, this process is not audited (too time consuming) which means that the file is no longer recoverable because of the *discontinuity* on the journal file. For this situation the database would maintain a *creation timestamp* on each structure which would be the time when the file was last initialized (or originally created if it has not been initialized). Thus, if there was a need to rollback (see Chapter 8) the database to a time before an initialization, the DBMS would report that this was not possible. Such a problem can be avoided by not using the initialize facility, but by deleting the records from the file programmatically (such changes would be audited, but would take much longer than an initialize), or by dumping the database immediately after an initialize.

A final type of timestamp is that of the *version timestamp* which is the time at which a given structure was last updated and is maintained by the DBMS as well as on the file itself. Load a wrong version of a file and the DBMS will notice the discrepancy.

Thus by maintaining a variety of timestamps it is very difficult to corrupt the database accidentally and the security of the system can be maintained.

Traditional views of privacy

Almost before data began being stored on computers, people were worried about how much data was to be stored and how unauthorized access could be prevented. In the early days of computing the privacy aspect was a much simpler problem than it is today. All the work carried out on computers was performed from within the confines of the computer room. Hence, prevent physical access to the computer room, and your data were safe.

Unfortunately (from a privacy point of view), data lines were developed along with terminals and modems (and these days telecommunications, satellites and lasers), so that nowadays computerized data are passing under, around and over us. Buy a relevant receiver and those data are yours (hence Teletext, Prestel, etc.). Therefore the only ways of securing privacy reasonably (though nothing is infallible) is to:

(1) introduce passwords into the system so that only authorized users can gain access
(2) encode the data whenever they are transmitted in such a way that they could be intercepted.

Since we are interested predominantly in data-storage

systems and not data communications, we shall study the first option.

Traditionally, therefore, access to a computer was/is by user-id and password. The former gives you your own area of disk to play with and the latter gives you access to that area. Alternatively, you might have a password to a more general area (not your own). Such passwords usually are maintained by the operating system: usually encrypted to prevent accidental disclosure in, say, a memory dump. And yet at most installations this set-up is not very secure; there are people who know other people's passwords (they have watched them type it in), both accidentally and deliberately. Passwords are, generally, fairly easy to change but there is apathy about changing them on a regular basis unless there is proof that they are known to other users. In addition, as outlined in Chapter 1, often there is only a single level of privacy. Thus, if the personnel department is a valid user, a single password will gain access to all of their programs and files and, as mentioned, sensitive data will have to be hived off into another system with a password only known to higher management with the problem that they will also want the non-sensitive data as a part of their system and so the danger of duplication and inconsistency looms large.

Levels of privacy

Referring back to the documentation requirements of data analysis outlined in the An entity, An attribute and A relationship sections, we notice the different levels with which access rights must be maintained (i.e. at attribute, entity and relationship levels). In general, we could define six distinct subsets of access constraints.

READ

Whether or not a user can access a piece of data and read its value.

CHANGE

There is a vast difference between simply being able to read a piece of data and being able to update it.

DELETE

Whether or not a user may delete a piece of data or record.

An employee may be allowed to see his bad conduct record, but to be able to delete it would be another matter!

CREATE/EXTEND
If the company has a special *bonus* record for staff eligible for a Christmas bonus then it is unlikely that you would wish anyone to be able to create one.

EXISTENCE VERIFICATION
Often overlooked in the matter of privacy, but a user may not need actually to access data to be able to ascertain important knowledge. A finance company would only need to know the existence of a client's bad debts record to decline them a loan.

EXECUTION
Execution is mentioned here because of the frequent occurrence of general-purpose Query languages (see Chapter 11) which can access the database, but also there is a requirement to restrict the usage of all programs which access data.

Of these, the traditional approach will, generally, only cater for the read/change constraints. Since all files and programs in a particular system are under a single password generally, having access to that password gives the user options to do all of the above. The read/change constraints are really only controlled by the valid user being able to describe a file as being Readonly, though this can be changed easily by the unauthorized user if he knows how.

Database approaches to privacy
Database systems that use submodels indirectly enforce privacy by only allowing the user to see that which he is allowed to see. This is very different to the all-or-nothing approach of the conventional system because by attaching a password to the submodel the user can ensure some form of privacy control.

In addition to this, most database systems allow the DBA to impose access constraints at the database/area/record/data item levels giving all round privacy control.
Again a CODASYL model has been used to illustrate this as shown in Figure 7.2.

```
SCHEMA IS PERSONNEL
ACCESS-CONTROL LOCK IS 'AXOLOTL'
AREA NAME IS GENERAL-AREA
ACCESS-CONTROL LOCK IS 'GENDETS'
AREA NAME IS WAGE-AREA
ACCESS-CONTROL LOCK IS WAGE-LOCK
RECORD NAME IS GENERAL-DETAILS
LOCATION MODE IS CALC EMP-INDEX USING EMP-NO
WITHIN GENERAL-AREA

02 EMP-NO                PIC 9(5);
02 EMP-NAME              PIC X(20);
02 EMP-ADDRESS           PIC X(40);
02 EMP-CONDUCT           PIC X(30)

ACCESS-CONTROL LOCK IS PROCEDURE CONDUCT-
LOCK;
RECORD NAME IS WAGES
LOCATION MODE IS CALC WAGE-INDEX USING WAGE-NO
WITHIN WAGE-AREA

02 WAGE-NO               PIC 9(5);
02 BASIC-RATE            PIC 99V99;
02 HOURS-WORKED          PIC 99V99;
```

Figure 7.2 *Example of a database source showing access control options*

The reader is directed to Chapter 13 for a fuller description of a CODASYL schema, but it is sufficient here to note the usage of the ACCESS-CONTROL locks. In this example they have been defined at the schema, area and data item levels. Since the areas GENERAL-AREA and WAGE-AREA each contain only a single file, an access-control lock at the area level is equivalent to one at the file level. Had the areas contained more than one file we would have had more options open. There are no sets defined here, but had there been we could have defined access-control locks on them (i.e. access control on relationships).

Of interest in the example are the three differing types of access-control lock available to the DBA. These are as follows.

(1) *Fixed constants*. In line 2 access control to the database (schema) is via the password 'AXOLOTL'.Obviously, this is easy to set up and maintain, but has two disadvantages. First, it is difficult to change without recompiling the schema and, secondly, it is available to anyone who gains access to the schema listing.
(2) *Variables*. In line 6 access to the WAGE-AREA is via a variable called WAGE-LOCK. This means that at run time the user

supplies a password which is checked against a value maintained by the DBMS in this variable. Such a variable can have its value changed easily by the DBA and is not visible in the schema listing.

(3) *Subroutines*. In line 15 the access control to the data item EMP-CONDUCT is via a procedure CONDUCT-LOCK. Such a procedure will, in general, have been written by DBA, and has the following advantages.

(a) At run time a user could be checked against a table of valid users; such a table would be easy to maintain.
(b) The procedure can be used to change dynamically the password on a day-to-day (or whatever) basis; for example, on a given day the password might be the day of the month plus the first three letters of the day of the week (an easy task for the computer and relatively easy for the authorized user). More complicated examples are possible certainly whereby an unauthorized user, seeing someone key in a password one day, could not possibly guess what the password will be the following day.

It is a pity that, in general, the tightest security is required at the lowest (i.e. data item) level. Subroutines offer by far the best access-control mechanisms, but their processor overheads are high, particularly if that subroutine has to be performed at every record access.

Summary

The definitions of integrity, security and privacy used within this book may not be the same as your own, but the principles are clear. Most database systems afford mechanisms whereby the data, records and relationships within a database, once set up, are not likely to be corrupted either deliberately or accidentally. Such mechanisms are likely to cause processor overheads, but decisions as to their employment will have to be considered carefully.

CHAPTER 8

Recovery and Backup

Introduction

If a survey were to be carried out on all database users and the question asked, what is the most readily visible advantage of having a database system?, then most would mention the recovery facilities. Recovery of a non-database system is a nightmare, fraught with difficulties and prone to many errors.

There is, unfortunately, no computer yet built that does not occasionally crash on hardware/software errors. In addition, there are precious few programmers who will write programs that will never go wrong, even if they are tested fully.

In this book I shall refer to a machine restart as a time at which the computer halts itself (self-halt) or is halted by operations (forced halt), for whatever reason, and then is booted up again. At such time, if programs are restartable then they should restart automatically (though some operating systems would suspend them awaiting a manual restart), otherwise they are terminated by the operating system. Note that most systems know which programs are running at the time of a halt and can therefore restart them automatically, though this does not mean that they can simply carry on from where they were; in most cases the program's environment is initialized and the program restarts from scratch.

The reasons for a machine restart (MR) are various, but a self-halt might, typically, be caused by a memory problem and a forced halt by operations being aware of a program looping. Whatever the reasons are, work is disrupted and clearly it is desirable to arrive back at a recovered state, ready for normal work to continue, as soon as possible.

It is unlikely that conventional programs will be restartable because:

(1) Unless every update is written to a restart file, it is impossible to know exactly which updates have been affected. If restart files are used, then in a conventional system it is difficult to restart at the correct point because of the following.
(2) When is the update completed? Is it when the updated record has been passed back to the main memory buffer? Or when that buffer has been written back to disk? If the former then some updates will be lost if an MR occurs while the update is being shuffled about in memory, and with the latter, the process of writing the buffers to disk is out of the control of the program. Therefore a program writing a restart record is not quite as simple as it seems.

Note 1: there are cases whereby a single program can be written in such a way that it can redo updates if that program merely does moves and not any arithmetic operations. Similarly, programs that create or delete records can be restartable if they contain some mechanism whereby records already created are not created again (i.e. a find is performed first). But in all these cases, the path is full of difficulties and it is often easiest to simply reload the last dump and rerun the programs.

Note 2: These problems really only apply to update programs. It is normally fairly easy to restart read-only programs. If they are random reads then there is no problem. For sequential reads it is straightforward to maintain a restart file by writing (1) the latest key value (2) any relevant totals to date every x records.

It is therefore one of the curses of conventional systems that so much time is wasted over (often relatively minor) errors as described in Chapter 1.

Transactions and checkpoints

Most database systems work on the basis that an application program is able to define when it is about to update the database (be that a single update or a collection of related updates), and similarly when the program has finished a particular update. These two times generally are referred to syntactically as a *begin-transaction* and an *end-transaction*. During the time in between the two the program is said to be in *transaction state*. As defined previously, all updates performed within a single transaction state (whether one or many) are called collectively a *database transaction*.

Now if an MR occurs whilst a program is in transaction state then the DBMS knows that an update was in the process of being performed and may or may not have been written to disk. It therefore knows that recovery is needed to maintain integrity (exactly how this is done is described in the following sections).

It would seem useful to define a point in time at which the DBMS knows that no updates are being performed currently and therefore no automatic recovery is needed (since the integrity is safe). Such a point is called a *quiet point*. Clearly, if no update programs are running then we have a quiet point, but what if update programs are running more-or-less continuously (such as during an on-line day). In the event of failure we would want the database to be recovered back to the last quiet point. If we then have to rerun all programs, then we are not much better off than the conventional reload and rerun. We therefore define a *checkpoint* to be a point in time when no programs are in transaction state.

The DBA can define a checkpoint as being so many transactions (see Chapter 10), such that after that number of begin-transactions, the DBMS will not allow any more programs to enter transaction state until all current ones have reached their end-transactions, thus forcing a checkpoint. This may mean that programs sometimes have to wait, but the advantages of this system will become apparent after the next section.

Journal files

Databases, generally, provide recovery mechanisms by the use of journal (or audit) files. On these are kept a record of all updates that have been performed against the database. Basically, this will comprise:

(1) a *before image*, or exact copy of the database record before it was updated.

(2) an *after image*, or exact copy of the database record after the update.

To each of these records will be appended the:

(1) exact time of the update (from the machine clock)
(2) name of the program which performed the update
(3) structure number/file name to which the update applies.

TIMESTAMP	PROGRAM	STRUCTURE	IMAGE + DETAILS
09:53:2604	A	06	BEFORE...
09:53:2643	A	06	AFTER...
09:53:2721	CHECKPOINT		
09:53:8912	A	06	BEFORE...
09:53:8931	B	07	BEFORE...
09:53:8967	C	02	BEFORE...
09:53:9002	B	07	AFTER...
09:53:9048	B	07	BEFORE...
09:53:9068	C	02	AFTER...
...ETC...			

Figure 8.1 *Example of the format of a journal file*

A journal file will therefore consist of many pairs of before and after images (though the after image corresponding to a particular before image may not appear juxtaposed if more than one update program is running), plus some checkpoint information. When the DBMS is able to signify a checkpoint, as just defined, it can write a special record to the journal file stating the time of the checkpoint. Thus an example journal file might contain records similar to those as shown in Figure 8.1.

Restart recovery

Supposing that, for whatever reason, an MR occurs after the last record shown above has been written to the journal file. The DBMS can detect that program A is currently in transaction state, but will not know whether the actual record has been updated and written back to disk. Therefore, to be safe, it will rewrite the before image from the journal file back to disk, overwriting any possible update, and thus undoing the update. In practice, the DBMS will reapply all before images from all programs by reading the journal file backwards until it reaches a checkpoint. Here it stops because it knows that the integrity is assured, for the following reasons.

(1) When a checkpoint occurs, the DBMS suspends all programs until all system buffers have been written back to disk (which is why a checkpoint can take some time). Once this is completed the integrity is maintained.

(2) If an MR occurs during a checkpoint then before images can be reapplied back to the last checkpoint.
(3) After this operation (which is done automatically), the DBMS knows the data to be consistent, but one of several things might now happen:

(a) if a particular program is restartable (and the ways of doing this within a database environment vary enormously) then it can be geared to restart from a checkpoint
(b) if it is not restartable then at least it can be terminated in a controlled fashion. Following this the DBA will have several options open concerning the recovery of that particular program (see later sections).

Program rollback

In the Concurrency section in Chapter 7 we looked at the problems of concurrency with its possible deadlock situations, and stated that to avoid it one of the deadlocked programs would have to have its updates undone. By reviewing the journal file it is possible to see how this can be achieved.

When a program is initiated (or terminated), a special record is written to the journal file to signal the beginning or the end (BOJ or EOJ). Thus given that the DBMS can determine a deadlock situation and has some method of choosing which program has priority, the other can be *rolled back* to its BOJ by scanning backwards through the journal file and reapplying all before images related to that program.

Exactly the same process applies if any program fails due to a run-time error: it will be rolled back to BOJ and, in general, this will be done automatically.

However, the two distinct approaches to journal file/locking management, as outlined in the Concurrency section in Chapter 7, must now be examined in more detail.

(1) Page locking is performed such that if program A updates a record on a page then that page is locked and remains locked until A terminates successfully. Basically, this means that A has exclusive use of the file in question (and in general this is forced by declaring USAGE IS EXCLUSIVE in the application program). Running against file F we have therefore the situation as shown in Figure 8.2.

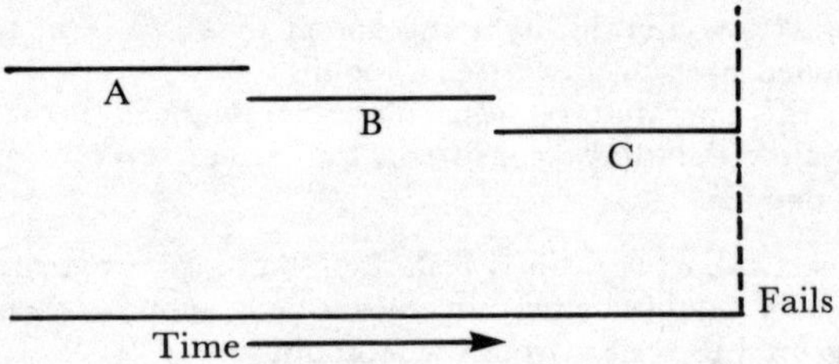

Figure 8.2 *Program run chart where true concurrency is not permitted*

The advantages clearly are that if a program C fails, the most that needs recovering is that single program's updates. The disadvantage is that only one update program can run against a file at any one time. This may not be a problem with batch work but it may be a huge problem with on-line updating.

(2) Page locking is performed as before, but the page is unlocked when the transaction is complete. Clearly, this means that several different programs can update the same file, as shown in Figure 8.3.

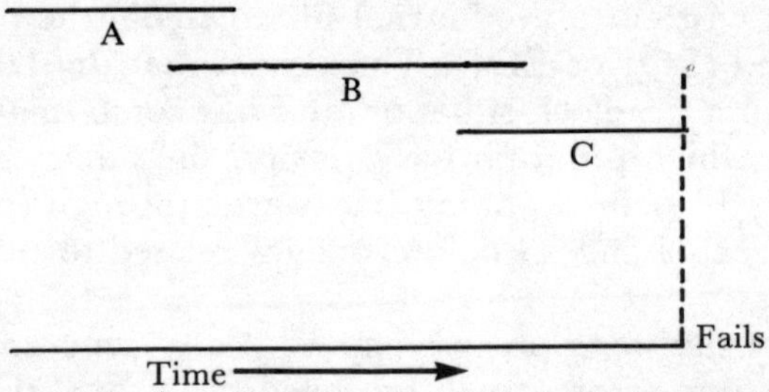

Figure 8.3 *Program run chart with true concurrency*

This now has the disavantage that if C fails then the file must be rolled back to the start of A. In general, this will mean that the whole database needs rolling back and not simply file F because the chances are that each of the concurrent programs will update different combinations of files on the database and not simply F, as is shown in Figure 8.4.

Program	Files updated						
A	1	2					
B		2		4	5		
C	1					6	Fails
D			3				

Figure 8.4 *Complexity of program/file usage*

In this diagram it would be impossible to rollback C without also A and hence B being rolled back. Program D should be unaffected, but in practice it too will be rolled back. Thus with this approach the most important aspect is to have frequent quiet points so that the database will not have to be rolled back too far.

Note: since the scanning of the journal file for relevant entries could be a lengthy process, some systems employ use of a *transient before image file*. Thus, while a program is active, its before images are written to its own journal file as well as to the master journal. If the program fails then its own journal file can be read and images reapplied quickly. If the program terminates successfully then the transient journal file is deleted.

Database rollback

Whichever journal-file method is adopted, situations will occur for which the entire database will need rolling back. Briefly, these include the following:

(1) A software failure occurs within the DBMS or operating system and it is possible that files may have been corrupted as a result. Of course, in general, it would not be known which data have been corrupted, if any, but the recovery mechanism will always assume the worst.

(2) Program errors are discovered after the program has completed: perhaps that two programs were run in the wrong order. In this instance it is not sufficient merely to rollback the offending programs and rerun because subsequent programs may have updated the same file. For the second journal-file approach it matters not because the entire database will need rolling back to a convenient quiet point anyway. Systems that employ transient journal files avoid any disparity by only allowing program rollback from this file. If the program finished and the journal file was deleted then the only course of action is to rollback the entire database, which is the desired result.

In both these cases, the operations/DBA usually are given the choice of manually specifying when the database is to be rolled back to (i.e. it is not done automatically, unlike the program-rollback mechanism mentioned in the last section). This can either be to a specific time (usually a 'not greater than' because the exact timestamp on the journal file will be unknown) or to a specific BOJ. The journal file is scanned backwards and all before images reapplied until the selection criterion is met. Usually, the journal file entries being used are destroyed as rollback proceeds thus making a subsequent rollforward (see the next section) impossible and necessitating the accuracy of the supplied time/BOJ parameter. As to how the operations/DBA know that the rollback has been completed successfully is described in the Recovery listings section where examples are given.

Note that, whereas program rollback should not affect any current programs other than those waiting to use the affected files, database rollback is an exclusive function meaning that as soon as the error is determined, all active programs (including read-only programs) must be terminated and cannot be rerun until the rollback has been completed successfully. In other words, if rollback fails for some reason and the DBMS is not sure of the integrity of the data, it will not allow any programs to proceed until it is sure.

Rollforward

The preceding sections have dealt with all forms of software error, but what of hardware errors? In the event of a disk crash or parity error it is not feasible to rollback because the disk would not be capable of having before images applied to it and, indeed, the DBMS may not be able even to apply the restart recovery. In the non-conventional file situation the only possibility was to reload and rerun. With the database approach there exists a far more efficient solution.

Again the last dump must be reloaded, but the journal file can now be brought into usage by scanning forward and reapplying all of the after images, thus reprocessing all updates performed since the dump. Such an approach must be faster than rerunning the programs. In the latter case there are the program's processor and I/O times to be taken into consideration as well as those of the database, whereas with the former there is, basically, just a simple read-write-read-write operation with very little processor time required. How much time is saved clearly varies, but a typical saving of 90 per cent in overall time is perhaps an underestimate.

Again the operations/DBA usually are given a choice of where to rollforward to in terms of time or EOJ, but again it is essential that the completed task leaves the database in an integral state, i.e. at a quiet point. Thus if our DBMS only allows the option of rolling forward to the end of the journal file, then it may be necessary to rollback to the previous quiet point subsequently.

Note: unlike rollback, the process of rolling forward does not destroy the journal file which means that if the operation is unsuccessful it can be tried again. This is useful particularly if we are trying to rollforward to, say, 10:47 and the DBMS encounters an error on the journal file at 10:42 and terminates. Since the integrity of the data is not guaranteed at 10:42 (not a quiet point) we might have to roll forward again to the quiet point before 10:42 (which will have been noted on the operator's log) and rerun subsequent programs.

As with database rollbacks, the rollforward process affects the whole database and is therefore an exclusive function.

Rebuilds

Some database management systems allow for the rolling forward of only parts of the database and this process is generally referred to as a *rebuild*. This is useful especially if the database is spread across several disks and one fails or perhaps just a single page is corrupted. It would seem a harsh overhead if all programs need terminating to rebuild just a few records.

First, we would expect the DBMS to be able to inform us of exactly which pages are corrupt, which may occur when an application program is trying to read data or when a piece of checking software detects errors (such as checksums; see the Physical data checking section in Chapter 7). A typical error message might be:

READ ERROR PAGE 17 OF FILE INVESTMENTS —
PAGE LOCKED OUT

The row locked out message would mean that no programs could access that page until the error had been removed. Other programs using other files would be allowed to continue.

Armed with this information it would be useful to be able to reload page 17 from the last dump and reapply any updates which have been applied subsequently to page 17 from the journal file. If the related area of disk is corrupted then often the page in question could be rebuilt on a separate area of disk with associated pointers patched up automatically (though the ease with which this could be done clearly depends on the complexity of the physical model). If any program attempts to access that page while it is being rebuilt then the DBMS can return a suitable error message, otherwise all programs can continue. In a similar fashion options usually exist to rebuild several pages, files, areas or whole disks with the minimum of disruption to users.

Clearly, rebuilds of this type must be continued to the end of the journal file (and to this end the DBMS eventually will have to suspend all user programs at a checkpoint while the rebuild catches up and finishes), since rebuilds to a particular time would not guarantee the integrity of the whole database.

Recovery listings

In both forms of database recovery in which the DBA/operations have specified their requirements, it is usual for the DBMS to provide a summary of exactly what it has done before allowing the normal running to proceed. For example, suppose that the request to rollback the database was

ROLLBACK TO LEQ AUG 16 AT 11:23

and produced the following listing as shown in Figure 8.5.

PROGRAM	BOJ		EOJ	
A	16/8/86	11:47		
B	16/8/86	11:42	16/8/86	11:49
C	16/8/86	11:37	16/8/86	11:59
D			16/8/86	11:39

Figure 8.5 *Example rollback listing with a missing BOJ*

Clearly, only program A was running at the time of the error (because B, C and D had reached EOJ), but where is program D's BOJ? It has not been found on the journal file and therefore the database has not been rolled back far enough and, hence, integrity is not guaranteed. The solution here would be to rollback again, having determined the time of D's BOJ. If the option exists to rollback to a BOJ then this should have been used to begin with in preference to the time parameter. If this is done successfully then we would have the listing as shown in Figure 8.6 (bear in mind that the records rolled back previously were destroyed).

PROGRAM	BOJ	EOJ
D	16/8/86 11:22	

Figure 8.6 *Rollback taken to completion*

At this juncture we would know that the database has been rolled back to a quiet point and that integrity is assured.

The printout for a rollforward would be similar except that BOJs and EOJs would be in a forward chronological order. On this occasion, if the listing is incomplete (i.e. a missing EOJ), two options would exist:

(1) to rollforward again to the corrected time/EOJ
(2) to rollback now to the prior quiet point and continue from there.

Where the time parameter is used then clearly mistakes can occur if the DBA/operations are relying on hand-written log entries and not machine timings. To this effect the BOJ/EOJ options are far more preferable. Sometimes the DBMS provides a print journal utility which lists all BOJ and EOJ times for a given period which can be used in manual forms of recovery.

It was stated in the Database versions and timestamps section in Chapter 7 that if the facility exists to initialize a file it results in a special record being written to the journal file which produces a discontinuity. If a rollback reaches a discontinuity it will terminate being unable to reconstruct how the file looked before it was initialized and the only alternative is to rollforward instead. However, if a rollforward reaches a discontinuity, it is possible to reconstruct the initialization procedure and then continue rolling forward afterwards.

Other recovery facilities

From what has been stated to date, it might seem as if the DBMS can recover all situations. What can possibly go wrong? For example:

(1) the disk or tape on which the journal file resides may crash or have parity errors
(2) recovery may fail because of errors on the journal file.

Both these cases can be catered for if the journal file is duplicated and many database management systems will allow this. It may seem a high overhead in backing storage and I/O time to duplicate, but it does mean that if recovery fails with one journal file in error then the DBMS can automatically switch to the other and continue. This means that lightning would have to strike twice in the same place (which it probably will at some time) for recovery to fail and, if this happens, the DBA still has the option to reload and rerun.

Whether or not the journal file is kept on disk depends on the tape unit's/operating system's ability to read tapes backwards as is needed with rollbacks. Usually, they are kept on disk (unless disk storage is at a premium) because:

(1) disks generally are more reliable
(2) recovery will be faster.

Certainly, any transient journal files will be kept on disk for quick access, but whenever keeping any journal files on disk it is always prudent to maintain them on separate disks to the database and the duplicated journal files on separate disks again.

In general, the maximum size of the journal file can be decreed by the DBA. Once this maximum is reached, some systems go into automatic restart recovery to the previous checkpoint and await instructions. The better management systems create a new journal file and, automatically, fire off a disk to tape copy to back up the old journal file to tape. In such cases continuity between the files is maintained by numbering the blocks on the file and by continuing the sequence on the new file. With the former database management systems a new journal file is created after each database dump, but it is left to the DBA to ensure that the old one is backed up and that the new one is large enough to last until the next dump. Whichever method is available, it is always advisable to maintain a library of previous journal files (usually on the grandfather, father and son cycle), because there is little point in keeping old database dumps for recovery if there are no journal files to go with them.

Thus recovery can sometimes involve the DBA/operations mounting a succession of tapes as and when needed (and the duplicate tapes if they are needed/available) until recovery is complete. If a good backup supply is kept then, even if a rollforward cannot be performed because of parity errors on the last database backup tape, it should be possible to rollforward from the last dump before that.

Backup facilities

It has been stated already how backup plays an important part in rollforwards or rebuilds, but it was also stated in Chapter 1 that backups infrequently are taken because of the inability to be updating files at the same time. Most database management systems have various dump facilities to alleviate both these problems and others.

(1) It has been shown already in the Physical data checking section in Chapter 7 how some systems recalculate checksums during the dump procedure and can therefore detect any disk errors (and hence allow them to be corrected) before application programs find them and crash.
(2) Other possibilities might include copying all the data from disk to tape as usual, but at the end reading the tape backwards and comparing it with the data on disk to verify that the dump has produced no errors. It must at this point be stressed that database dumps as performed by the DBMS or operating system are physical copies and that there is no logical ordering to the records. Therefore they cannot be used when restructuring the database (see Chapter 9).
(3) Some DBMSs will allow different parts of the database to be dumped to different destinations. Thus all files on diskpack A will be dumped to the first tape, all those on diskpack B will go to the second tape and so on. Often the two can be dumped concurrently (assuming two tape drives), which will increase efficiency if there is more than one I/O channel available from the diskpacks and to the tape drives. Such a dump will be useful particularly when rebuilding packs, because the recovery mechanism will not have to search for the 'data that goes on pack B', but merely ask for dump tape 2.

(4) Another useful facility is the option of only dumping parts of the database instead of all of it. This facility, generally, only extends to whole files being dumped and not merely odd pages. Thus if we are pursuing currently the mortgage processing then at the same time we could be dumping the investment files, and vice versa.
(5) Perhaps the most useful backup function (unfortunately only offered by a few database management systems at present) is the ability to perform on-line dumps. The problems outlined in Chapter 1 meant that 24-h on-line work/batch processing was impossible with conventional files, but if on-line dumping is available then all problems are removed. Whatever the recovery mechanisms available, it is still advantageous to dump as frequently as possible to reduce recovery times. Whereas with the conventional approach, on-line dumps are impossible because we would not know which updates are on tape and which are not, with database systems we do because they are also on the journal file. Thus if the time of the commencement of the dump is noted then we can always reload the tape dump and rollforward the database to the end of the dump and thus reapply all after images created while the dump was taking place and hence the integrity is maintained.

In practice, most database management systems only require the previous dump reloading in the event of a rollforward or rebuild, and so the above procedure is being performed anyway.

With both on-line dumping and partial database dumping, mechanisms must exist whereby the integrity of the database can be assured. In Chapter 1 it was stated how easy it was to corrupt conventional files by reloading wrong versions at recovery time. In the next section it will be shown how the database approach counters this problem.

Timestamps revisited

This section uses the Burroughs DMS-II as an example. Other database management systems which allow on-line or partial dumping have their own mechanisms.

The whole database is controlled dynamically by a *control* file which contains data pertaining to the current state of the:

(1) Audit (journal) files
(2) usage of the database, whether it is in normal use currently, or exclusive use by rollback or rollforward, etc.
(3) update level of the database
(4) creation, format and version timestamps of all structures within the database.

The timestamps are also maintained on the files themselves and, at a database open, all such statistics are cross-checked. If any discrepancies are found, then no processing is permitted until the errors have been corrected.

Suppose that we have reloaded a partial dump of the mortgage files. The version timestamp (i.e. the time of the last update) on that reloaded file will not match that on the control file (assume that the mortgages have been updated since the partial dump), and so we cannot continue with any processing until we have rebuilt the mortgage file. (While rebuilding takes place the after-image timestamp will be written as the version timestamp on the file. Thus when the last image is applied the version timestamp on the file will equal that on the control file.) In other words, yet again, we cannot use the database unless it is consistent.

Note that if the file had been restructured since the dump (see Chapter 9) then the DBMS would not let us rebuild because the format timestamp on the file would not equal that on the control file.

As a more complex example, suppose that we have taken an on-line dump of the whole database as that shown in Figure 8.7.

END OF DUMP

DUMPED CONTROL FILE VERSION TIMESTAMP FOR FILE F	17/08/86	14:27:3802
DUMPED VERSION TIMESTAMP ON FILE F	17/08/86	14:31:2639
ON DISK CONTROL FILE VERSION TIMESTAMP FOR FILE F	17/08/86	14:58:2914
ON DISK VERSION TIMESTAMP ON FILE F	17/08/86	14:58:2914

Figure 8.7 *Example timings of an on-line dump*

Note that at the end of the dump, the version timestamps on the disk control file and the disk file F are consistent but not those on the tape because the control file was dumped before the file.

Suppose that for some reason we now have to reload the dump in its entirety. In doing so the disk control file and file F will be overwritten by the dumped versions. When we now come to open the database, the DBMS will flag that the control file's and file F's version timestamps do not match and will not let us continue until the database has been rolled forward. Moreover, since the control file contains a pointer to the audit file and the control file is dumped first, by reloading the control file the DBMS will know where on the audit file to start the rollforward.

Clearly, this involves an overhead of having to use rollforward recovery every time we wish to reload a prior on-line dump, but against that is set the very great advantage of being able to dump files while they are in use and hence be able to have an uninterrupted flow to the data processing.

Summary

In general, the actual recovery procedures afforded by any one database management system vary in detail, but all provide similar basic features of rollback and rollforward, and, more importantly, ensure that following the recovery mechanism the user can be assured that the database's integrity is guaranteed otherwise they would not be allowed to proceed. If all recovery procedures fail then there is always the original option of reload and rerun.

CHAPTER 9

Restructure and Reorganize

Introduction

To design a database system and hope that it will for ever remain constant is a very blind outlook and, at most installations, flexibility is considered to be one of the main goals of database design (see the Design objectives section in Chapter 5). Future changes can be varied in nature and most of these will be unpredicted at the time of the initial design. In particular, an organization may decide to:

(1) take on new areas of business (for example, our bank may launch a new type of account or a new type of mortgage insurance)
(2) change existing areas of business (for example, the way in which interest is calculated or the way in which insurances are handled)
(3) computerize existing manual systems, possibly through new innovations in technology (for example, there may become a need to computerize management expenses once the accounting side of the business has been computerized successfully)
(4) change the volume of business, either by external factors or by a conscious decision to market certain products more fully, increase advertising, etc. (alternatively, a merger with another business might double the volume of data required to be stored).

All of these are likely to affect the existing database and the ease with which such changes can be incorporated might be critical. Suppose that government legislation means a radical change to the way in which tax is paid on investment interest which involves changes to the investment file. The organization cannot say that it cannot be done or that it will take x amount of time; the change will have to be done as and when decreed.

There will also be times when the efficiency of the database is suffering because the way in which data are stored has changed. This may be because:

there are varying volumes of data
deletions have left many holes in the file
insertions have led to overflow problems
patterns of access may have changed such that, for example, there is no longer a business requirement to access records from files A and B together and hence there is no longer a need to group related records on the same page.

The overall result of any of these would be, to a lesser or greater extent, that the neat efficient database which was set up carefully by the load programs, has degraded in performance with an overall loss in efficiency. (As to how such a degradation might be noted, see Chapter 10.)

The general desire in such a situation might be to 'shuffle the data around a bit' such that spare space is consolidated, overflows are eliminated and natural groupings restored. Any approach to shuffling the data around has to be considered carefully.

Again, the terminology varies from database system to system, but the definitions used in this book will be as follows.

(1) If changes are required to the logical structure of the database, i.e. by adding or deleting areas, structures, records, sets or data items, or by changing the size/type of data items, then these will be performed via a *restructure*.
(2) If changes are needed to the physical storage of the database, then these will be performed by a *reorganize*.

Restructure

Changes to the logical structure of the database could involve the addition, deletion or amendment of

(1) record types
(2) data items
(3) set types.

It must be stressed that these changes initially will be made known to the business as changes to

(1) entities
(2) attributes
(3) relationships

and it is the DBA's task to decide how such changes will affect the existing database.

For example, it may be decided to include the address code as a separate item on all stored address data, perhaps because the post office has decided on a postal rebate if all mail is sent with address code included. The DBA must find all occurrences of an address field and make decisions as to how the extra field will be implemented. For example:

(1) is the address code already in existence, perhaps stored on the end of a data item called

03 COUNTY PIC X(20)

(2) is it to be implemented as a separate item or can COUNTY be broken down into two separate items?
(3) would it be useful to have the address code as a key item such that all customers living in a particular area can be identified quickly?
(4) what are the consequences of there not being an address code available immediately (such as on new housing developments)?

It is important that the DBA looks to the conceptual model and its associated documentation to map out any proposed changes, because it is here that the changes affect on the organization will show. To this end he should be aided by the data dictionary (see Chapter 11) if one exists.

It is likely that the systems analysts will have been informed (and they may even be the originators) of the proposed change, such that it will be left to them to decide which existing application programs require amendment or whether new ones will need to be written (and again the data dictionary will be able to help them with the former) but it is very important that they liaise with the DBA about the new submodel requirements and the timescales involved in pursuing the change.

Unload and load

The actual processes involved with restructuring vary from system to system. With many, the data must be unloaded logically from the database. This entails a special dump program being written which copies the data from disk to tape (usually), in some predefined sequence which will make the reloading as efficient as possible. Once the data are dumped, the old file can be destroyed and then recreated in its new format. Generally, this process is supervised by the DBMS which will create and store a new format timestamp for the structure and also increment its update level by one. The dump tape can then be used by a specially written load program to load the data back onto the new file. Such a load program will be written with similar considerations to those outlined in the Load programs section in Chapter 6.

A database dump is unsuitable for this process for two reasons:

(1) the update level is changed by the restructure which means that the DBMS will not allow a prior dump to be loaded at the wrong update level
(2) even if the first problem could be overcome, a database dump will neither be in a logical ordering of records, and will hence make the load inefficient, nor will it be in a form easily readable by an application program since it will contain checksum data, page control data, pointers, etc., which are invisible normally to the user program.

Clearly, such a process can be very time consuming and for a large file the timescales could be of the order of days rather than hours. Moreover, a restructure is an exclusive function which means that all application programs will have to be excluded while it is being performed. Thus we are considering weekend schedules at the best and for some restructures we may have to be planning for the next 3-or 4-day public holiday.

Owing to the possible size of the task, the onus clearly is on the dump and load programs to be as efficient as possible. To that end they will have to be written very carefully and tested thoroughly before they are actually employed, preferably with testing against a database of similar data volume to be able to gauge an approximation for the timescales.

Some database management systems broach part of this problem by using fourth-generation software. The DBA feeds the proposed changes to the DBMS (usually in interactive mode) and the latter generates code which will dump and reload the required file. Usually, it is source code that is generated which means that the DBA has the opportunity to modify it before compilation. For example, normally the DBMS will generate code to dump and load a file in the order of its prime key. There may be reasons why the DBA wishes to reload in a secondary key order and this can be achieved easily. Generally, the dump will be directed to tape, but there is often the option of the restructure being performed *in situ*. Thus a new structure is generated by the DBMS and the old data physically mapped on to it without needing a secondary medium. At the end of the process (if successful) the original file is removed and the new one becomes a part of the database. In the event of failure the original is still there and can be used.

From the data dictionary, the DBA should have been able to compile a list of application programs which will require amending and/or recompiling as a result of the restructure. Those of the former category will be passed to the programming teams, but there may be difficulties in recompiling and testing such programs before the actual restructure is done. This is simply because the testing is, as usual, essential before usage but there is no suitable database to test against. A possible solution to this problem, using test databases, is outlined in Chapter 12.

At the end of the restructure, the DBA can at least rest assured that, if the DBMS uses timestamps or some equivalent, then any programs which slip through the net and are not recompiled will not be allowed to run against the database and will therefore not be capable of corrupting the database.

It should be noted that some restructuring exercises will not require the unloading and loading of data nor the recompilation of programs. For example, the addition of a new file or record type will probably only entail the recompilation of the DBMS code to flag that it exists and provide the new accessing code, followed by the structure's initialization and readiness for use by (usually) new programs.

Change of record layouts

Perhaps the most common form of restructuring exercise revolves around one of the following:

(1) change of the format of an existing data item, e.g. addition of an extra digit to a numeric field
(2) addition of new data items to an existing record.

Deletion of data items is a process seldom contemplated. If items are used no longer then, because of the large amount of time required to restructure and remove them, often they are left unused on the record. Similarly, the change of data-item names (which would make unused items reusable) generally is avoided because usually it means deletion of the old item and addition of the new via a restructure, even if the two are of the same length and type (though, of course, there is no reason why the unused item cannot be renamed in subschemae).

Suppose that a record for a customer appeared as that shown in Figure 9.1. Note how the two odd number of digit items have been grouped together to minimize storage requirements if numeric data can be packed. The total number of bytes required for storage is 73 (with packing). Suppose that the computer is a word machine with four bytes to a word. This means that the customer record actually will be allocated 19 words of physical storage. In other words, three bytes are wasted (this assumes that there are no pointers on the record which, generally, add one word to the length for each pointer). Some database management systems allow us to use those three bytes by declaring them as a *filler* item (similar to the COBOL *filler*, except that they must appear at the end of the record). If now we wish to restructure the record by adding a two-digit code then we can simply redefine the existing *filler* into a two-digit identifier plus two bytes of *filler*. In this way the physical size of the record has not changed and hence no dump and reload is necessary. Also the only programs that will need changing are those which will want to use the new item whether or not subschemae are used.

```
02 CUSTOMER-NUMBER          PIC 9(7).
02 SEX                      PIC 9.
02 NAME                     PIC X(20).
02 ADDRESS-1                PIC X(20).
02 ADDRESS-2                PIC X(20).
02 POST-CODE                PIC X(8).
02 AGE                      PIC 99.
```

Figure 9.1 *Example customer record*

If such a provision as *fillers* is allowed for by a DBMS generally it is sensible to make the record size into a whole number of words and, if the structure of the record is likely to be particularly volatile, then there is no reason why we should not add on a *filler* of any number of bytes and, as long as it does not increase storage overheads vastly, it will be worth the saving in future work.

Reorganization

This is the process whereby, for a variety of possible reasons, we wish physically to move data around on disk. The usual reason is either to consolidate space or to resituate data which has become less ordered or grouped than we would like and is therefore impairing the efficiency of the database. Other reasons might be as follows:

(1) As a direct consequence of a restructure. By adding new records/data items or by deleting or amending them we may have more/less data on each page than we require.
(2) Patterns of storage and access may have changed. For example, there may now be a business requirement to produce an important report daily. Such a report might involve files F1 and F2 which before were unrelated. It might be decided that there is just cause to represent the new relationship by storing associated records of F1 and F2 on the same page physically.
(3) Volumes of data have changed and the efficiency of the database has degraded. For example, a file originally may have been created with Calc access in the belief that it would not contain more than 1000 records. With that value in mind, table and/or page sizes were set accordingly. Over a period of time the number of records goes up to 5000 and the result is many overflow pages being used. (When designing a database the DBA should predict what will happen to the business over the subsequent five years or more. In practice this is extremely difficult.)

The actual reorganization (sometimes called *physical placement reorganization* or *garbage collection*) often requires a logical unload/reload of the data in similar manner to the restructure (although again some database management systems allow this to be done *in situ*). The difference between a restructure and a reorganize is that, with the latter, no user programs will need recompiling (in general).

Restructure/reorganize timetable

The timescales for the restructuring/reorganizing processes must be thought out/estimated meticulously as soon as possible after the request for change is given, such that everyone who has a part to play can draw up their own timetables. The following is an example of the processes required.

(1) Check with the conceptual model to decide on how the proposed changes will affect the database structure as a whole.
(2) Use data dictionary, if available (otherwise it's down to a manual search of program documentation), to derive a list of application programs which will be affected by the changes. Pass the list to the systems analysts who will decide which programs need amending, and which simply need recompiling, and will then allocate the work to programmers.
(3) Write or generate the unload/load programs. The unload program can be compiled immediately, but the load program cannot until a test database has been created.
(4) Update the live database to create a test version (see Chapter 12) and syntax run the proposed update against it to clear any possible syntax errors. Compile the load program against this version and test the reload for run-time errors/timing estimates. Allow the programmers to use this version to test their amended programs (bear in mind that their programs must be compiled against this test version).
(5) Dump the existing live database software to tape if it was not done already after the last update. It has not so far been mentioned, but in updating the database it is usual to have to recompile some or all of the DBMS software to reflect the changes. Thus the software also has an update level to match that of the database and it is impossible to run a database with out-of-date software.

At this point we are ready to proceed once all necessary application programs have been amended and once a suitable time slot has been agreed with operations.

(6) Dump the database. As with (5) this is a security measure such that if things later go wrong, we can always return to the original database and continue with normal processing.
(7) Logically dump the database or generate the restructuring program using the DBMS software if available.
(8) Physically perform the restructuring by either creating a new file manually or allow the restructuring program to do so.
(9) Recompile the new database software.
(10) Reload the database from tape (if the restructuring program has not done so already by mapping across from the old file in 8).
(11) With similar considerations as outlined in Chapter 6 it may be possible to turn the journal file off for this reloading or perform any of the other time-saving ideas. This is the time for silent prayer because an error in the load program half-way through a long run generally will mean that the exercise should be abandoned and tried again the following weekend.
(12) While the database is reloading, all relevant programs can be recompiled against the new database software. Note that this cannot be done against the test version because the format timestamps would be different.

(13) If the previous two steps are successful then dump the database again (physically). This is because the restructure will cause a discontinuity on the journal file through which the database will not be able to rollforward/rebuild and so it is essential to have a new dump to recover from.

(14) Dump the new database software to tape ready for the next restructure.

Note:if we were contemplating a reorganize rather than a restructure, then essentially we would have only to be concerned with points (3), (6) – (8), (10), (11) and (13).

Summary

The problems of change outlined in Chapter 1 may not have been removed completely by the database approach. Certainly, for many database systems, we still have to dump off the data and then reload them again as before, but because of the devices of data dictionary and timestamping, we can be assured that all programs which require amendment will be flagged as such and that if any slip the net they will not be allowed to run, and hence corrupt the data. Thus, once again, the integrity of the system is being maintained.

CHAPTER 10

Tuning the Database

Introduction

The efficiency of the database we have constructed would soon degrade if we simply loaded it up and let it run, and every time it crashed, for whatever reason, find out what the trouble is and fix it. It is a part of the DBA's job to try to foresee problems (particularly with regard to future restructures and reorganizations) and to try to cure or circumvent them before they have had time to develop. To this end, most database management systems supply (usually at extra cost!) a set of software designed specifically for monitoring the performance of the database.

This software can take the form of any of the following three.

(1) Software that is run occasionally to scan the physical database and produce a report of disk usage, wasted space, overflow situations, etc.

(2) Software that runs concurrently with the database (and usually is a part of the DBMS code) and produces statistics on the dynamic workings of the database such as the memory management, read times and physical I/O times for each program which runs against the database.

(3) A combination of the above two.

Given a piece of software of this nature, clearly it is up to the DBA to run it as and when required, in the case of (1), and how to interpret the results produced and decide:

(a) what has caused the results (if unusually good or bad)? Was it a special year-end or one-off program the efficiency of which we may not be too bothered with? Were there known hardware problems at the time to account for the results? Was the program itself inefficiently written? Could the database design be at fault?

(b) based on the deductions from (a), what can be done to improve the situation (be those improvements to the program or database)?

Much of this chapter concerns parameters which on some database management systems are easy to change dynamically, while others require a reorganize and possibly a database recompilation. It is essential that the DBA is aware of exactly what they can or cannot do at a dynamic level, when the database is designed initially as, clearly, this may affect the design. For example, if they cannot add extra space to an area without having to recompile the database, then that spare space will have to be designed into the original model.

Program statistics

Many DBMSs produce program statistics which can, if taken independently of any other information, produce results which are very misleading. Database processor and I/O times can vary enormously from one run of a program to another, depending very largely on what else the computer is doing at the time (this is contrary to most theory). The DBA must collect together several sets of statistics for a single program, determine (usually from the statistics) whether the same volume of work was carried out by each run of the program, and weight the results accordingly to produce an average.

For example, if an on-line inquiry program performs a single inquiry, the database statistics might produce an I/O time of 1.07 s, which might make it appear that the DBMS took 1.07 s to locate a single record. Running the same program with two inquiries might show a time of 1.09 s. From this the DBA could deduce reasonably that a database I/O takes 0.02 s and the rest of time is taken in the database being fired up, buffers initialized and all the necessary DBMS code read into memory. Of course, in practice, the number of inquiries in a true sample would be very much greater than one or two. A typical set of statistics produced by a program run might appear similar to those as shown in Figure 10.1.

Given that there is one MTG-CNTRLS record for each of the 200 branches, that MTG-CNTRLS is a Calc file whereas mortgages and customers are both index sequential, and that a physical read (from disk) does not take place if the record is already extant in memory, we can deduce what the program which produced these results probably does and analyse its inefficiencies (of course the DBA would know what it does).

PROGRAM – MTG04

Total DB processor	time	00:02:23	(2 min 23 s)
I/O	time	00:31:21	
elapsed	time	00:47:53	

STRUCTURE	RECS READ	PHYS READS	TOTAL I/O	AVE (ms)	RECS WRTN	PHYS WRITES	TOTAL I/O	AVE (ms)
MORTGAGE	7283	4283	00:03:29	49	7283	4283	00:04:12	59
MTG-TRANS	21426	48	00:00:03	62	7291	52	00:00:03	58
MTG-INDEX	7283	3741	00:02:11	35	0	0	0	0
MTG-CNTRLS	7283	6108	00:05:54	58	7283	6108	00:04:10	41
CUSTOMERS	7249	7041	00:05:11	44	0	0	0	0
CUST-INDEX	7249	6914	00:04:09	·36	0	0	0	0

Figure 10.1 *An example set of program statistics*

(1) There were no mortgage records created, otherwise there would be writes to the MTG-INDEX, but the mortgages are being updated.
(2) The number of mortgage records being written is very similar to the number of MTG-TRANS records being written.
(3) Customer information is only being read.

The most likely scenario is therefore that the program is adding mortgage transactions to the file (amending existing transactions is far less likely given the nature of the business and the quantities being written), updating the mortgage record, updating the MTG-CNTRLS record and reading related customer information (for a printout?).

There is evidence in the results to show that mortgages are being read in random order:

(a) were the mortgages being read in sequential order, we would expect far less reads on MTG-INDEX

(b) if the input file was in branch order, we would expect a maximum of 200 physical reads for MTG-CNTRLS (less if they are blocked).

All of this the DBA should know from the program documentation, but their conclusions should be the same, as follows.

(1) It would appear that, in all but 48 cases, the existing mortgage transactions are on the same page as their owners (since no further physical reads were required to access the transactions). This is good news as it shows that our physical-placement strategy is still reasonably efficient, but from the number of logical transaction reads it is clear that the program is having to chain through the existing transactions (i.e. do a FIND NEXT) before the new one is inserted. This problem will worsen as the number of transactions grows throughout the year. It implies that either no mechanism exists to FIND LAST (see the Linked lists section in Chapter 6), or else one exists but the programmer is not using it (i.e. the program is inefficient and not the database). It is hoped that it is the latter because to correct the former will involve a restructure and should have been foreseen when the database was designed.
(2) A general conclusion might be to presort the transactions before running the program (into account-number order). If the account-number ranges are linked to particular branches, then this will not only cut down on the number of mortgage and MTG-INDEX physical reads, but also those for MTG-CNTRLS. We would not expect the customer statistics to be improved because they will always be random, the number of physical reads being slightly less than the number of logical reads purely because of the occasional chance siting of two consecutive (as processed) records being on the same page (which was therefore still in memory).

The result of this might be to save up to 10 min of I/O time, but consideration must be made of how long the presort will take. It is likely to take several minutes, so would we be saving really? An alternative might be as shown in the next section.

Buffer management

Supposing that our database has had two buffers allocated for each structure (the extra one to allow for READAHEAD if the accessing is sequential). If we could change this aportioning of memory at run time dynamically, then certainly we could improve the efficiency of the database. For example, the MTG-CNTRLS record is 50 bytes long, is blocked in 10s, and there is a total of 200 records.

In the normal running of the above program, with two buffers, there would be 20 records in memory at any one time. If the next required record is not one of those 20 then one of the buffers will have to be flushed (discarded or written back to disk if it has been updated) and the new page read in. Thus for a random reading we have a 0.9 probability that a physical read will be needed for each required record. Suppose now that we could alter the number of buffers to 20 dynamically. The memory overheads are fairly small (10 k) but only 20 physical reads are necessary to read all pages into memory such that no more physical reads are necessary thereafter (although the buffers will still need flushing at checkpoints; see the Transactions and checkpoints section in Chapter 8). The difference between records being read from disk to being read from memory is enormous (approximately 40 ms – 5 μs). So the result of the number of buffers being increased will save 4 min of I/O time directly without the need to presort transactions.

Other programs might only require a single MTG-CNTRLS record and so it would be inappropriate to read all 200 into memory. Therefore it is highly advantageous for the buffering to be controllable dynamically (and perhaps to be included in the operating instructions for the program).

Were the MTG-CNTRLS records each 500 bytes long, it might be less feasible to have them all in memory at once (100 k) but even here, by just doubling the number of available buffers, we arc increasing the hit rate and reducing the I/O time.

A further example of memory management might be seen with the investment index. If we allow 20 investments per page (with their transactions), then we would need 50 000 table entries in the index. By dividing these into 50 entries per table (see Appendix B), we need a 1000 tables. For these we would need 20 subtables and one sub-subtable (in other words three levels of table). Thus to access an investment record via the index takes four reads. If we only have two buffers available then we would need to:

(1) read in the sub-subtable
(2) read in the relevant subtable
(3) flush out (1) and read in the relevant table.

Clearly, it would be advantageous to allocate at least three buffers to the index such that the sub-subtable can be kept in memory permanently (since the sub-subtable is needed for every find it will never be flushed out except at checkpoints).

Readaheads

If a program is reading a file sequentially, then it will read in a page of data, process it and then read the next. However, there will be a certain delay while the next page is being read in, a delay which could be avoided if the computer could pre-empt the call for the next page and read it in while the previous page is being processed. Such a device is called *readahead* and, clearly, requires a minimum of two I/O buffers in memory. The question now is, how does the DBMS know that the file is being read sequentially? On some systems there is a special DDL syntax for sequential reading which flags the programs intentions to the system. On others, a record is kept of the I/O requests. If three or four consecutive pages are read into memory, one after the other, then the DBMS assumes that accessing is sequential, switches to a readahead mode and reads in the fourth or fifth page before it is requested. (It should be noted that this is not exclusive to database management systems and many operating systems perform readaheads on non-database files.)

If the records on a file are blocked (block = page) correctly, then most sequential programs will be processor bound, i.e. having read a block into memory it will take longer to process every record on that block than it will to read in the next block. However, if the program involved is doing very little processing (for example, perhaps just dumping the records to tape), then it is more likely to be I/O bound and time can be wasted waiting for the next block to be read in, even taking readahead into consideration.

A useful weapon in the DBA's armoury might therefore be the ability to alter the unit of physical access from a block into a superblock dynamically when performing sequential reads. Thus, instead of reading in

10 records at a time (or whatever the blocking factor is), the DBA can specify a superblock to be equal to 10 blocks, and thus 100 records are read in at one time. Again the memory overheads are high, but this feature is of great use on a dedicated task where time is of the essence.

Memory management
Those database management systems that produce program statistics usually also produce a summary listing of the database usage every time the database is opened (if various programs overlap in their running then the database will only be opened once by the first and closed once by the last to finish). As well as a summary of I/Os against each structure used, as shown in Figure 10.1, there might also appear a summary of the memory usage. Examples of these, and their significance, follow.

(1) MAXIMUM ALLOCATED MEMORY = 100 000 WORDS
MAXIMUM MEMORY USED = 96 329 WORDS
NUMBER OF OVERLAYS = 2386
NUMBER OF FORCED OVERLAYS = 487

When creating the database, the DBA often has to specify a maximum amount of memory that the database will use. Too much and other programs, utilities and/or system software may not have enough memory to function. Too little and the following problems may occur. If more than the maximum is used, the system should not fall down but the number of forced overlays will increase. A forced overlay occurs when the system has to write a buffer back to disk at a time when it would not normally do so to make room for another page to be read in. This means an increase in I/O time and a decrease in efficiency.

The DBA should therefore be aware of times at which memory usage peaks: at certain times of the day or with certain programs. To aid them, many manufacturers provide software which will produce memory maps of usage over a given period. Using this information the DBA may decide that the memory allocation should be increased dynamically at certain times. (The actual database memory usage, clearly, depends on the buffer sizes and any use of superblocks may affect it radically.)

(2) TOTAL NUMBER OF PHYSICAL READS = 4206
TOTAL NUMBER OF PHYSICAL WRITES = 683
AVERAGE WAIT TIME PER I/O = 54.3 ms
CHANNEL 1 – NUMBER OF READS = 1032
NUMBER OF WRITES = 293
AVERAGE WAIT TIME PER I/O = 79 ms
CHANNEL 2 – ...ETC...

The DBA can use these statistics to determine whether certain I/O channels are being overloaded. (*Note*: there may only exist a single channel between the processor and three or four disk packs, though the number varies and some do have a separate channel to every disk and every tape.) In general, it is wise to not have databases on the same disk (or string of disks) as the operating system or any often-used system files if it can be at all avoided, because that channel will be in constant use and the DBMS will have to wait for its I/Os. The DBA must therefore be careful as to which files are stored where.

In the same way care must be taken that disk head movements are kept to a minimum. Normally, this is achievable by spreading the database across several disks such that structures likely to be in use at the same time are on different disks. For example, we might have:

DISK 1 INVESTMENTS
CUST-INDEX
DISK 2 MORTGAGES
INV-INDEX
DISK 3 CUSTOMERS
MTG-INDEX

Clearly, the restriction on efficiency is the number of disks available.

(3) CURRENT JOURNAL FILE NUMBER = 97 (28% FULL)
CURRENT JOURNAL FILE PAGE NUMBER = 3842
CHECKPOINT = 10 TRANSACTIONS
AVERAGE TIME FOR CHECKPOINT = 0.9 S

General journal file information can be very useful to the

DBA. The journal file is a file written to just as any other file and so its I/O times are equally as important, particularly with regards to checkpoints. A checkpoint can take the DBMS a considerable length of time (comparatively speaking), largely because all updated buffers are written back to disk. If the current work being carried out is mostly on-line with perhaps 10 or 15 transactions/min, then we can afford to take one or two checkpoints during that time (an extra second or two in a minute is a relatively small overhead). However, if the work is batch and we are processing, perhaps, five transactions/s, then 30 per cent of our time is now taken up in checkpointing and will drastically increase the program's run time. Certainly, it would be beneficial if the DBA could alter dynamically that value of 10 transactions per checkpoint to, say, 100. Now only 3 per cent of the time is taken in performing checkpoints.

Summary of run-time statistics

What must be stressed at this point is that features mentioned to date in this chapter certainly are not general features, available with every database management system. Moreover, other systems have their own, equally useful features. Those given here are merely representative of the kind of options that can be open to the DBA and which, if used correctly, can increase the efficiency of the database greatly. In particular, the database can be altered dynamically to improve the throughput of every program if desired by changing its own environment.

Clearly, if it is necessary to restructure or reorganize the database merely to change the memory allocation or buffer sizes, then tuning of this nature is severely restricted.

If it is possible, then the database statistics, as shown, provide the DBA with the best indication of how the database is performing, structure by structure, on a day-to-day basis. By maintaining these statistics over a period of time, the DBA can ascertain whether the efficiency of the system is degrading. For example, if the average I/O time to read a record of a particular file shows a marked increase over a period of weeks, then problems with the file's structure are likely and the DBA may have to resort to another piece of software to determine what the problems are: the database analyser.

Database analyser

Such a piece of software will, generally, be manufacturer supplied and will read through the whole, or selected parts, of the database to analyse the content of each structure. The report produced will show the DBA where inefficiencies lie and can point out where possible restructure or reorganize requirements are likely.

The reports generated vary from system to system but given here are two examples which display some of the information produced and the action required.

(1) FILE – INVESTMENTS
ACCESSED BY INDEX – INV-INDEX
TOTAL RECORDS = 978 326
RECORDS PER PAGE = 50
TOTAL PAGES = 37 286
% SPACE PER PAGE = 16.4 (AVERAGE)
INVESTMENT FILE IS 78% IN THE SAME ORDER AS INV-INDEX
INV-INDEX TABLESIZE = 100 ENTRIES

NUMBER OF TABLES –	LEVEL 1	9
	LEVEL 2	420
	LEVEL 3	20983

NUMBER OF OVERFLOW TABLES = 904

In this example, investment transactions are not stored on the same page as their owner investments for simplification. The DBA could glean some important information from these results. First, each page is only 83% full, presumably the space coming from deleted records (unless some spare space was pre-allocated at the design stage). The DBMS may maintain available space tables in which case the space will be re-used eventually, but if this is so then the ordering will suffer with a corresponding increase in I/O time when the file is read sequentially. If this is the case then the DBA may consider a reorganization to recreate the investments file in index order, which will also have the benefit of consolidating any space spare on the file.

A second observation would be the number of overflow tables in the index, which is far too high. The DBA may therefore consider it worthwhile reorganizing the index, such that each contains 150 entries but that each is only 75% full initially, thus allowing room for future expansion without the need for overflow.

(2) AREA – MORTGAGES
AVERAGE MORTGAGES RECORDS PER PAGE = 9
AVERAGE TRANSACTIONS PER PAGE = 67.81
UNUSED SPACE PER PAGE = 58.19
TRANSACTIONS

In this database system we have allocated space for nine mortgages plus 126 transactions (14 per account) on each page (the DBMS allows for physical placement). This means that each page should be full at the end of the year (although the mortgages with 54 transactions clearly will cause overflow problems) but, at the beginning of the year, most of each page will be empty. The DBA might therefore decide initially to define a page as holding 15 mortgages, but each with only six or seven transactions, and then, part way through the year, reorganize the data into the above framework.

Thus, by using the analyser program, the DBA should be able to monitor the physical state of the database and be able to predict any future problem areas and efficiencies, so that they can be amended before the performance degrades too seriously.

Note: it is here, in particular, that we see the advantages of having disjoint logical and physical models. If this is so then we can afford to change blocking factors, page sizes, page contents and the like without affecting user programs.

Summary

Many facets of database tuning exist and it must be stressed that, no matter what options are available, it is still highly desirable to consider all future possibilities and run-time criteria when the database is designed and implemented initially.

The features mentioned in this chapter are by no means available on all database management systems, but they are described here to show how the DBA often has quite close control over the running environment of the database and often can vary the run-time parameters dynamically. Compare this with the conventional file approach where, with the exception of being able to specify block sizes, it is largely a matter of a program being run, with the hope that the operating system will make best use of the memory available.

CHAPTER 11

Data Dictionary and Query Languages

Introduction

This chapter is divided broadly into two halves: in the first the general features of a data dictionary are described and in the second general-purpose Query languages are looked at. However, as will be seen, there are strong connections between the two.

The previous chapter stated that a piece of software called a data dictionary could aid the DBA in mapping out the effects of change at the business level and determining how those changes would affect the existing database and programs. By reading back even further, it was stated in Chapter 3 that the user's view was defined to be the conceptual model, whereas the logical model was the implementation of that conceptual model. It might appear that there is no link between the two models other than the obvious one derived by searching through the data analysts documentation. Clearly, this is time consuming and error prone, and yet definitely it would help the DBA to be able to determine easily what effects on the logical model a change to the conceptual model would have.

The task of performing this vital function is given to the data dictionary system. This is not to say that a data dictionary cannot be a manual system, indeed this is certainly better than no system at all, but most DBMS manufacturers have now provided machine-based data dictionaries, although arguably too late to be of maximum use. Compare the current developments in micro database systems which nearly all have in-build data dictionaries which were designed concurrently with the database management system, and which generally are more beneficial (see Chapter 16).

Need for a data dictionary

As early database systems were developed and implemented, the DBA largely had to rely on manual forms of documentation to maintain their own data about the database. As such the DBA suffered because the manual system's tendencies were to be:

(1) incomplete
(2) out of date
(3) difficult to read and extract information
(4) difficult to update
(5) unable to provide quick cross-referencing.

Such a system might comprise the collection of data-analysis documentation as outlined in Chapter 3. If a particular attribute needed to be checked on then the only solution was a visual scan through all such documentation for all required references. Restructures were (and still are) often such hectic worry-producing exercises that there were no guarantees that the DBA would remember to update the documentation fully. As soon as one inconsistency slipped in then more would soon follow by a ripple effect. The results were too often a loss of integrity and a database administrator suffering from nervous exhaustion.

For this reason, pressure was placed on manufacturers to provide a machine-based solution to these problems which, in particular, would:

(1) retrieve information about the database in interactive mode
(2) update similar information in interactive mode
(3) guarantee completeness by means of checking procedures
(4) cross-reference data (by the normal database ability to express relationships).

The result of this pressure was many data dictionaries being produced: not all by manufacturers, some by independent software houses who 'tailor-made' them for specific database management systems. Before looking at the success of these systems, we must study what they should contain at least theoretically.

Meta-data model

It has been stated already that the DBA needs to keep data concerning the data on the database. This is known as *meta-data*. By using techniques described within the first few chapters of this book, the meta-data can itself be analysed in terms of entities, attributes and relationships and a database designed and implemented. This derived database is the data dictionary system.

The relationship between an entity and its attributes can be shown by:

However, if more than a single entity were to be considered, then an m:n relationship would develop as shown in Figure 11.1.

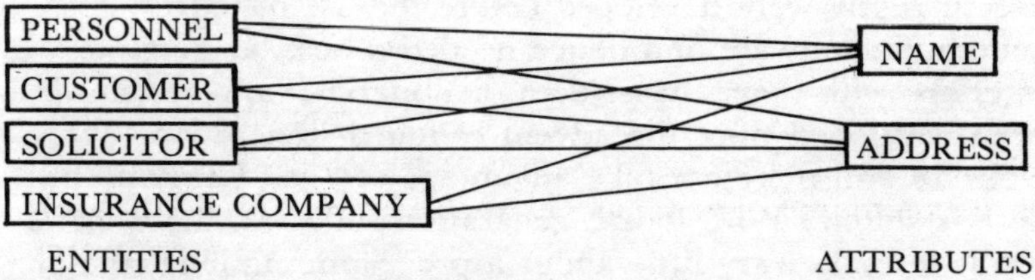

Figure 11.1. *Possible complexity of entity/attribute relationships*

Note: at the conceptual level the attributes take on a very generalized nomenclature as has been mentioned previously, and at this level certainly we would not want PERS-NAME, SOL-NAME and CO-NAME as three distinct identifiers.

Using this m:n relationship we can define the occurrences of the meta-entity ENTITY to be the entities of the conceptual model, i.e. investment, mortgage, customer, etc., and the occurrences of the entity ATTRIBUTES to be the attributes of the conceptual model, i.e. account number, customer name, address, etc. Thus a data dictionary is the implementation oı this meta-model where files have become records and data items have remained the same. This meta-database can be navigated just as any other such that given an entity (file), then all of its attributes can be obtained and, conversely, given an attribute all of the files in which it resides can be obtained.

Suppose that, for example, an organization wishes to implement a post code on every address field. If the database is large and complex, without a data dictionary the DBA must check visually through the logical database listing and pick out such items as CUST-ADD, CO-ADDRESS, PROPERTY-ADD, etc., and hope to find them all. On occasions it may not be at all obvious that a field is an implementation of an address item. Using a data dictionary, the DBA can sit at a terminal (nearly all data dictionaries work in interactive mode, but with hardcopy report facilities also), key in the word ADDRESS and obtain a listing automatically, via the meta-database, of all implementations of the attribute address.

To the reader this may appear as a sudden departure from what has gone before. Aren't databases accessed by host languages in general? Where is the host language here?

The answer lies in the fact that most database systems in use currently were developed before the use of fourth-generation software and hence needed a host language to interface with them. Most data dictionaries, however, have been developed since the advent of fourth-generation software and therefore take advantage of this. The concept here is simple. With fourth-generation software, the user needs to know very little about a programming language or the workings of a particular DBMS. He simply enters a command on a terminal declaring the data he requires and the system software is able to generate code to perform the retrieval from that request. This is the underlying philosophy of Query languages as described later in this chapter.

Meta-process model

By reverting to the data analysis exercise, as well as being able to feed details of entities and attributes into the data dictionary, it is also possible to collect data about the processes involved. By referring back to Figure 3.2, a truncated version might appear as shown in Figure 11.2. If

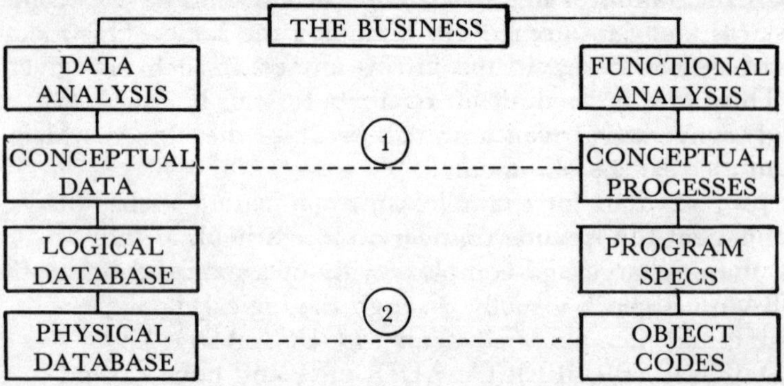

Figure 11.2 *Summary of the data analysis exercise*

the relationships between conceptual data and conceptual processes (1) can be incorporated into data dictionary, then clearly it will be possible to determine which processes (and hence which programs) act on which data items.

Again, if this information can be extracted from data dictionary interactively, then the DBA will have a very useful tool for restructuring exercises. In other words, given a data item that is going to be changed, data dictionary can inform the DBA of all programs which will be affected.

Data dictionaries in practice

As has been mentioned previously database management systems were developed long before data dictionaries in general. For that reason most data dictionaries were designed to adapt to existing database implementations, and therefore seldom follow the development stages from data analysis through the design stages, and thus much of what has been described to date in this chapter is not available in practice (at least on non-relational models).

As an alternative, a dictionary generator is run against the compiled logical database model, and all data relating to records, relationships and data items are extracted and stored to form a data dictionary. Moreover, since in all current database management systems, the physical database design is incorporated into the logical model, the 'how and where' of data storage also can be extracted in the same pass through the database definition.

In this way the meta-data database is constructed along with the physical model such that, for example, if a diskpack crashes, the data dictionary can inform the DBA/operations exactly which pieces of data were on that disk (in a contents sense, the actual value of those contents is, of course, unknown to the data dictionary).

There is a more difficult task of creation of a meta-process database because all the data cannot be extracted from a single source. Instead, all application programs must be passed, at a source level, through a precompiler which can extract the required details before the source code becomes object code. The information extracted in this way will be such as:

(1) whether the program is update or inquiry
(2) which files are accessed

(3) how the files are accessed
(4) are the records read/updated/created/deleted
(5) which sets are used.

By using a system of timestamping or similar methods, it can be ensured that programs cannot run against the database unless they have been passed through the preprocessor, thus negating the possibility of omissions and future inconsistency. In this situation, given a change to the database, the DBA can use the data dictionary to determine:

(1) the result of the change on the logical database
(2) which records need changing
(3) which submodels need changing
(4) which programs need changing
(5) which programs need recompiling without change.

It must be noted therefore that these kinds of data dictionary systems do not possess many of the aims and advantages outlined previously in this chapter. Because they deal exclusively with the implemented logical database and implemented programs, links with the conceptual data and process models are lost with the resulting product being of use solely to the DBA, there being no bridge between the implemented database and the user's (conceptual) viewpoint. In these systems, it is unlikely that you could type in the word address and obtain a list of all associated implementations, which is something of an anticlimax after the theory that has gone before.

Nevertheless, the data dictionary does often form a foundation for the type of software that does provide the desired bridge: the general-purpose Query language.

Query languages

A Query language is such that people can retrieve information (not simply data) from databases without having to write special application programs. Thus no knowledge of, or skill at, programming is required and the user can be anyone who wishes to, or is allowed to, extract facts and statistics from the database.

Most database management system manufacturers now supply Query language facilities (at extra cost) and the principles involved have much in common. The Query program is compiled against the database description of a particular database and thereafter will only run against that particular database. If the database is changed (through a restructure), then the Query language will need to be regenerated. Indeed, a timestamp facility often prevents an old Query program from running against a database of a different update level, especially if updates are allowed (see following).

In its compiled form, the Query program should provide a true computerized management information system which can present management with facts at their fingertips and thus overcome most of the problems highlighted in Chapter 1 concerning their decision making. To this end, Query will normally work in interactive mode, but generally there is a report-writing feature (see the Report generators section at the end of this chapter) to provide hardcopy.

Privacy is an important aspect and it is essential that the DBA is strictly aware of who should be allowed to use Query facilities. There is a world of difference between having to write a program, by using a high-level programming language to be able to bypass access controls, and being able simply to sit at a terminal and gain the same information through Query. To prevent problems partially, the DBA may be able to construct Query on a Readonly basis if the software allows this. Alternatively, the DBA may decide that they want update rights and can set relevant access controls accordingly. (Being able to update through Query may be of great benefit to the DBA. If, for example, a control field such as an interest rate is wrong and is holding up processing, then changing it via Query is a 2-min job as opposed to writing a one-off program which would take hours.)

If updating is allowed then it is important that the Query facility also uses the normal database recovery facilities (i.e. journal files). Otherwise, Query updates will not be audited and recovery may cause serious inconsistencies.

Query-language examples

The examples given here relate to non-relational databases, and in particular to CODASYL models. The reason for this is that nearly all relational models have been developed around interactive technology and are mainly accessible in this way. Therefore the Query-language method of relational algebra or calculus is commonplace (see Chapter 16).

Most Query languages allow input to be spread across more than one line. In this instance a continuation character is necessary at the end of any unfinished lines. Such a character varies from system to system. I have used a %.

```
(1) SELECT MTG-ACC-NO MTG-LOAN-AMOUNT
FROM MORTGAGE %
WHERE MTG-LOAN-TERM > 25 %
DISPLAY
```

This would find the first mortgage occurrence, which satisfies the conditions given by performing a linear search on the structure mortgage (no indexes are used), and displays the account number and loan amount on the screen.

If we wanted to see all mortgage details for the chosen account we could have used:

```
   SELECT MORTGAGE WHERE MTG-LOAN > 25 %
DISPLAY ALL
```

```
(2) DISPLAY MTG-ACC-NO MTG-LOAN-AMOUNT
WHERE MTG-LOAN-TERM > 25
```

Here, because we are using DISPLAY instead of SELECT, all record occurrences satisfying the conditions will be selected momentarily and have their account numbers and amounts displayed before Query moves on to look for the next.

```
(3) DISPLAY COUNT(MTG-LOAN-TERM > 25
```

This will display nothing except the total number of record occurrences satisfying the condition.

```
(4) SELECT CUSTOMER WHERE CUST-NAME=
'[ENTER SURNAME]' %
AND '[ENTER FIRST NAME]' %
DISPLAY ALL
```

Most Query implementations will allow this to be saved as a procedure (FINDCUST, for example). When needed, the user types in

```
FINDCUST
```

and gets the response

```
ENTER SURNAME> COULSON
ENTER FIRST NAME> NEIL
```

Query then searches for the required record and displays it. The procedure can be saved permanently and reused as required. In this way quite complex conditions and navigational paths can be stored to avoid excessive retyping.

```
(5) SELECT INVESTMENT WHERE INV-ACC-NO=
1076548302 %
SELECT INV-TRAN VIA I-T WHERE INV-TRAN-NO
=6 %
UPDATE INV-TRAN-SOURCE=09
```

This would find the required investment (if the Query in question is worth its salt it will detect that INV-ACC-NO is the key field and therefore use the Calc or index method of access, or whichever is declared in the database description), find the required transaction via the set and then update the INV-TRAN-SOURCE field to the given value. Of course, if any NOTFOUND errors are detected en route then the user is informed immediately.

```
(6) DEFINE AVE-PREMIUM=%
SUM(INSURANCE-PREMIUM)/COUNT(INSURANCE)
%
DEFINE AVE-CALC %
SELECT INSURANCE WHERE INS-NUMBER > 0 %
SUM(INSURANCE-PREMIUM) %
COUNT(INSURANCE) %
REPEAT %
AVE-CALC %
DISPLAY AVE-PREMIUM
```

In this example AVE-PREMIUM is defined in terms of how it can be calculated. Line 2 defines a procedure which comprises the next four lines. The next line calls the procedure and executes it (note the use of REPEAT to keep reiterating the procedure) and the final line displays the result.

In all of these examples, which are general and do not

relate to any specific Query implementation, it should be noted that all access and storage mechanisms used by the database are totally transparent to the user who requires minimal training to be able to obtain the desired information. The examples also only show a small subset of the capabilities of most Query implementations which, generally, allow far more complex procedures and functions than are shown here.

Of note is the comment made in (6) concerning access methods. Most Query programs will use the defined access paths whenever they are appropriate, but it is important to realize that many desired requests will not lend themselves to standard access mechanisms, and the only alternative is the linear search which may tie up the terminal for long periods while it is being performed, unless Query can be run in background mode.

Report generators

A possible counter to the above problem is to direct the Query output to a printer and thus release the terminal for other use while the various searches, etc., are taking place. This brings up the question of output formatting and it is to address this area that the report generator has been developed.

Actual syntax for the various Query-language systems varies widely, so here I shall give some of the general features available and follow up with a single example.

(1) Automatic titling including headings and footings.
(2) Automatic page numbering.
(3) User-defined variables such as subtotals and quantities.
(4) Control over columnation of output (i.e. which output items will appear where on the page).
(5) Sorting of output into a defined sequence.
(6) Editing of output to provide zero suppression, floating monetary symbols, etc. (by using similar notation to COBOL).
(7) Provide column headers.
(8) User-defined control breaks to allow for the printing of subtotals, statistics to date, fresh headings, etc.

For an example, suppose that we were looking through all mortgage records associated with a particular branch, reading through their insurance details and summarizing which insurances belonged to which companies and for how much they were for. The actual selection expression need not concern us here, but the output could be reported in an agreeable form by using the following:

```
SORT ON COMPANY CODE
TABULAR DETAIL
MTG-ACC-NO PIC 9(10)
MTG-INS-TYPE PIC 9
MTG-INS-AMT PIC ££,£££.99
GROUP HEADING FOR COMPANY EJECT
'COMPANY CODE' COMPANY CODE SKIP 1
SUMMARY FOR COMPANY-CODE SKIP 1
TOTAL MTG-INS-AMT
FINAL SUMMARY SKIP 3
TOTAL MTG-INS-AMT
```

Note: the term EJECT will cause a page throw; the term SKIP 1 will skip one blank line; if no heading values are declared within quotes then the heading will default to the variable name.

From this an output might appear as:

```
COMPANY CODE 107
MTG-ACC-NO        MTG-INS-TYPE        MTG-INS-AMT
8670903108               1             £15 000.00
8685463203               1              £6 500.00
8649445110               2              £9 750.00
SUMMARY FOR COMPANY CODE 107
                                       £31 250.00
COMPANY CODE 108
MTG-ACC-NO        MTG-INS-TYPE        MTG-INS-AMT
8344222109               2             £18 250.00
8420087803               3              £7 000.00
867189400                1             £12 000.00
8769435502               1             £17 250.00
SUMMARY FOR COMPANY CODE 108
                                       £55 500.00
SUMMARY FOR BRANCH 194
                                       £86 750.00
```

CHAPTER 12

Database Administration

Introduction

Throughout this book to date I have referred to the database administration as the DBA without defining who, exactly, they are or if, indeed, there is a team rather than a single person. In this chapter I have tried to remedy that deficiency by looking at the actual role played by the DBA within an organization.

By listing the tasks performed by the DBA, it might be possible to understand the sort of person(s) required for the job. They must have sound knowledge of:

(1) data analysis
(2) database-design methodologies
(3) how to implement the database on the particular machine in question
(4) imposition of privacy rights as access controls
(5) definition of backup and recovery strategies
(6) control of changes to the database
(7) how to monitor the database on a day-to-day basis
(8) prediction of future changes needed to maintain efficiency and minimize storage requirements
(9) applications support
(10) operations support
(11) how to tune the database
(12) creation of test databases

Clearly, from this list, it can be seen that if a database exists already then the first three items will have been performed already (though the DBA will still need the documentation as produced at the time); presumably, the applications department will be familiar with database accessing techniques, documentation for operations will have been written and recovery strategies thought out. This may sound as if there is nothing left for the DBA to do, but this is not the case. As with all other system software, the DBMS will be updated by the manufacturers every so often, some features will be phased out, some added, and these enhancements will need passing on to the programmers and operations. More areas of the business may be computerized which may, in turn, involve the design of further databases. (Although, as mentioned, the original data analysis should not need repeating, because it should have covered the entire organization. There are still also the important areas of monitoring, tuning and changing the database.)

It may be possible for all of this to be carried out by a single individual, but in a large business a team is more likely and if there is no database in existence then one would expect the task of data analysis and design to be too much for one person.

Database team

Having opted for a team approach, we must enrol some members and look at the special skills that they will need.

First, in charge of the team we would need a database administrator to co-ordinate the development of the database in much the same way that the systems analyst co-ordinates the development of a project. This implies that the database administrator should possess the usual management qualities of:

(1) planning
(2) co-ordinating
(3) motivating
(4) communicating (with many other people).

He/she should also have a specialist knowledge of the systems software and hardware available and, in particular, an intimate knowledge of the database management system and its utilities. He may or may not have a detailed knowledge of the workings of the organization (certainly it would be useful, but is not essential). If he hasn't then there is, clearly, the need for someone close at hand who has. In general, this will be a systems analyst, though it must be borne in mind that many systems analysts tend to specialize in one particular area of a business (especially in a large organization) and thus all of the analysts are likely to be called on individually at some time. As they will each have their own work to do as well, they will not be permanent members of database administration.

A diagrammatic representation of a database team might therefore be similar to that as shown in Figure 12.1.

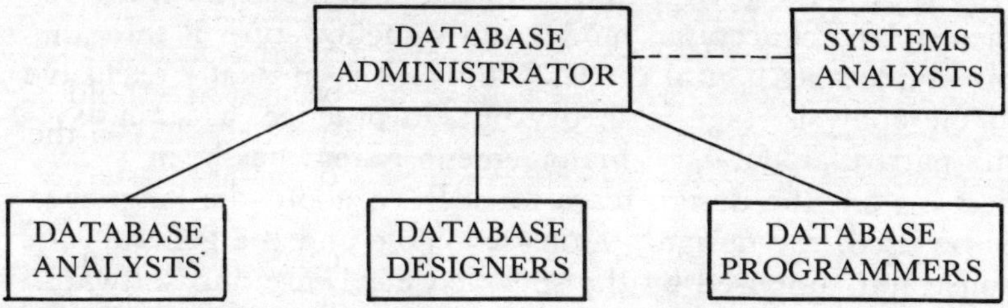

Figure 12.1 *The database administration team*

The database analyst(s) will be responsible for the collection of data in the analysis stages, for interviewing users re their requirements, for searching out existing documentation and/or programs, files, etc., and by the process of normalization or by any other methods, eventually creating a conceptual data model.

Concurrently with this process, the same or, more likely, a different database analyst will be looking at the functional areas of the business and will be drawing up lists of the events and operations involved. Eventually, this should lead to a conceptual process model. (It may have been decided to extract the data requirements for the business from this study of the functional analysis, as outlined in the A solution section in Chapter 4, in which case probably only a single database analyst will be required.)

These two processes should generate reams of paperwork (unless the data can be fed directly into a data dictionary), which should be properly maintained and kept in a readable form for future reference.

From what has been said, it is likely that the database analysts will extract their information by working in small teams, the members of which will vary depending on the various systems analysts available and also the user department being looked at currently, at any one time, because that user department usually will supply a member.

Following the successful conclusion of the data-analysis

stage, the database analysts should be needed no longer. This is not to imply instant redundancy; it is more likely that they were recruited from existing programming staff on a temporary basis and can now return to their former duties.

It is now the turn of the database designers who must pick up the conceptual model and somehow turn it into an implementable logical model. This task is mutually exclusive of the analysis stage in theory but, in practice, as soon as the particular database management system has been decided on, the design team must learn about the languages to be used, the design options available and the general constraints imposed by the specified hardware and software. To this end they will tend to be a different set of people to the database analysts though by no means does this have to be the case. Having designed an appropriate database, then probably they will liaise with operations over a relevant load and testing strategy.

Since future changes to the database, or even the day-to-day monitoring, affect the aims and objectives of their database design, it is likely that at least one database designer will be a permanent member of the DBA.

In conjunction with the designers, there may exist database programmers who will be asked to write various pieces of software to support the database. These might include data-validation or access-control procedures which eventually will be bound into the DBMS. Once the database is designed it will be their task to write and test the load programs (as outlined in the Load programs section in Chapter 6) and, indeed, any other one-off programs needed to create and initialize the database. For this obviously they will need to be good experienced programmers who have been taught the workings of the DBMS and who will be able to interface with it, generally by using a high level programming language such as COBOL.

As mentioned, the database team may only be temporary in nature (with the exception of the database administrator) and may be drawn from existing data processing (DP) staff. For example, the database analysts may be existing systems analysts or senior programmers who should already know much of the workings of the organization (though their own concepts should not cloud the important data-analysis task of interviewing user departments). The design team might also consist of programmers and maybe even operators (who better would know the shortcomings of an existing machine?). The database programmers could also be existing programmers. However, it may be necessary for them to be versed in more than a single high-level language. The load programs almost certainly will be written in the host language, but the various DBMS subroutines may well be written in the operating system language, such as ALGOL or FORTRAN.

Having finished their allotted tasks, the various members may be allowed to return to their original jobs, hopefully having gained from their experience. This would leave the database administrator plus, possibly, a single designer/programmer, to perform the remaining tasks and generally monitor the database.

In this section the stages of analysis, design and implementation (bar the tasks mentioned in subsequent sections) have been covered. Most of this work directly will be the responsibility of the database administrator.

Privacy

Privacy, as an important consideration in both the analysis and design stages, was dealt with in Chapter 8, but there are still a few points which need clarifying.

First, it is not the database administrator's task to decide who can see which data, or what they can do with them. These are organizational decisions which must be taken at a higher level than the DBA. Given those constraints, the administrator must then find ways in which to guarantee that the access controls which he/she imposes on the data will uphold those constraints.

The real problem here is that the constraints rarely are written down in practice. Given a manual system, it is, usually, a matter of 'who has the key to the filing cabinet'. Also, access controls generally are on an all-or-nothing basis with no regard for individual data items. A member of staff either has access to all of the contents of the filing cabinet or none of it. Thus the DBA can gain something by knowing who has the keys, but may not know whether all such data are at the same level of privacy. Indeed, there may well be members of staff whose own jobs would be simpler and more efficient if they had immediate access to some of the data in that filing cabinet, but who are denied access because of the confidentiality of some of the data. This is identical with the problems of the conventional computerized filing system as outlined in the Privacy section in Chapter 1. To avoid these problems, and also the related ones of data duplication (see the Application views section in Chapter 1), the DBA must clarify all access-control decisions at the analysis stage, for example by filling in correctly the privacy parts of the forms shown in Figures 3.3–3.6.

Backup and recovery

Before the database becomes a 'live' concern, the DBA must have drawn up some form of recovery procedures. Preferably, they will have tried and tested as many of the error conditions as they can manufacture, and will have documented the outcomes. The operation department may well have been through some initial training courses relating to the usage of the particular DBMS (and, indeed, these courses may have been given by the DBA themselves), but courses are second best to experience, and experience in recovery techniques will be essential. This is perhaps the strangest area to operations, whose natural instincts may well be to reload and rerun.

At some sites, the recovery of a database is only ever carried out by the DBA no matter what time of day or night, but I can see no reasons why, after an initial period of a few months, operations cannot perform this (usually) relatively simple task, especially if they have a good set of documentation. There are, after all, few options open. Either the database will recover itself (as in restart recovery; see the Restart recovery section in Chapter 8) or not. If not, then it is a case of one of the following:

(1) rollback and retry (if rollback is not automatic)
(2) rollforward and retry
(3) rebuild a disk/page (or whatever is necessary)
(4) reload and rerun if none of the above work.

Given the actual syntax for the three types of database recovery, there is no reason why the nearest operator should not perform them. Moreover, operations are far more likely to know exactly what work has been done and when the last dump was than the DBA.

Some decisions will only come from experience. For example, given the following timetable

5 p.m. Database dump ends
6–7 p.m. A single update program is running
7–11 p.m. Various concurrent programs

If a program crashes at 11 p.m., clearly it will be necessary to recover to the last quiet point (7 p.m.). Will it be quicker to rollback, or reload and rollforward?

Occasionally, events will occur that cannot be solved by recovery easily. Possibly the worst thing, is an unknowing operator performing a non-DBMS controlled disk to disk copy of a database file while it is in use, and then start using the new disk. This would be non-recoverable because the DBMS has no knowledge of the copy and cannot therefore mark the journal file (compare with on-line dumping in the Other recovery facilities section in Chapter 8). The only solution is to reload and rerun. This emphasizes a general point not discussed yet. Given a database, it is essential that general housekeeping duties (such as copying) are performed only by DBMS routines and not by normal operating system commands, otherwise all integrity checking and guarantees are bypassed.

The DBA should have impressed on operations the need to dump the database as frequently as possible. Clearly, exactly when they do so is up to them and a lot will depend on whether on-line dumping facilities are available, and what their workload is on a day-to-day basis.

The DBMS will dictate whether manual recovery is required to the last quiet point (in which case there should be frequently scheduled quiet points), or whether the DBMS will rollback the faulty program automatically. Whichever, operations should be aware of all forms of automatic recovery and what they achieve, and what the options are once they have finished.

It is very likely that, as well as the database(s), there also will be some conventional files in use which will not be recoverable in the database fashion. Operations should be clear therefore as to which files these are, when they will need dumping, and which to reload in the event of failure.

Changes

When restructures or reorganizes are forced on the database through changes to the business or by degradation of database efficiency, the DBA needs to control these changes and co-ordinate all other people involved.

RESTRUCTURES

These changes will have been passed to the DBA from elsewhere, usually from a user department via a systems analyst. It is the DBA's task to evaluate these changes and plot the effect that they will have on the database and existing programs.

Normally, this will be done in conjunction with the data dictionary (if one is available), which should be able to project proposed changes across the breadth of the conceptual and logical models and supply listings of all structures/programs affected. The DBA can decide therefore on how long the work will take (by experience or guesswork), and arrange a proposed timetable. The list of affected programs can now be passed to programming with timescales of writing and testing (the latter clearly will revolve around when a test database will be available; see the Test databases section at the end of this chapter).

Come the day of the restructure, a detailed schedule must be drawn up for operations (if the DBA is not present). Probably, this will show a critical time after which the exercise must be abandoned and the old database and its software reloaded (to be able to carry on with the day-to-day work).

REORGANIZES

Essentially, the programming department will not be involved with this exercise in theory, but with the merging of the logical and physical models, a change of (for example) blocking factors may well involve the recompilation of programs. A similar schedule is needed for operations.

Monitoring

The process of monitoring the database has been dealt with extensively in Chapter 10 and so little will be said here other than the fact that it is the DBA's most important role on a day-to-day basis. Statistics must be collected and collated such that future problems can be detected and, ideally, corrected before they have time to develop. The DBA should also provide the run-time parameters for each program relating to allowed memory, blocksizes, checkpoints, etc., to operations, to ensure the maximum efficiency of the database.

Applications support

While the database is being designed and implemented, the DBA is likely to spend some time instructing the applications programmers on what the database will mean to them, and how they should use it. (This option generally will be cheaper than sending them all on a manufacturer-supplied course and the results will be comparable.)

The most common type of application's usage is through a host language. If this is adopted then it should not be too difficult for the programmers to gain the syntax requirements for the extra dozen or so verbs involved and their usage. If not, then the interface to the database is likely to be through CALL routines (i.e. the program calls the relevant DBMS routines to access the database). In this situation the routines may well have been written by the DBA and it will be necessary only for him to inform the programmers as to the parameter passing involved.

In either case it is vital that the programmers are taught how to trap DBMS errors within their programs and how to deal with them. It is not uncommon to have a set of standard error routines which can be compiled into a program by the use of a library call. In particular, each update program must be able to handle a deadlock situation [the DBMS itself will resolve the deadlock, but the program must decide whether to terminate and await rolling back or simply to wait a few milliseconds, depending on the mechanisms available (see the Program rollback section in Chapter 8)].

If it were merely a case of syntax learning, the DBA's instruction task would be simple, but there is also the more important job of teaching the programmers how to make the most effective and efficient use of the database; this may be more difficult because the DBA may not, at this stage, be aware of the full workings of the DBMS.

The programming department also will need to be informed of:

(1) any proposed changes to the database in terms of restructures (if they are not the originators of them)
(2) any reorganizations if they are likely to affect the running of programs
(3) any changes to the DBMS software (i.e. new releases), which may affect programs or else provide new techniques of interest to the programmer
(4) how to use any existing Query languages (subject to any access constraints).

Note: it may be appropriate also for the DBA to teach the usage of Query languages to any other user groups who are allowed to view certain areas of data and who may wish to extract information quickly without resorting to a new program request (see Chapter 11).

Operations support

Recovery and backup strategies have been mentioned already, but operations will also want information about the day-to-day running of the database; for example, as follows.

(1) How and when to change and dump the journal file (if it is not automatic).
(2) How and when to change the database dynamically (if it is possible). It may only be feasible to restrict these changes to the differences between on-line and batch work, but if it is possible on a program-to-program basis then details should be incorporated in the program's operating instructions.
(3) How the DBMS interacts with the on-line control program (if there is one), particularly with regard to recovery. (Many on-line systems revolve around sophisticated message control systems which pass data from the communications network directly to the application programs and, as a result, often have their own mechanisms for recovering messages in the event of failure.)

Test databases

At most sites there is a distinct need for a test database on which the programmers can develop and test application programs before 'putting them live'.

While they are becoming accustomed to using databases it is probable that any database vaguely similar to the live version will suffice but, as their confidence grows and the various systems develop, there will become an ever increasing need for the test model to be as near as possible to the live version. This would allow full testing of all possible data and error variations. Clearly, the main problem is resources. If the site can afford the processor power and disk-storage capacity to be duplicated entirely, then the programmers will benefit. It is more likely that the database administrator will be asked to create a submodel containing enough data for reasonable testing to be performed (though the actual loading of data to this test database may be left to programming who will know exactly what they require).

Most database management systems provide the facility for the DBA to update the live database to form the test model. Since the new schema and its software are moved elsewhere (usually to another machine) the live model is not actually affected. The advantages of this clearly are that the programmers are working on the most up-to-date version. Other considerations are outlined in the Database versions and timestamps section in Chapter 7. If the live database is restructured (though not if it is reorganized), a new test database will need to be created as soon as possible.

Other database systems allow the live DBMS software to be used for the test versions directly without having to regenerate it. This is made possible by the fact that the variable data concerning the database, such as resident disk names, journal-file information, memory allocation etc., are not compiled into the DBMS code but are maintained elsewhere (for example, in the control file). The DBMS is thus a combination of the logical and storage models, but not the device model. Generate a new control file with the test database disk names and run-time parameters and the DBMS itself will not need recompiling.

The actual loading of the test database is a complex task. It is not sufficient usually merely to dump and reload every tenth record (or whatever) from the live version. The test model will have to be consistent, all member records in a particular set occurrence will have to exist and all control totals will have to balance. In a complicated network model, such as CODASYL, it is often very difficult to separate out records which are not linked to others which are themselves linked to others, etc.

In such cases, it is often wisest to allow the programmers to populate the test database with their own contrived data, rather than try to extract any from the live version. This may be achievable through a Query language (see Chapter 11), if one exists and allows the creation of data.

Whatever the method, this will be a very slow process if the amount of data loaded is to be significant, because there is little sensible testing that can be carried out on half a dozen accounts if the live database contains half a million. Moreover, it will not be just the programmers who will use the test database. The DBA will also want to experiment with future restructures, monitoring and tuning exercises and the results may not be meaningful unless the volume of data throughput is a significant proportion of the live situation.

Part 3:
Database Systems

CHAPTER 13
CODASYL: A Network Approach

Background

Throughout the first two parts of this book, many of the theories, definitions and examples have used the concepts of the CODASYL database. This is not to say that all CODASYL approaches are identical, indeed they are not, but they are all bound together under a common architecture and a common philosophy and, as such, are used widely throughout the world of commercial databases (see Appendix A). For that reason, the brief history of the CODASYL database, as outlined in the CODASYL: historical backgound section in Chapter 2, is expanded here to show its full relevance.

Following its success with the rationalization of COBOL, the CODASYL group decided to extend its activities to related areas, and in 1965 formed a List Processing Task Force to look at the list-processing capabilities of COBOL. Two years later they were renamed the Data Base Task Group (DBTG). In October 1969, the DBTG submitted a report to the Programming Language Committee (PLC) proposing a data description language (DDL) to describe a set of linked structures, and a data manipulation language as an extension to a host language (COBOL), to be used for the access and manipulation of the data.

This report was revised in 1971 to incorporate two DDLs: one for the global model or schema, and one for the submodels or subschemae, which was accepted by the PLC. In the same year the Data Description Language Committee (DDLC) was formed and within 2 years had produced a journal of development outlining its proposals. In 1973 two task groups were set up by the DDLC: the Subschema Task Group (SSTG) in the USA and the Data

Base Administration Working Group (DBAWG) in the UK (for the development of tools for use by the DBA). The latter's preliminary report in 1975 included work on a data strategy description language (DSDL) for reorganizing the database, and for the provision of concurrency and data protection. This was included as an appendix in the CODASYL journal of development in 1978. In 1976 a CODASYL Fortran database facility was published and incorporated into a journal of development in 1977. The 1978 report was important in that it included, for the first time, a data storage definition language which would provide the physical data independence lacking in the earlier models. However, as mentioned previously, there are as yet no commercial implementations of a CODASYL 78 model (most are still based on the CODASYL 73 model).

From this brief history it will have been observed that CODASYL is run by a selection of committees and task groups. They are not a manufacturer of databases, but rather a group of users, manufacturers and software houses which was established to try to rationalize and standardize the concepts of database design and current technologies, by producing a set of system specifications. Since they were brought into existence, CODASYL have influenced the thinking of all of the major manufacturers (though some have since deviated from the CODASYL architecture; for example, see the next chapter on IMS).

CODASYL architecture

CODASYL is a network model with structures grouped as shown in a Bachman diagram (see the Data model diagrams section in Chapter 3) of which a simple example is shown in Figure 13.1, with some records (owners) related to others (members) in a 1:n relationship. Member records can themselves be owners in other relationships (mortgages and investments in Figure 13.3).

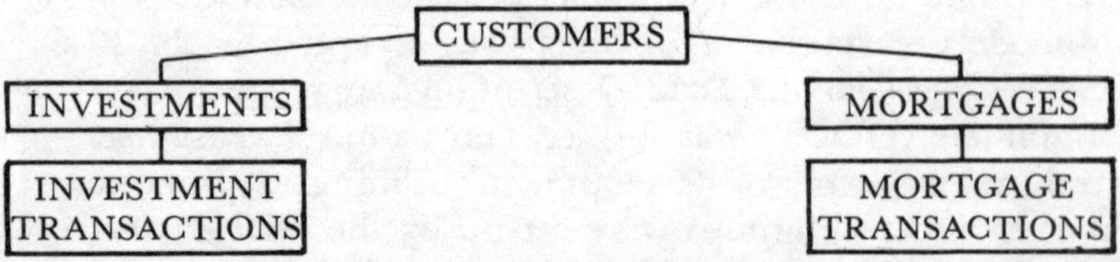

Figure 13.1 *A simple CODASYL network*

The logical data model is defined by the name schema, which is itself written in a special language, the *data definition language* (DDL), which describes the various records, their constituent data items and the relationships between them (implemented as *sets*). The schemae of CODASYL 73 models also describe the storage data model, but the CODASYL 78 proposals put forward an independent data storage definition language.

The logical data submodels are defined as being subschemae which are derivable from the schema. A subschema essentially is an application-orientated view of the database. It is not possible to restructure the data within the subschemae: for example, to define new sets which do not exist in the schema.

The CODASYL approach to data manipulation is one of a host language (COBOL or FORTRAN in general), with extensions to allow for communication with the database, and the manipulation of the data in the subschemae. The programmer invokes the relevant subschema at program compilation time and the user work area (UWA) is copied into the object code for that program.

Thus, overall, we have the architecture as shown in Figure 13.2.

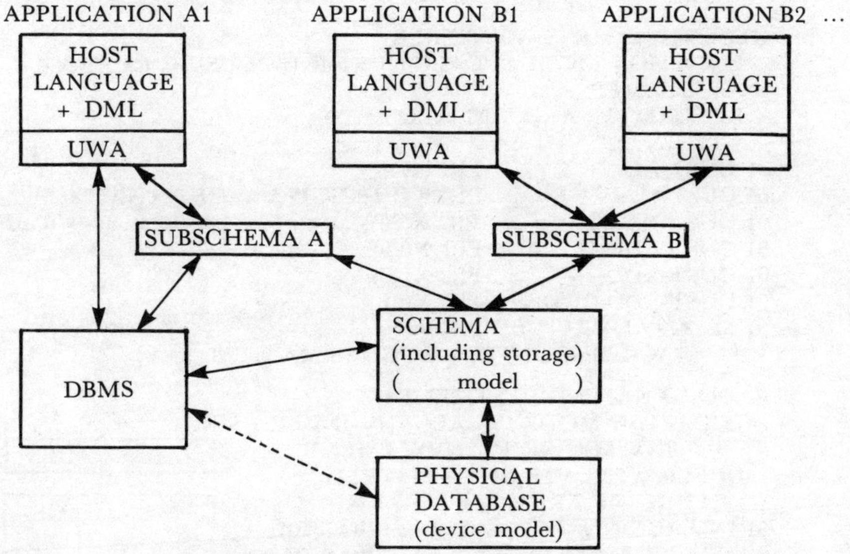

Figure 13.2 *A generalized CODASYL architecture*

Schema

The schema is written by using the DDL which describes records and sets. Records can be equated readily to COBOL records, whereas sets describe relationships between records, generally on a 1:n basis. (M:n or n:1 are not maintainable directly on most CODASYL implementations, as mentioned in the An intersection entity section in Chapter 4.)

The schema itself should always be representable by means of a Bachman diagram (see the Data model diagrams section in Chapter 3), though the processes of normalization, collapse and fragmentation are still highly relevant.

To describe the data definition language itself really requires an example (Figure 13.3); the one used here is a basic study of the customer/investment/transaction set of relationships as shown in the left-hand half of Figure 13.1.

```
SCHEMA NAME IS ACCOUNTS
ACCESS-CONTROL LOCK IS DB-KEY

AREA NAME IS CUST-AREA
     ACCESS-CONTROL LOCK IS CUST-KEY
AREA NAME IS INV-AREA
     ACCESS-CONTROL LOCK IS INV-KEY

RECORD NAME IS CUSTOMER
   LOCATION MODE IS CALC CUST-INDEX USING CUST-NO
IN CUSTOMER
   DUPLICATES ARE NOT ALLOWED
   WITHIN CUST-AREA
01 CUST-NO              PIC 9(7);
01 CUST-SEX             PIC 9 CHECK IS VALUE 0 THRU 4;
01 CUST-NAME            PIC X(20);
01 CUST-ADD-1           PIC X(20);
01 CUST-ADD-2           PIC X(20);
01 CUST-ADD-CODE        PIC X(8);
01 MARITAL-STATUS       PIC 9
          ACCESS-CONTROL LOCK IS MARITAL-KEY;

RECORD NAME INVESTMENTS
   LOCATION MODE IS CALC INV-INDEX USING
          INV-ACC-NO IN INVESTMENT
   DUPLICATES ARE NOT ALLOWED
   WITHIN INV-AREA
01 INV-ACC-NO                  PIC 9(10);
01 INV-OPEN-BALANCE            PIC 9(6)V99;
01 INV-CURR-BALANCE            PIC 9(6)V99;
```

(continued)

```
01 NO-OF-OWNERS          PIC 9 CHECK IS VALUE 1 THRU
4;
01 ACCOUNT-TYPE          PIC 99 CHECK IS TRAN-TYPES;

RECORD NAME IS INV-TRAN
  LOCATION MODE IS VIA I-T SET
  WITHIN INV-AREA
  ON STORE CALL IT-CHECK
01 IT-NO                 PIC 999;
01 IT-DATE               PIC 9(6);
01 IT-TYPE               PIC 99;
01 IT-SOURCE             PIC 9;
01 IT-AMOUNT             PIC 9(5)V99;

SET NAME IS CUST-INV
  OWNER IS CUSTOMER
  ORDER IS PERMANENT
  INSERTION IS FIRST
MEMBER IS INVESTMENT FIXED AUTOMATIC
SET SELECTION IS THRU CUST-INV OWNER IDENTIFIED
BY CALC-KEY;

SET NAME IS I-T
  OWNER IS INVESTMENT
  ORDER IS PERMANENT
  SORTED BY DEFINED KEYS
MEMBER IS INV-TRAN FIXED AUTOMATIC
SET SELECTION IS THRU I-T OWNER IDENTIFIED BY
CALC-KEY;
```

Figure 13.3 *An example of schema listing*

SCHEMA ENTRY

The schema name must be a unique identifier within the system (i.e. there cannot be two databases with the same name). An access-control lock is optional, the various options having been discussed in the Database approaches to privacy section in Chapter 7.

AREA ENTRY

The total storage requirement for the database is divided into areas. For each record defined in the schema, an area name must be specified using the WITHIN clause, in which the record will be placed when created. In fact, more than one area can be defined for each record, in which case the decision as to where to store the record could be made by the:

(1) DBMS
(2) DBA-written procedure
(3) application program storing the record.

This could be an important concept for larger files. For example, the investment file could quite easily be spread across several areas, and in which particular one a record is stored might depend on the account type which itself could be determined by either the second or the third options above.

As to what an area is in physical terms, this varies greatly from machine to machine (e.g. it could be disk, platten, cylinder, etc.). It is perhaps with the concept of an area that it is shown how much physical database design has encroached into the logical model, since it is both related to how and where the record is to be stored.

As mentioned previously in the Database approaches to privacy section in Chapter 7, the area clause can also contain access-control locks.

RECORD ENTRY

The main difference between the schema record definition and that of a COBOL record definition is the specification of a *location mode* to state how and/or where the record is to be stored (again a direct relationship with the physical data model).

An important concept in CODASYL is that of the database key. In theory this is defined as being the uniquely identifying key which distinguishes one record from any other. However, in CODASYL it is synonymous often with the physical address. At run time, a program can supply this key and hence gain fast and efficient access to the requested record.

The problem with the physical-address approach is that if the programmer obtained such a value and stored it as a data item for an application's usage, a subsequent restructure would change the physical address of the record but not that in the data item. Current DBTG proposals would mean that the database key is available to the programmer solely on a read-only basis and cannot be moved or manipulated.

By bearing this in mind, there are four possible location modes.

(1) *Direct*. Each record has a unique database key (equating to the physical address) which the program supplies when it wishes to access that record. The advantage is that a very quick access is afforded. The disadvantage is that a restructure necessitates program amendments.
(2) *Calc*. A data item or group of data items within the record form the key which is passed through a hashing algorithm (Appendix B) to produce a physical address. This algorithm is either provided by the manufacturer or written by the DBA. This is probably the most common form of access method in CODASYL databases since it combines a relatively fast access method with physical data independence (the program does not need to know the physical location).
(3) *Via*. A record can be stored depending on its relationship with another record type (i.e. through a set). This is very useful for storing member records physically close to their owners and thus reducing I/O overheads.
(4) *System*. The access/storage method is by means of DBMS-supplied software. This is the default value, if the DBA is not bothered how the record is to be stored or accessed, and leaves the decision to the DBMS.

Note: it is important to realize that location modes are not the only access methods. A serial read can always be performed by a

FIND NEXT WITHIN Areaname

clause.

DUPLICATES

In most CODASYL databases it is possible to have two keys having the same value: for example, if a mortgage is covered by two endowment policies (as is often the case), the key for each occurrence of the endowment record would be the mortgage account number. If duplicate keys are not required then the DBA must specify

DUPLICATES ARE NOT ALLOWED

and the system will guarantee that no two records will be stored with the same key value.

ON STORE

The ON STORE CALL procedure name can be used to invoke a prewritten procedure when the record is stored, and this is useful particularly for data validation. As with other CALLed procedures, this one will be written by the DBA.

For example, if the possible values of an item are fixed then each can be assigned check values such as those for CUST-SEX and NO-OF-OWNERS, but if the values are likely to change (perhaps tax rates or hourly payments), then it is wiser to incorporate them into a procedure which can be changed readily without having to update the schema. In the schema example given, such a procedure might check that the:

(1) transaction number (IT-NO) is one higher than that of the last stored transaction
(2) date is valid
(3) account type has a correct value
(4) source is valid
(5) amount is within predefined limits.

SETS

The distinguishing feature of CODASYL databases is the set concept by which relationships between differing record types can be expressed. In general, only 1:n relationships can be represented directly using owners (1) and members (n), for which the following rules apply.

(1) A record type may be an owner in one or more set types (e.g. a customer can be an owner in both customer-mortgage and customer-investment sets).

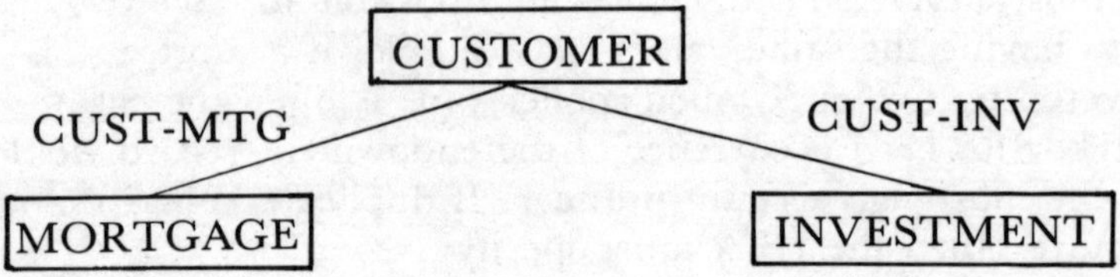

(2) A record may be a member in one or more set types (e.g. an insurance record can belong to both an insurance company and a mortgage record).

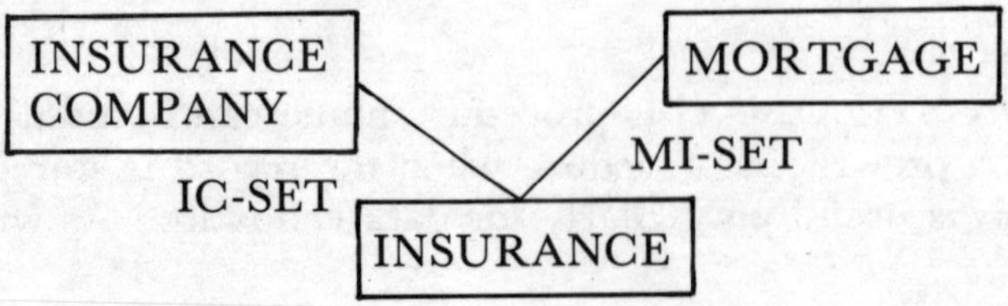

(3) A record can be an owner in one or more set types and a member in one or more set types. This provision allows for true networking facilities.

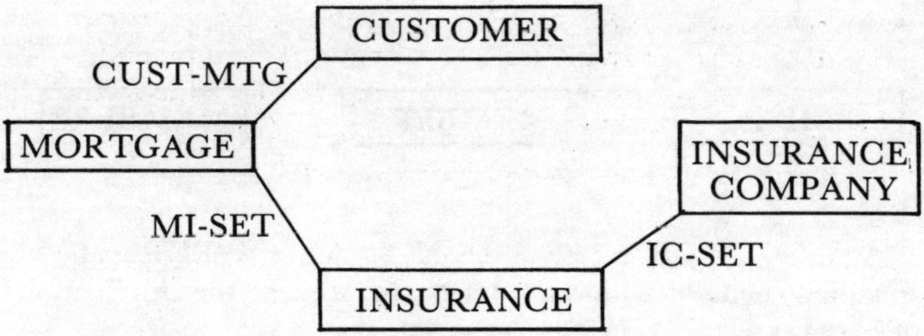

(4) A set occurrence contains an owner and any number of member records (including none).
(5) A record cannot be both an owner and a member in the same set type. This condition means that we cannot have directly:

(6) A record cannot appear in more than one occurrence of the same set type. This prevents, for example, a transaction belonging to more than one account at any one time.

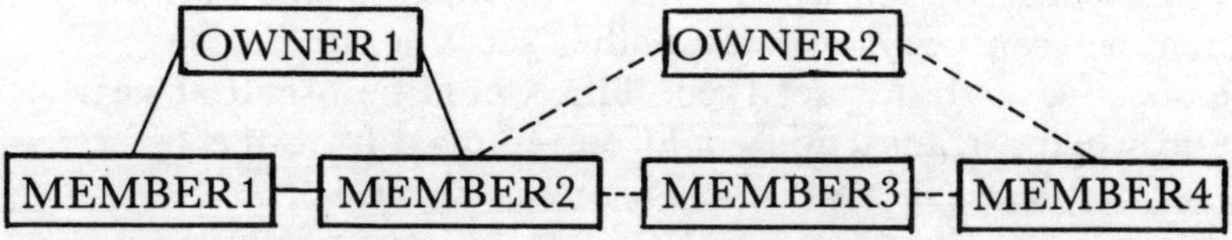

For every set defined, an ORDER IS clause must be specified to define where the DBMS is to insert a new member record when created (if the AUTOMATIC option is used; see later). The options are:

(1) FIRST, immediately after the owner
(2) LAST, immediately before the owner
(3) NEXT, immediately after the currently accessed record
(4) PRIOR, immediately before the currently accessed record
(5) SORTED, the members are sorted into some pre-defined ordering (via the KEY IS ASCENDING option)
(6) IMMATERIAL, the decision is left to the DBMS.

These can be shown on the following diagram:

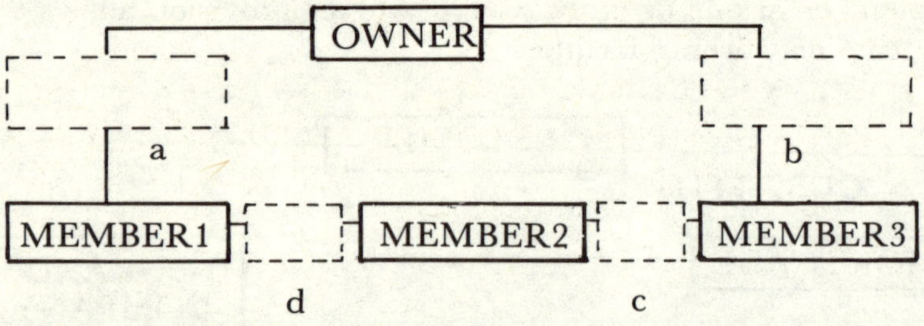

Again, DUPLICATES ARE NOT ALLOWED can be specified, usually with sorted sets, to prevent the duplication of sort keys.

EXISTENCE
The FIXED entry states that the particular occurrence of a member record can exist only in that particular set occurrence (i.e. it cannot be moved to another owner) and must be deleted from the entire database to remove it.

The second alternative is MANDATORY which means that the member can be removed from a set occurrence, but only to another occurrence of the same set type. For example, an investment transaction could be moved to another investment account, if desired, but it must belong to an investment somewhere.

The third option is OPTIONAL which means that the member can be moved to another set type, or not be associated with any set type. This would be useful at year end when a transaction could be removed from the I-T set and be placed in an historic transaction set.

INSERTION
The AUTOMATIC entry refers to how the record will be stored, in this case a member will be inserted automatically into the set by using the guidelines of the ORDER IS clause without need of a specific INSERT within the application program.

The alternative is MANUAL which implies that the insertion point within the set is determined by the application program (which must read through the members until it finds the required point).

SET SELECTION

This clause states how a particular occurrence of a set is to be identified. There are many possibilities of which only one is used in the example OWNER IDENTIFIED BY CALC KEY. This means that the application program will provide a key value for the CALC KEY routine. This format is often used when the member record does not itself contain the key of the owner record.

Another useful alternative is the OWNER IDENTIFIED BY CURRENT OF SET. If we have the example

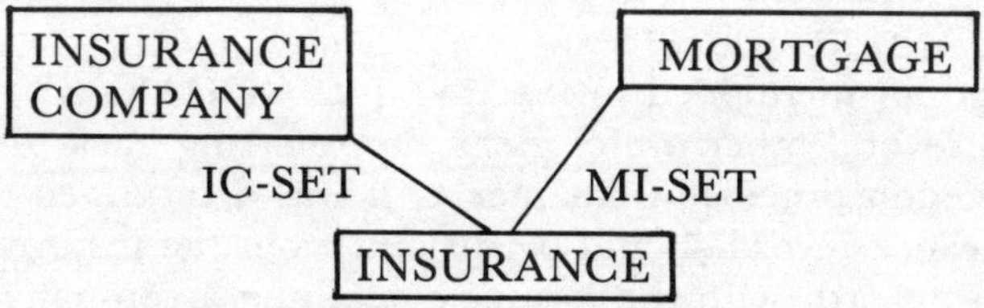

then having accessed the insurance record through the MI-SET, and then wishing to access the insurance company record, the rules defined dictate that each insurance record can belong only to a single insurance company record, and thus the required insurance company record automatically will be CURRENT OF IC-SET. By using this the insurance company record can be located.

SINGULAR SETS

The advantages of sets lie in the fact that the application program can navigate through all associated records in some predefined way by using pointers. It might also be considered advantageous to navigate through all customer records in some predefined manner by also using pointers. From what has gone before, the only way to do this would be to define a new record type called (for example) CUST-OWNER which owned all customer records in a new set type. The way in which this is achieved in practice usually is to define a *singular* set which has the system as an owner. Thus we could add to our schema definition:

```
SET NAME IS CUSTS OWNER IS SYSTEM
   ORDER IS PERMANENT INSERTION IS LAST
MEMBER IS CUSTOMER FIXED AUTOMATIC
SET SELECTION IS THRU CUSTS SYSTEM;
```

IDENTIFIER
As a further step away from the equation

database key = physical address

CODASYL 78 has introduced the concept of *identifiers*. This equates to the candidate key concept of the A strong third normal form section in Chapter 4, the syntax being

IDENTIFIER IS INV-ACC-NO IN INVESTMENT

A record could have many, one or none such identifiers.

SOURCE AND RESULT ITEMS
Although not mentioned in the example, CODASYL includes several other useful ideas. By referring back to the normalization process of Chapter 4, it was determined that the insurance record should be disjoint from the insurance company record, with the former containing a company code which was the key to the latter. It was also stated that, although this was data redundancy, it was at least a controlled redundancy. In CODASYL there is no need to store physically the same item twice. If it exists already in the insurance company record then within the insurance record itself we could state

```
01 CO-CODE IS VIRTUAL SOURCE IS
COMPANY-CODE OF OWNER OF IC-SET
```

To an application program the CO-CODE appears actually to be stored in the insurance record and is made available as if it were. However, to obtain physically the value for CO-CODE, the DBMS must access the current owner of set IC-SET and find the value there. Again, there has to be a trade-off between storage space and possible duplication with inconsistencies, against an increase in I/O and processor times.

A second example of virtual items is as follows: Suppose that the insurance record contains a field called PREMIUM which is the yearly premium amount due. We could now define an item TOTAL-PREMIUM in the insurance company record as:

```
01 TOTAL-PREMIUM       PIC 9(6)V99 IS VIRTUAL
RESULT OF ADD-PREMIUMS ON MEMBERS OF
                                        IC-SET;
```

PREMIUMS would be some prewritten procedure. No item TOTAL-PREMIUM is stored physically, but when a particular set occurrence is accessed, an item is created. The procedure ADD-PREMIUM is then called which reads through all the insurance (member) records, accumulating each PREMIUM amount and finally storing the result in TOTAL-PREMIUM (in memory, not on disk) which can then be accessed by the application program (on a readonly basis of course).

Note: if in this example, it was necessary to store the field TOTAL-PREMIUM on disk, then it could be defined as above but using the term ACTUAL instead of VIRTUAL.

Subschema

The application's view of the schema can be defined as a subschema such that a database will contain one or more subschemae (all implementations insist on at least one subschema even if that one defines the whole of the schema for a single application), with the possibility that a particular subschema could be shared by more than one application program. The various subschemae will not, in general, be disjoint. In particular, a subschema can omit (from the schema definition):

(1) one or more areas
(2) one or more record types
(3) one or more set types
(4) one or more data items.

In addition, certain amendments to the schema definition are allowed:

(1) areas, sets, records and data items can be renamed in the subschema
(2) access-control locks can be changed (affording different passwords for different users)
(3) the ordering of data items within a record can be changed
(4) data items can be omitted
(5) data items can be given different data types (for example, a PIC 9(6)v99 can be redefined as a PIC X(8) in the subschema)
(6) different SET SELECTION clauses may be defined.

In general terms, the subschemae of a CODASYL database provide the logical data independence, as defined in Chapter 2, that is missing in non-database approaches.

At present, CODASYL subschemae usually are written in either COBOL- or FORTRAN-orientated languages.

COBOL SUBSCHEMA

Supposing that we have a schema as defined in Figure 13.4 and also that we have an application which reads through the investment file and checks the current balance (INV-CURR-BALANCE) against the sum of all of the transaction amounts added to the opening balance (INV-OPEN-BALANCE); whether the amount actually is added to or subtracted from the total depends on the value of the transaction type (IT-TYPE). For this application we could define a subschema similar to that as shown in Figure 13.4.

```
TITLE DIVISION
SS BALANCE-CHECK WITHIN ACCOUNTS

MAPPING DIVISION
ALIAS SECTION
AD INVESTMENTS BECOMES INVS
AD INV-TRAN BECOMES TRANS

STRUCTURE DIVISION
REALM SECTION
RD INV-AREA

SET SECTION
SD I-T

RECORD SECTION
01 INVS
    03 INV-ACC-NO            PIC 9(10)
    03 INV-OPEN-BALANCE      PIC 9(6)V99
    03 INV-CURR-BALANCE      PIC 9(6)V99
01 TRANS
    03 IT-TYPE               PIC 99
    03 IT-AMOUNT             PIC 9(5)V99
```

Figure 13.4 *An example of COBOL subschema listing*

We have thus defined everything that the particular application requires (in fact if we had defined a virtual item TRANS-AMOUNT-TOT within investments and had written a subroutine as described previously, then there would be no need to have the program other than to print out discrepancies). If any other database items change via a restructure, then this program would not be affected (i.e. it is as logically data independent as it can be).

TITLE DIVISION
This is used to give the subschema a name (which must be unique) and to state to which schema it belongs.

MAPPING DIVISION
This is used to give any alternative names if used. Thus long self-explanatory names within the schema definition can be shortened for the programmer's convenience.

STRUCTURE DIVISION
Within this division, which is used to define the logical structure of the subschema, are the:

(1) *realm section*, because area is a reserved word in COBOL, the word realm has to be used as a synonym in the subschema definition; a realm does not have exactly the same connotations as the schema's area because it can contain subsets of the records in one or more areas
(2) *set section* names the required sets
(3) *record section* describes the records and data items to be used within the subschema.

Note: the FORTRAN subschema (not described here) affords very similar features but for one major difference. In COBOL, access-control locks can be specified in the subschema definition, and these will take priority over any conflicting locks specified in the schema definition. In the FORTRAN subschema, the reverse is true.

Data manipulation language
As mentioned previously, the CODASYL approach to data manipulation language (DML) is one of a host language (i.e. extensions to an existing language, in this case usually COBOL or FORTRAN). Before defining the various extension verbs, it is important to grasp the concept of *currency*, which forms a central part of the CODASYL DML philosophy.

CURRENCY
Since a database is likely to be composed of many record occurrences and many set occurrences, it is important that the DBMS can keep track of where an application program is with respect to the database at any one moment. The basic concept of currency therefore is that the database key of the current record is stored.

This concept extends to other portions of the database. In particular, currency status indicators are maintained for the following:

(1) *realm*, for each realm accessed by a program, the most recently accessed record within that realm is termed the *current of realm*
(2) *record type*, for each record type accessed, the most recently accessed is termed *current of record*
(3) *set type*, for each set type accessed, the most recently accessed, owner or member, is termed *current of set*; this is because a set itself does not have a database key but, by bearing in mind the rules for sets (the Sets subsection in this chapter), either an owner or a member will identify uniquely a particular set occurrence
(4) *any record*, the most recently accessed record of any description is termed *current of program*. (In CODASYL terminology, a program is often alternatively termed a run unit.)

ACCEPT

This is similar in principle to the normal COBOL accept statement. In DML it allows a program to read into its user work area any of the currency-status indicators (clearly on a Readonly basis). For example, if a record R has just been stored and the program wishes to note exactly what database key has been assigned to that record, then it can use

```
    STORE R.
ACCEPT WS-RKEY FROM {CHOICE} CURRENCY.
```

where {CHOICE} is the realm name, record name or set name of the required currency indicator. The data item WS-RKEY (or whatever) must have been declared with a USAGE IS DB-KEY clause.

CLEAR

As mentioned previously, not all database management systems zeroize the error-status field after the next successful database instruction. To avoid possible confusion therefore the task must be performed by the application program. For example:

```
IF DBERROR > 0 PERFORM
               CHECK-ERROR-TYPE
               CLEAR DBERROR.
```

Note: the actual data item DBERROR can have different names on different systems.

CONNECT (INSERT)

Suppose that we have just created an investment record and wish to relate it to an existing customer record (i.e. place it in the set CUST-INV). To be able to do this we need three operations:

(1) FIND CUSTOMER
(2) FIND INVESTMENT
(3) CONNECT INVESTMENT TO CUST-INV

Note: the set CUST-INV must not be specified as AUTOMATIC unless it is also OPTIONAL, in this instance.

DISCONNECT (REMOVE)

This statement (not surprisingly) does the opposite to the connect verb. If we wished to remove an investment record from an occurrence of the CUST-INV set we could use:

(1) FIND INVESTMENT
(2) DISCONNECT INVESTMENT FROM CUST-INV

With this done, then the investment record can still exist within the database if CUST-INV is specified as OPTIONAL.

ERASE

This option is used basically for deleting records. There are four possible suboptions:

$$\text{FIND INVESTMENT}$$
$$\text{ERASE INVESTMENT} \begin{Bmatrix} \text{PERMANENT} \\ \text{SELECTIVE} \\ \text{ALL} \end{Bmatrix}$$

(1) If no qualification is specified, then the investment record will be deleted only if it is the owner of no member records in any set occurrence, otherwise an error is returned.
(2) If PERMANENT is used then the investment record is deleted along with all MANDATORY and FIXED members for which the investment is an owner in all set occurrences. Note that OPTIONAL members only will be removed from the set occurrence and not deleted from the database.

(3) If SELECTIVE is employed, then the effect is the same as that when PERMANENT is used except that OPTIONAL members are also deleted, but then only if they are not members of other set types.
(4) If ALL is specified then the investment record and all of its members are deleted no matter what their standing.

It is important to note that if any deleted members are themselves owners, then the same ERASE statement applies to their members and so on. Thus great care must be taken! With a complex network database, it is possible to delete half of the database (or more) with a single ERASE ALL statement. If ERASE is used then the current of program is set to null. No other currency indicators are affected.

FETCH (OBTAIN)
This command combines a FIND and a GET (see subsections following) into a single statement. Thus

```
MOVE 1234567890 TO INV-ACC-NO.
FETCH ANY INVESTMENT.
```

FIND
This is the most complicated DML statement because there are several distinct possibilities. For all options the FIND locates a particular record in the database and makes it the current of program, current of realm, current of record type and current of all set types in which the record participates. The options are as follows.

Direct access

```
FIND INVESTMENT DB-KEY IS INV-KEY
```

In this statement INV-KEY is a program data item (i.e. in the data division in COBOL and not in the database) which has been declared as USAGE IS DB-KEY. At the time the above statement is executed the program must have placed a valid database key into that item.

Calc key access

```
MOVE 1382941603 TO INV-ACC-NO.
FIND ANY INVESTMENT.
```

Here the key field INV-ACC-NO must appear within the subschema. The DBMS applies its hashing function to the key value to provide a physical address.

Linear searching
Suppose that there existed a need to scan through all transactions for a particular account, adding the individual amounts together in passing. We could use

```
      MOVE 1384216803 TO INV-ACC-NO.
      FIND ANY INVESTMENT.
      IF I-T EMPTY GO NO-TRANSACTIONS.
LOOP.
      FIND NEXT INV-TRAN WITHIN I-T.
      IF END-OF-SET GO END-ACCOUNT.
      ...PROCESSING ...
      GO LOOP.
```

When the first line after loop is executed for the first time, the current of set I-T will be the investment. Thus a FIND NEXT will locate the first transaction. The word NEXT can be replaced by PRIOR, FIRST, LAST, an integer or the name of a data item having an integer value. In the last two cases, a positive number indicates the number of occurrences of the transactions to be read in a NEXT context, and a negative number would be the equivalent for the PRIOR. Thus if we knew that the transaction we required was the third from the end, then we could specify

```
      FIND -3 INV-TRAN WITHIN I-T
```

(This of course assumes that backward pointers are available.)

Current record
This is used to make the current of a set the current of program (which may not necessarily already be the case).

By assuming the current of I-T to be a transaction and not the investment

```
      FIND CURRENT INV-TRAN WITHIN I-T
```

This situation would be possible if, for example, we had found an investment, found the relevant transaction and then gone off to read the customer record. This would make the transaction the current of set but the customer would be current of program. The latter could revert to the transaction by using the above. In this sense, this is not a true FIND because the record was found already: it is merely a means of updating currency indicators.

Find owner
If the current of program was an investment record and we wished to find its owner customer record (in the CUST-INV set), then we could use

```
FIND OWNER WITHIN CUST-INV.
```

Another linear search
To illustrate this mechanism, the example must be changed to that of the insurance company and mortgage records which both own insurance records via the IC-SET and the MI-SET respectively.

Suppose that we wished to find the premium on the contents record for company 014 for mortgage number 9876543211. Clearly, we could either find the mortgage record and scan the MI-SET until we found the contents record with insurance company code 014, or we could find the insurance company record and scan the insurance records through the IC-SET. In this instance, the former would be far more efficient in general, because the mortgage will own less insurance records than the company. Thus we could use:

```
MOVE 9876543211 TO MTG-ACC-NO.
FIND ANY MORTGAGE.
IF MI-SET EMPTY GO NO-INSURANCES.
MOVE 014 TO IC-CODE IN INSURANCE.
FIND INSURANCE WITHIN MI-SET CURRENT
USING
    IC-CODE IN INSURANCE.
```

If current is omitted from this example then the SET SELECTION statement would be performed. There are other possible variations on the FIND statement which will not be discussed here.

FINISH
When a program has finished work on a particular realm, it

is most efficient if it releases that realm for use by other programs. Thus:

```
FINISH INV-AREA.
```

FREE

This statement nullifies a KEEP statement (see the subsection following).

GET

We have looked at the FIND verb which locates a required record, but does not return it to the user work area (UWA), although the outcome of the FIND can be checked (i.e. a NOTFOUND condition would be returned to the program). To obtain the record, the program must contain a GET verb. Thus

```
MOVE 1234567890 TO INV-ACC-NO.
FIND ANY INVESTMENT.
IF NOTFOUND GO NO-FOUND.
GET INVESTMENT.
```

In this example, the final noun INVESTMENT is spurious, because GET acts on the current of program (i.e. just GET. would have sufficed).

KEEP

Some CODASYL systems allow concurrency by placing the onus on the application program to maintain integrity. In this situation, the current of program is said to exist in a 'monitored mode'. If a second program wishes to update a record after it has become current of the first program, then the first program will terminate with an error. In other words, MONITOR is as it sounds and not a locking device. The monitored mode ends when a record ceases to be current of program. However, a program may extend monitored mode by KEEPing the record until it is explicitly FREEd.

If a program requires a set of records for a set of consistent updates, then it could FIND all records and KEEP them until it has finished. However, if while doing this one of them is updated by another program, an error will occur. To prevent this happening a REMONITOR command can be used which effectively KEEPs all the desired records, but only after the last has been accessed.

The general idea behind this old-fashioned method of allowing concurrency (generally used before page locking became common practice), is that a program using KEEP and/or REMONITOR can detect whether a record, which it has obtained as current of program, has been updated by another program since that time and can act accordingly, i.e. can decide whether to terminate or simply to reread the record. This prevents the possible loss of integrity problem outlined in the Concurrency section in Chapter 1, although the onus is on the application program.

MODIFY

This verb is used to alter existing records within the database. For example:

```
FETCH INVESTMENT.
ADD TRANS-AMT TO INV-CURR-BALANCE.
MODIFY INVESTMENT.
```

Thus the record must have been found previously, moved into the UWA and updated, and then MODIFY stores the record back onto the database. If MODIFY specifies a record name then the entire record is written. Alternatively, if MODIFY specifies certain data items then only those items are replaced. Thus in the example, the same effect could have been achieved by using

```
MODIFY INV-CURR-BALANCE.
```

ORDER

The ORDER statement can be used to impose a new ordering on the member records of the current occurrence of a particular set. This can only be done if the program has exclusive retrieval or protected retrieval declared against the relevant realm (see the Integrity section in this chapter).

For example, if ORDER IS SORTED is specified in the schema definition, then an application program could use

```
ORDER I-T LOCALLY ON ASCENDING KEY IT-
TYPE IN INV-TRAN.
```

Note: the change is only temporary and the ordering reverts to its original state whenever the realm is FINISHed.

READY

Before a program can use a realm it must READY it and declare its required usage type. This can be:

UPDATE
RETRIEVAL
UPDATE EXCLUSIVE
UPDATE PROTECTED
RETRIEVAL EXCLUSIVE
RETRIEVAL PROTECTED

The differences between these are highlighted in the Integrity section following. An example would be

```
    READY INV-AREA USAGE-MODE IS
RETRIEVAL.
```

STORE

This command is used to create a record occurrence (as opposed to MODIFY which is used to change an existing record). Thus to create a transaction record we would use

```
MOVE 15 TO IT-NO.
MOVE 010786 TO IT-DATE.
MOVE 37 TO IT-TYPE.
MOVE 2 TO IT-SOURCE.
MOVE 26.38 TO IT-AMOUNT.
MOVE 1234567890 TO INV-ACC-NO.
STORE INV-TRAN.
```

The sixth line is necessary because the set I-T was declared as AUTOMATIC which means that when an INV-TRAN is stored the DBMS will store it automatically within the I-T set. The SET SELECTION clause states that the owner is located by CALC KEY and so we must supply the DBMS with a key value.

USE

This DML statement implies usage of named procedures, perhaps to action database error reporting or to control privacy locks or validation routines. For example:

```
IF I-T EMPTY USE NO-TRANS-ERROR.
```

Example

It is perhaps difficult to visualize the construction of a DML program without a full example to reference. For that reason an example is given in Figure 13.5, the program in question being one which checks through all investment transactions, checking the balance against that stored on the investment record itself.

Please note that the program is not structured in a program-design sense, and also that the syntax is not standard across all computers employing CODASYL products. The subschema does not appear in the listing but would be invoked in the subschema section by a precompiler or during the compilation itself. It is, however, the same format as that described in the COBOL subschema subsection in this chapter.

```
IDENTIFICATION DIVISION.
PROGRAM-ID. INV/01.
ENVIRONMENT DIVISION.
INPUT-OUTPUT SECTION.
FILE-CONTROL.
    SELECT PRINTOUT ASSIGN PRINTER.
DATA DIVISION.
SUBSCHEMA SECTION.
DB BALANCE-CHECK WITHIN ACCOUNTS.
FILE SECTION.
FD PRINTOUT.
01 P-LINE                       PIC X(132).
01 PR-LINE.
    03 ACC-NO                   PIC 9(10).
    03 FILLER                   PIC X(5).
    03 ACTUAL-AMT               PIC Z(5)9.99.
    03 FILLER                   PIC X(5).
    03 CALC-AMT                 PIC Z(5)9.99.
    03 FILLER                   PIC X(96).
WORKING-STORAGE SECTION.
01 CALC-TOTAL                   PIC 9(6)V99.
PROCEDURE DIVISION.
OPEN-UP.
    OPEN OUTPUT PRINTOUT.
    READY INV-AREA USAGE-MODE IS PROTECTED
RETRIEVAL.
    FIND FIRST INVESTMENT WITHIN INV-AREA.
    GO GET-INV.
INV-LOOP.
    FIND NEXT INVESTMENT WITHIN INV-AREA.
    IF END-OF-FILE GO CLOSE-DOWN.
```

(*continued*)

```
GET-INV.
    GET INV-ACC-NO INV-OPEN-BALANCE INV-CURR-
BALANCE.
    MOVE INV-OPEN-BALANCE TO CALC-TOTAL.
TRAN-LOOP.
    FIND NEXT INV-TRAN WITHIN I-T.
    IF END-OF-SET GO CHECK-BAL.
    GET IT-TYPE IT-AMOUNT.
    IF IT-TYPE < 20 ADD IT-AMOUNT TO CALC-TOTAL
        ELSE SUBTRACT IT-AMOUNT FROM CALC-TOTAL.
    GO TRAN-LOOP.
CHECK-BAL.
    CLEAR DBSTATUS.
    IF CALC-TOTAL = INV-CURR-BALANCE GO INV-LOOP.
    MOVE SPACES TO P-LINE.
    MOVE INV-ACC-NO TO ACC-NO.
    MOVE INV-CURR-BALANCE TO ACTUAL-AMT.
    MOVE CALC-TOTAL TO CALC-AMT.
    WRITE P-LINE BEFORE 1.
    GO INV-LOOP.
CLOSE-DOWN.
    FINISH INV-AREA.
    CLOSE PRINTOUT.
    STOP RUN.
```

Figure 13.5 *An example of COBOL host language program*

Note: the items END-OF-FILE and END-OF-SET would be defined as 88 levels on the field DBSTATUS which would be added to the program with the subschema. The actual numerical values of DBSTATUS implying end-of-file or end-of-set vary enormously from machine to machine.

Data storage description language

As mentioned previously, the CODASYL 78 report introduced a separate language for the storage model which was to become independent of the logical model.

By referring back to the schema definition earlier in this chapter, it was of particular note that:

(1) a database key relates to how and where a record is to be stored, even more so if it is a physical address itself
(2) location mode clauses are concerned with how a record is to be stored and accessed
(3) virtual or actual clauses state how a record is to be derived and from where (thus giving them physical data dependence).

Not surprisingly, CODASYL 78 has sought to remove these from the DDL. Instead, within the DSDL, it has implemented the following three constructs.

(1) A storage record. This is 'a variable length addressable container for data and pointers associated with a single schema record'. Basically, what this entails is a 1:n mapping with each storage record relating to a single schema record, but one schema record possibly producing many storage records.
(2) A mapping which is defined by a MAPPING DESCRIPTION entry and is the mapping between schema and storage records. If the mapping is 1:n then the storage records for a particular schema record may overlap with duplication of data items. The DBMS will be able to control such duplication (e.g. a mortgage record could be stored in two parts, one current data and one historic data, but each might contain the account number, customer number, etc.).
(3) An index which is defined as 'a set structure which supports access paths to storage records'.

There is no mention of set storage constructs in the CODASYL 78 report. Any set associations are defined via pointers and indexes in the storage record definition. In particular, location mode has been replaced by a PLACEMENT clause for which there are three possible values:

(a) RANDOM used for quick accessing
(b) SEQUENTIAL used for accessing by key sequence and randomly
(c) CLUSTERED used for storage of associated records on the same or adjacent pages.

Privacy

In a CODASYL database all access to the data must be done through subschemae (except for Query languages; see Chapter 11), which themselves afford a considerable amount of access control. The DBA can allocate a subschema to an application program which contains exactly what the application wants (or is allowed to see). In addition, the DBA can also specify access-control locks at the schema, realm, set, record and data-item levels, and it is possible for different locks to be applied for different users (through the use of subroutines). It is also possible to set different locks for different operations (e.g. insert, remove, delete, etc.).

At the schema level the functions which can be controlled are ALTER (updating facilities), DISPLAY (Readonly),

LOCKS (displaying the access-control locks in the schema) and COPY (to define a subschema).

At the other levels, the possibilities are:

SUBSCHEMA	ALTER DISPLAY LOCKS COMPILE
AREA	RETRIEVAL (PROTECTED OR EXCLUSIVE) UPDATE (PROTECTED OR EXCLUSIVE)
RECORD	DELETE FIND GET INSERT MODIFY REMOVE STORE
SET	FIND INSERT ORDER REMOVE
DATA ITEM	GET MODIFY STORE

For all the possibilities, the relevant access-control key must be supplied by the application program before the function can be performed.

Note: the COMPILE subschema option simply implies the ability to invoke the subschema at compilation time.

Integrity

In the last section how access-control locks can be used to maintain privacy (and hence maintain that aspect of integrity) was dealt with. The DBA can also define various validation procedures which can be invoked (usually at the time of a STORE or MODIFY) to check that the content of the current record obeys predefined rules. These procedures can be CALLed either by the application program or by the DBMS (if they are defined in the schema).

Loss of integrity by concurrent updating can be avoided by use of the USAGE-MODE clause as outlined in the previous section. The meanings of EXCLUSIVE and PROTECTED are as follows:

(1) EXCLUSIVE means that once a program has used READY on a realm in exclusive mode, no other program can ready that realm (and thereby use it), be it for update or retrieval
(2) PROTECTED means the same except that other programs may ready the same realm for retrieval only.

A program that has readied a realm for UPDATE or RETRIEVAL only (i.e. without the EXCLUSIVE or

PROTECTED clauses) must cater for the fact that another program may be updating the same realm at the same time. In this instance, the DBMS uses the notify protocol to inform the program if, after it has made a record current of program, another program updates that record (see the Keep subsection in this chapter).

Such a system has come under severe criticism because there is no locking mechanism and no guarantee that integrity cannot be lost if the programs have been written badly. For this reason, most CODASYL implementations have taken to realm/page/record locking as an alternative and, since this is a far neater and safer methodology (the onus for maintaining integrity is placed on the DBMS), this trend is likely to continue.

Restructure/reorganization

It is perhaps in this area that the CODASYL implementations have been traditionally weak. Because of the complex relationships afforded by a network model, in particular the reliance on database keys as physical addresses and physical-address pointers, it is often very difficult to restructure a file without having to 'fix up' the pointers of all related record types.

The result of this is that too often large parts of the database have to be dumped to tape programmatically, the database restructured and then the data reloaded (i.e. recreated) in its new format by another user written program.

For example, in our customers/investments/transactions network, if we wished to restructure investments we would have to bear in mind that pointers exist on both customer and transaction records which are dependent on the physical location of an investment record. If the latter are moved physically, as they would be in either a restructure or reorganize, then the related pointers would need to be changed. To do this we would need to:

(1) dump the investment records logically
(2) delete all investments, leaving all occurrences of CUST-INV empty, and leaving all transactions without owners (only possible if I-T is OPTIONAL which is not what we would normally want)
(3) restructure investments

(4) reload the investments and hope to patch them into the relevant CUST-INV occurrences along with all their related transactions, a process that is not easy when each transaction does not have a unique identifying key (the reason it does not is that it is not needed in a network model).

By bearing these factors in mind it would be condonable to:

(1) dump customers, investments and transactions logically
(2) restructure
(3) reload and recreate all three (assuming that they were dumped in such a way as would facilitate this).

Those of you who are observant will have realized that the customers also are connected physically to the mortgages which are connected to their own transactions, insurances, endowments etc. Therefore we cannot dump and delete customers without mortgages and, by extension, nearly every other file on the database.

These problems stated, it must also be said that CODASYL currently are working on a common restructuring language which hopefully will alleviate these problems when implemented.

CHAPTER 14

IMS: A Hierarchical Approach

Background

One of the most widely used database systems, IMS, was first developed in conjunction with the Apollo space programme; the acronym IMS standing for information management system. The system has been evolved by IBM over the years, from an IMS/360 version I through version II and on to an IMS/VS (VS = virtual storage) under the operating system OS/VS. In its basic form, IMS is suitable only for batch applications, but it can be extended (via the data communications feature) to support on-line applications also.

Architecture

With reference to Figure 14.1, the first point of note with the IMS architecture is that the stored database consists of several physical databases. (The term 'physical' here does not have its usual meaning as defined in Chapter 2. Instead it refers to a system of files as will be described later.)

Each physical database is defined by a database description (DBD) which also specifies the mapping of physical database to storage structure. However, the user sees very little of this structure which means that IMS offers very good physical data independence (as defined in Chapter 2). In fact the user interfaces through submodels which, in turn, are a collection of logical databases. Each logical database is defined, together with its mapping to the physical database, by means of a program communication block (PCB). Since a user can access a set of PCBs then that set is termed a program specification block (PSB).

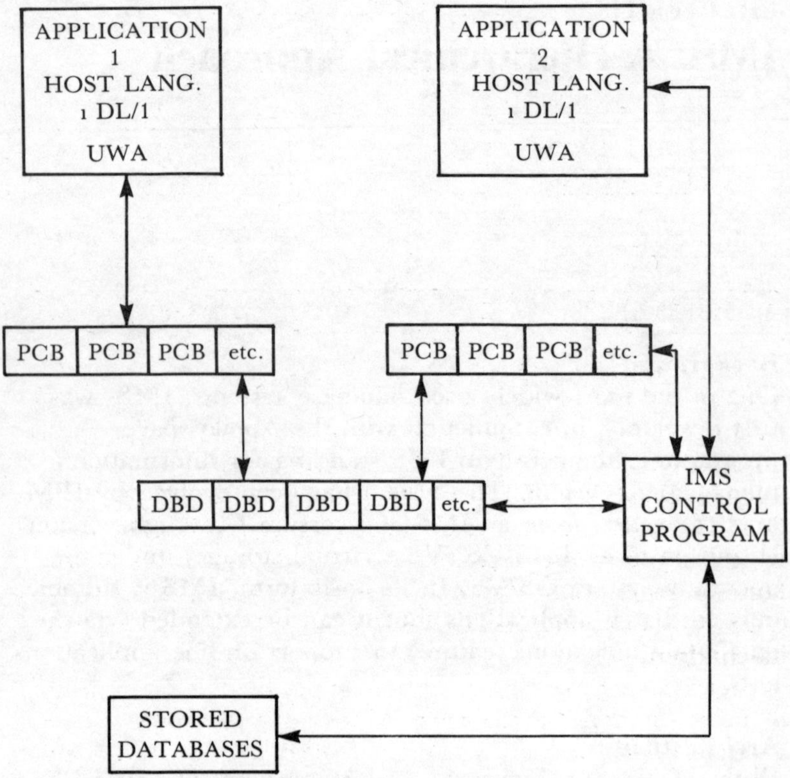

Figure 14.1 *The IMS architecture*

The data manipulation is carried out by the host-language approach (PL/1, COBOL or IBM 360 Assembler) from which the IMS sublanguage DL/1 (Data Language One) can be invoked by subroutine call.

Physical databases

In the last section we have defined a physical database as being an ordered set of all occurrences of a single type of physical database record (PDBR). This in turn consists of a hierarchy of fixed (or variable) length segment occurrences, each of which comprises a set of fixed (or variable) length field occurrences.

Consider the hierarchy of Figure 14.2 (which is a PDBR).

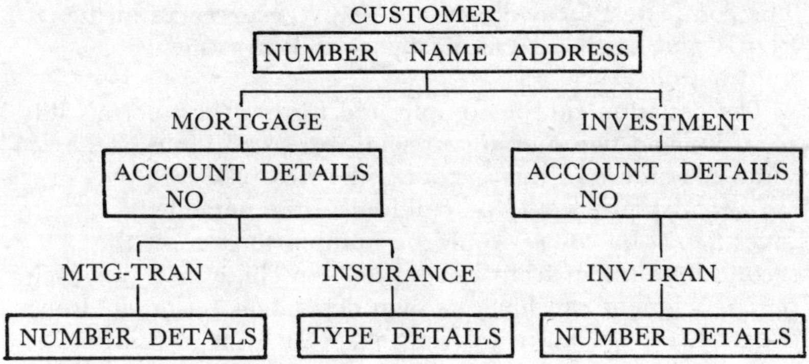

Figure 14.2 *Physical database record*

In this example we have six types of segment: CUSTOMER, MORTGAGE, INVESTMENT, MTG-TRAN, INSURANCE and INV-TRAN. The CUSTOMER segment is defined to be the *root segment* on which all others are dependent. These dependencies form families/generations. Thus the parent of MORTGAGE is CUSTOMER while MTG-TRAN and INSURANCE are its children.

Clearly, each parent occurrence must be able to own one or more (or none) occurrences of its children. For example, a single PDBR occurrence might appear as shown in Figure 14.3.

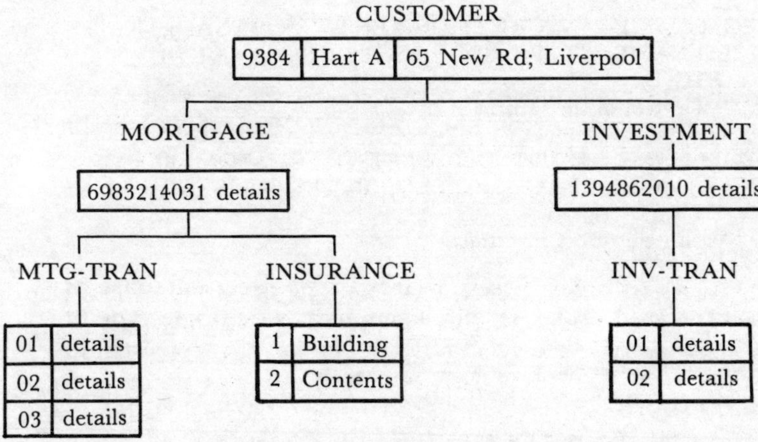

Figure 14.3 *Single physical database record occurrence*

The complete PDB will contain many occurrences of the PDBR and hence all the mortgage and investment information.

The situation can be complicated further (and permissibly so) if we had two investment segments as children of the same customer. In this instance, the two INV-TRAN segments shown would be children of the named investment, but there would be nothing to prevent the second investment from having its own children. Thus each parent segment can have its own dependent set of children occurrences (i.e. a 1:n relationship). Each set of children occurrences having a common parent occurrence are said to be *twins* (no matter how many of them there actually are).

```
DBD   NAME = ACCOUNTS
SEGM NAME =CUSTOMER, BYTES =10
FIELD NAME =(CUST-NO, SEQ), BYTES = 6, START =1
FIELD NAME =CUST-NAME, BYTES = 20, START = 7
FIELD NAME =CUST-ADDR, BYTES =74, START =27
SEGM NAME =MORTGAGE, PARENT =CUSTOMER, BYTES = 36
FIELD NAME =(M-ACC-NO, SEQ), BYTES =10, START = 1
  ... ETC. ...
  ...each item of the mortgage segment ...

SEGM NAME =MTG-TRAN, PARENT =MORTGAGE, BYTES = 20
FIELD NAME =(M-TRAN-NO, SEQ), BYTES = 2, START = 1
  ...ETC. ...
  ...each item of the mortgage transaction ...

SEGM NAME = INSURNCE, PARENT =MORTGAGE, BYTES = 50
FIELD NAME = (TYPE, SEQ), BYTES =10, START = 1
  ...ETC. ...
  ...each item of the insurance ...

SEGM NAME =INVSTMNT, PARENT =CUSTOMER, BYTES = 40
FIELD NAME = (I-ACC-NO, SEQ), BYTES = 10, START =1
  ...ETC. ...
  ...each item of the investment ...

SEGM NAME =INV-TRAN, PARENT = INVSTMNT, BYTES = 20
FIELD NAME = (I-TRAN-NO, SEQ), BYTES =3, START = 1
  ...ETC ...
  ...each item of the investment transaction ...
```

Figure 14.4 *Example of database description*

Note: each parent may have any number of types of children and each child may have any number of segment types as its own children up to a maximum of 15 in any one hierarchical path and up to a total of 255 for the whole PDBR.

Data description language

System 360 Assembler is the language used to describe each physical database. The database descriptions are then assembled into machine (object) code for immediate usage when called by IMS.

By omitting the physical/storage mapping, the description for our banking example as shown in Figure 14.2 would appear similar to that shown in Figure 14.4.

Notes:

(1) The first line simply gives a unique name to the database description (DBD).
(2) All identifiers are limited to eight characters.
(3) The second line defines the name of the root segment and states its length in bytes.
(4) The following three lines define the fields which make up customer giving their name, length and offset from the beginning of the segment (note that the key item is defined within parentheses).
(5) The remainder of the description is concerned with defining all other segments, their parents and their constituent fields.
(6) The term SEQ is used on the field description of each segment's key item to declare that the segment occurrences (if there are more than one) should be maintained in ascending key sequence. If any of these were allowed duplicate key values, then we would specify (I-TRAN-NO, SEQ, M), the M standing for multiple.

The duplication here refers to that within a certain parent/child hierarchy. Thus without an M, an investment could not have two transactions of the same transaction number, but other investment occurrences could.

(7) The ordering of SEGM statements is very important and must follow the overall hierarchy pattern from top to bottom and left to right.
(8) The field items may overlap by specifying the START location accordingly. Hence with

```
FIELD NAME = DATE, BYTES = 6, START = 23
FIELD NAME = DAYS, BYTES =2, START =23
FIELD NAME = MONTH, BYTES = 2, START = 25,
FIELD NAME = YEAR, BYTES = 2, START = 27
```

we are, in effect, redefining the date as three distinct two-digit items.

With

```
FIELD NAME = (SEG-KEY, SEQ), BYTES = 10, START = 1
FIELD NAME = ITEM-1, BYTES = 8, START = 1
FIELD NAME = ITEM-2, BYTES = 2, START = 9
```

we are defining a 10-byte key as the concatenation of two separate fields.

Internally, IMS identifies each segment type by its position in the hierarchy. In the example above we would have:

CUSTOMER = 1, MORTGAGE = 2, MTG-TRAN = 3,
INSURNCE = 4 INVSTMNT = 5, INV-TRAN = 6

This number is important in identifying the 'hierarchical sequence key value', which consists of the concatenation of the

root type code + root key + parent type code + parent key + child's type code + etc.

From the above list and the example shown in Figure 14.3 we can derive the sequence key for the second insurance record which would be

1 + 9483 + 2 + 6983214031 + 4 + 02

As can be imagined, the larger the hierarchy the larger the number, producing a key which is not wholly memorable.

The hierarchical sequence for an IMS database is that sequence of segment occurrences defined by ascending values of the hierarchical sequence key. This is an important concept because the databases are stored in hierarchical sequence.

IMS submodels

As defined in the Architecture section in this chapter, a user's view of the hierarchy basically consists of a group of logical databases each of which is an ordered set comprising all occurrences of an LDBR. This, in turn, is a subset of some PDBR. The subset can consist of the omission of any PDBR segment and its associated children.

Again by referring to Figure 14.2, as a logical

database we could have customer only, customer and investment only, customer and mortgage only, customer and mortgage and investment only, etc. However, we must include the root segment and we cannot omit any intermediate generation.

Segments included in an LDBR are said to be *sensitive* to the user of that LDBR. That user can only view those segments within his LDBR though if he deletes a parent record, its associated children will also be deleted whether or not they are in the LDBR. Such a scheme provides a reasonable amount of logical data independence (as defined in Chapter 2) and protects the application from change to other areas of the hierarchy. In particular, a new segment could be added in many places without affecting a user, but not if it interferes with their particular subhierarchy.

For example, if an LDBR contained the full hierarchy as shown in Figure 14.2, then we could change the PDBR by adding a segment as a child of:

(1) MTG-TRAN
(2) INSURNCE
(3) INV-TRAN

or as another child of customer (at the same level as mortgage or Invstmnt), mortgage (at the same level as Mtg-Tran or Insurnce) or Invstmnt (at the same level as Inv-tran). None of these would affect the LDBR and hence the user. However, if we wished to insert a new segment between customer and mortgage, or between mortgage and Mtg-tran (i.e. at a new hierarchical level), then the user would certainly be affected because the hierarchical sequence key would change. Users also would be affected by changing or adding fields in the appropriate existing segments.

As stated previously, each logical database is defined by a program communication block which includes a specification of the mapping between the LDB and the corresponding physical database (PDB). The PCB is, again, written in System/360 Assembler. A PCB for an application's view of customer, mortgage and insurance from the example of Figure 14.2 with a DBD of Figure 14.4 could be written in similar fashion to that shown in Figure 14.5.

```
    PCB TYPE = DB, DBDNAME = ACCOUNTS, KEYLEN = 16
    SENSEG NAME = CUSTOMER, PROCOPT = G
    SENSEG NAME = MORTGAGE, PARENT = CUSTOMER,
PROCOPT = G
    SENSEG NAME = INSURNCE, PARENT = MORTGAGE,
PROCOPT = R
```

Figure 14.5 *Program communication block definition*

Notes:

(1) TYPE + DB in the first line specifies that this is a database PCB (as opposed to terminal PCBs which are used for on-line applications).
(2) The physical database for which the PCB is a subset is named using DBDNAME.
(3) The length of the key is stated as 16 (as derived at the end of the Data description language section in Chapter 14), but without the segment-type codes.
(4) The second line specifies the root of the hierarchy (note that no renaming is allowed).
(5) The PROCOPT clause stands for PROCessing OPTions and specifies the functions that the user is allowed to perform on the segment. The legal values are

G = Get = Retrieval only
I = Insert
R = Replace = Update
D = Delete
L = Load [this may be used only at the PCB level (see following) and is used for the initial loading of data]
K = Key sensitivity [this is useful if, for example, the user only required customer and insurance details; as stated previously, the mortgage segment cannot be omitted from the LDB but the DBA can specify K as the mortgage PROCOPT and this acts as a 'dummy segment invoker' declaring that only the mortgage segment key actually is required (for accessing insurances)]
E = Exclusive use.

One or more of these options may be specified for a particular PCB. If the PROCOPT has the same value for all SENSEGs, then it is worthwhile putting that PROCOPT option(s) on the PCB statement itself. If this were done it would cover all segments save those specifying a different PROCOPT option.

(6) The remaining statements within the example define the dependent segments and their own processor options. Again these segments must be defined in a top to bottom, left to right order.

Data manipulation language (DL/1)

When an application program uses a particular LDB, the related PCB is kept in memory to act as a communication area between the program and the IMS. The program, by using DL/1 subroutines, must specify the storage address of each LDB's PCB that it wishes to use. At run time, IMS is given control and determines the program specification block (PSB), which is specified in a job control language (JCL) statement, and hence the database definitions (DBDs) required. It then calls on the appropriate libraries and loads them into memory. Finally, control is passed back to the application program along with the PCB addresses (as parameters).

As stated previously, the application program invokes a particular DL/1 command by calling on a subroutine to which it passes relevant parameters. These parameters are:

(1) the address of the relevant PCB
(2) the operation required (see below)
(3) the address of the input/output area
(4) sometimes, qualification conditions.

The actual DL/1 procedures are as shown in Figure 14.6.

Full name	Abbrev.	Meaning
GET UNIQUE	GU	Direct retrieval
GET NEXT	GN	Sequential retrieval
GET NEXT WITHIN PARENT	GNP	Sequential retrieval under the current parent
GET HOLD UNIQUE	GHU,GHN,GHNP	Retrieve for update
GET HOLD NEXT	GHN	Sequential retrieval for update
GET HOLD NEXT WITHIN PARENT	GHNP	As GNP but for update
INSERT	ISRT	Add new segment
REPLACE	REPL	Replace an existing segment
DELETE	DLET	Delete existing segment

Figure 14.6 *DL/1 procedures*

An example of their use in an application program, by assuming that the PCB is defined as in Figure 14.5, might be:

```
GU CUSTOMER (NAME = 'LINFORD')
MORTGAGE (M-TYPE = 4)
INSURNCE (PREMIUM = 48.63)
```

Note: this is not true DL/1 syntax because it is missing the PCB address and the I/O area address.

This example basically is requesting IMS to perform a linear search. It will do this by searching the CUSTOMER segment for an occurrence with the required name. It will then search the MORTGAGE segments dependent on that customer occurrence for one in which the M-TYPE = 4 (M-TYPE being not explicitly named in Figure 14.4 but being one of the mortgage items). Having found that occurrence, IMS will scan the related INSURNCE segments for one in which the PREMIUM = 48.63.

By referring to the example, the conditions in parentheses are known as segment search arguments (SSAs). If a particular SSA is not found (for example, if no MORTGAGE segment is found where M-TYPE = 4), IMS will go back up one level and carry on searching (i.e. in the example, for another segment occurrence where the name is Linford). The operation will be successful only when all conditions are met. If this occurs then only the lowest segment is retrieved (the INSURNCE segment here). If the operation fails, the user has a STATUS area assigned (as with other database systems) into which a non zero number is returned. If an SSA is not specified then any occurrence for that segment will suffice. For example, if we required any insurance premium greater than £100 for any customer, we could use:

```
GU CUSTOMER
   MORTGAGE
   INSURNCE (PREMIUM > 100.00)
```

Further examples, with other DL/1 verbs, are now given.

(1) Retrieve all INSURNCE segments for mortgage 9238611407.

```
    GU CUSTOMER
          MORTGAGE (M-ACC-NO = 9238611407)
          INSURNCE.
    process first insurnce
 LOOP.
    GN INSURNCE.
          process subsequent insurnces
    GO LOOP.
```

The first INSURNCE statement will find the first INSURNCE segment for the defined mortgage. Thereafter the loop will retrieve all subsequent segment occurrences. *Note*: again an apology for those readers familiar with structured programming; my aim here is solely to illustrate the database syntax.

(2) Retrieve all CUSTOMER segments.

```
    GU CUSTOMER.
 LOOP.
    GN.
    GO LOOP.
```

In this example, only GN is needed within the loop because CUSTOMER is the only segment specified.

(3) Get all transactions for the customer whose name is Thompson and whose mortgage account number is 9238666410.

```
    GU CUSTOMER (NAME = 'THOMPSON')
          MORTGAGE (M-ACC-NO = 9238666410).
 LOOP.
    GNP MTG-TRAN.
    GO LOOP.
```

(4) Add a new transaction (number 14) for the customer 'Casey' to his mortgage 9138218604. First, the MTG-TRAN segment must be set up within the user work area. Then:

```
 ISRT CUSTOMER (NAME = 'CASEY')
          MORTGAGE (M-ACC-NO = 9138219604)
          MTG-TRAN.
```

Note that the CUSTOMER and MORTGAGE segments must exist already. Hence, despite the appearance of the above statement, we are only inserting the lowest segment occurrence, the first two lines merely being a hierarchical

route to that segment.
(5) Delete an insurance type 3 record for the customer 'TELFER' whose mortgage number is unknown.

```
GHU CUSTOMER (NAME = 'TELFER')
   MORTGAGE
   INSURNCE (TYPE = 3)
DLET.
```

The desired record can be deleted only if it has already been the subject of a GET HOLD command. Were we to have used

```
GHU CUSTOMER (NAME = 'TELFER')
      MORTGAGE
DLET.
```

then not only would the first MORTGAGE have been deleted, but also its associated transaction and INSURNCE segments.
(6) Update the amount on transaction 10 of the mortgage account 9133674502 belonging to customer 'Ritchie'.

```
GHU CUSTOMER (NAME = 'RITCHIE')
   MORTGAGE (M-ACC-NO = 9133674502)
   MTG-TRAN (MTRAN-NO = 10)
(change amount field in the I/O area)
REPL
```

(7) Find the MORTGAGE segment 9224746308 and its associated customer record.

```
GU CUSTOMER * D
     MORTGAGE (M-ACC-NO = 9224746308)
```

The result of this would be to find the specified mortgage and its parent customer, and concatenate both within the I/O area. The * D means 'get the customer data also'.
(8) Insert a new CUSTOMER segment, a MORTGAGE and an INSURNCE record. First, the three segment occurrences must be set up in the I/O area. Then:

```
ISRT CUSTOMER * D
      MORTGAGE
      INSURNCE.
```

The * D need only be specified for the top hierarchical

segment because that is created first. Thereafter the MORTGAGE can be inserted and finally the INSURNCE.
(9) Find the transaction which paid the buildings insurance premium (type 01) for mortgage 9264383700 belonging to customer 'Walsh'.

```
GU CUSTOMER (NAME = 'WALSH')
     MORTGAGE (M-ACC-NO = 9264383700)
     INSURNCE (TYPE = 01).
GNP MTG-TRAN * F.
```

First, we need to find the INSURNCE segment of the required type to ascertain the amount of premium paid (and possibly the date of payment). Next it is a case of going back ('back' because transactions precede INSURNCE segments in the hierarchical sequence) to search for one with the corresponding amount (and date). To do this we can use * F which tells IMS to start searching from the start of the specified segment type (since no SSA is specified for MTG-TRAN).
It is noteworthy in this example that had we wished to progress from transactions to insurances and not the other way round, * F would not have been required. By using GNP, once IMS had read the last transaction occurrence, it would have progressed automatically on to the INSURNCE segments.

Storage model
IMS provides four different storage structures which are known as HSAM, HISAM, HDAM and HIDAM. The interface between physical database and stored database consists of the following four access methods:

(1) OS/VS sequential access methods (QSAM and BSAM)
(2) OS/VS indexed sequential access method (ISAM)
(3) OS/VS virtual storage method (VSAM)
(4) overflow sequential access method (OSAM) which is a special IMS method (all the others being general IBM storage methods).

The relationships between these and the storage structures are as shown in Figure 14.7.

Every PDB segment within the stored database consists of a stored segment occurrence which contains the data as the user sees it plus a prefix (except HSAM and HISAM)

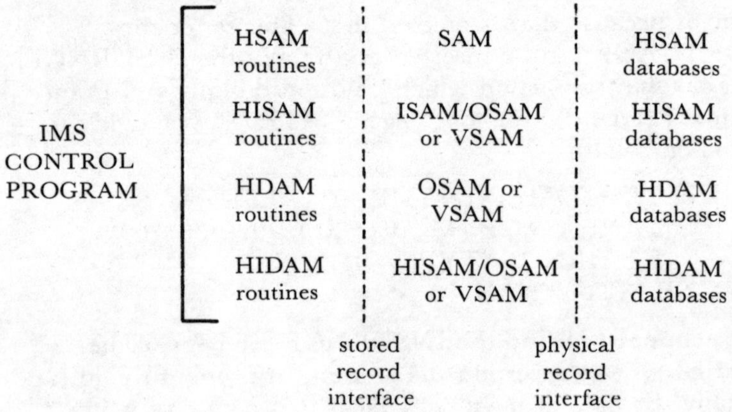

Figure 14.7 *Relationship between access mechanisms and storage structures*

which the user does not see. This prefix contains control information for the segment such as the segment types and various pointers.

For each of the four structure types the PDB segments essentially are the same. Where the structures differ is in (1) the means to connect PDB segment occurrences together to form PDBR occurrences and (2) the means to connect PDBR occurrences together to form the PDB.

HIERARCHICAL SEQUENTIAL ACCESS METHOD (HSAM)

This method is best observed as equivalent to a tape-based file which is read and written sequentially (indeed an HSAM database may actually be stored on tape). The data are kept in hierarchical sequence in a top to bottom, left to right manner. Thus:

> customer 1, mortgage, Mtg-tran 1, Mtg-tran 2, Insurnce 1, Insurnce 2, Invstmnt 1, Inv-tran 1, Invstmnt 2, Inv-tran 1, Inv-tran 2,,customer 2, mortgage, etc.

Each hierarchical occurrence contains any number of stored segments, but the total is a fixed-length record, a size chosen by the DBA. Thus inevitable gaps will be left between records since the DBA must allow for the maximum possible number of segments. Thus this particular storage approach would present similar problems to the large-record approach of Chapter 1, and is therefore likely to be used only when the hierarchy is of a fairly fixed (or variable within narrow limits) nature.

An HSAM database is created as a one-off exercise using ISRT and thereafter can only be used for retrieval (GU, GN or GNP). The only method of updating it is to read through and create a new file along the way.

HIERARCHICAL INDEXED SEQUENTIAL ACCESS METHODS (HISAM)

The actual details of HISAM storage methods can be complicated but, basically, once the database is loaded it contains an index for the root segment based on its defined SEQ item plus sequential access to all its dependent segments. HISAM uses either a combination of ISAM and OSAM, or VSAM as its access method.

(1) Using ISAM/OSAM the database consists of an ISAM dataset and an OSAM dataset each of which is divided into fixed length records. Within each, stored records are created sequentially and then accessed either sequentially or by (a) the index (ISAM) or (b) the relative address (OSAM).

Whenever a root segment within a HISAM database is created, a new ISAM stored record occurrence is also created followed by the subordinate segments in hierarchical sequence, as many as will fit in the stored record. If the record becomes full before all related segments are loaded, then a new OSAM record is created and filled (a pointer links an ISAM record to its related OSAM record, if there is one).

A segment is deleted by setting a flag within the segment prefix, it is never removed physically from the storage record. A new root segment is inserted by creating an OSAM record and by linking it to the previous sequence field value record and the subsequent one, as shown in Figure 14.8.

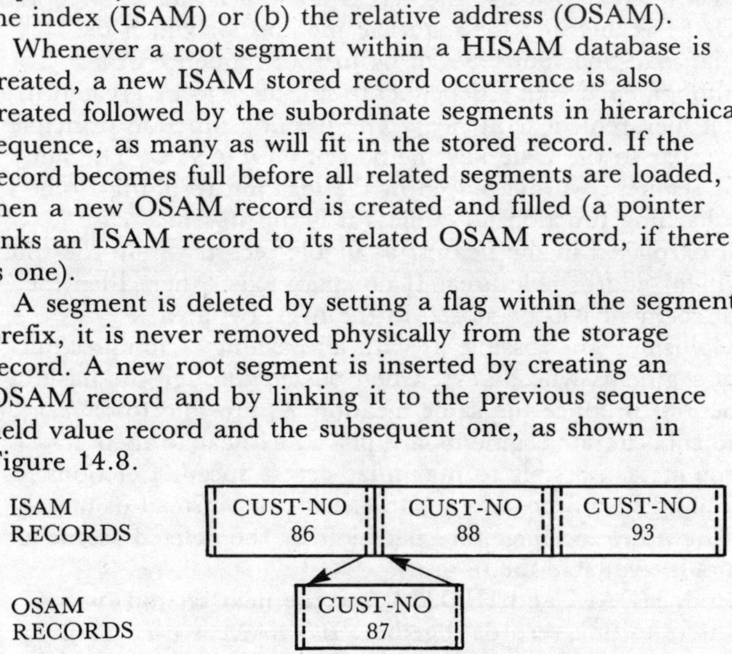

Figure 14.8 *Insertion of a new root segment in HISAM*

To insert a new dependent segment, first the storage record is scanned to find its logical predecessor. The segment is then inserted and all subsequent segments are shifted right. If this causes an overflow situation, then all overflow segments are placed in a new OSAM storage record.

(2) With VSAM the important differences from ISAM/OSAM are that (a) the ISAM records are replaced a VSAM key sequenced data sets and OSAM records are replaced by VSAM entry sequenced data sets and (b) all root segments, including insertions, are stored in the VSAM key sequenced data set.

HIERARCHICAL DIRECT ACCESS METHOD (HDAM)

HDAM provides a direct access to the root segments by the sequence field value by using hashing and chaining techniques plus a pointer access to the root's dependent segments. The database is divided into fixed-length records (either OSAM or VSAM), some of which form a 'root segment addressable area' and the remainder form an overflow area. Because the access is via a hashing function, HDAM is the only IMS storage method for which the initial load does not have to be in root sequence order (although each root's dependents still have to be created in strict hierarchical sequence). The hashing function principle is similar to the Calc key method of CODASYL. The new root segment will be placed in the location resulting from the hashing function (X) unless it is full in which case it will be placed in the nearest available record within the root segment addressable area. If no space exists there then the root segment will be stored in the overflow area.

Collisions are possible as with all hashing techniques (all root segments whose keys, when passed through the hashing function, produce the same location X, are said to *collide*). The subordinate segments are placed as near to their root segments as possible to maximize access speed. Deletions are handled differently to HISAM in that instead of merely setting a deleted flag, the space left by the deleted segment is made available for re-use.

Both HDAM and HIDAM (see the next section) use pointers to link records together. If VSAM is used then data are stored in one or more VSAM entry sequenced data sets. If OSAM is used then data are stored in one or more OSAM data sets. The pointers are stored in the segment prefix and are used to show two separate things.

(1) The hierarchical sequence within a PDBR. These are linked as a chain with either (A) each segment having a forward pointer to the next segment in the hierarchical sequence or (B) with each parent having a pointer to the first occurrence of each of its children. The difference between these two approaches is shown in Figure 14.9.

With both approaches there are backward pointers also available and which approach is chosen depends largely on the processing requirements. Sequential processing would certainly be faster with A and random processing with B. It is worth noting that the two types can be mixed within a PDBR type.

With approach B there is also the possibility of a parent having a pointer to the last of its child segment types (shown by broken lines).

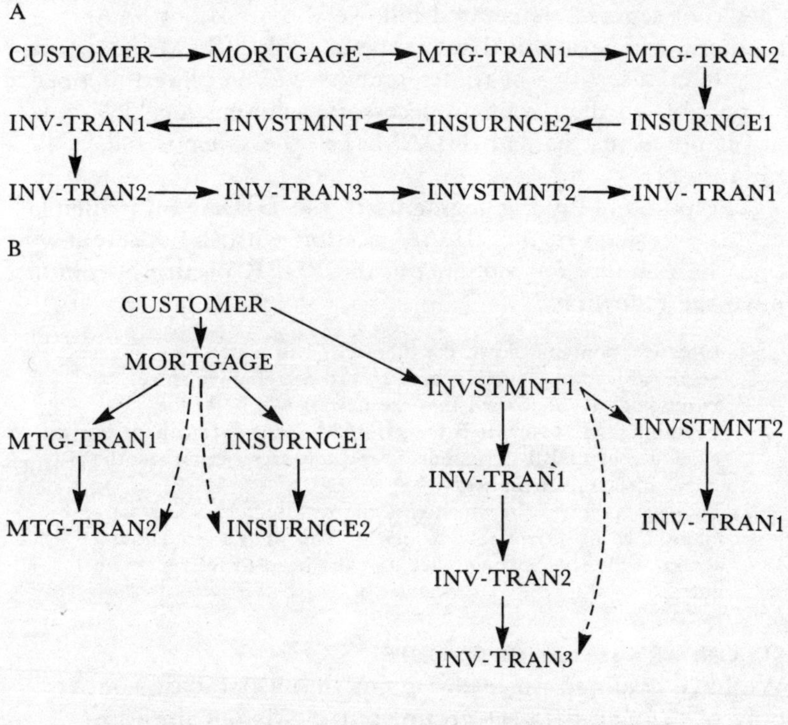

Figure 14.9 *Linked chain of segment occurrences (A) and hierarchical chain mechanism (B) for HDAM or HIDAM*

(2) To show the sequence of PDBRs. The pointers here are twin pointers kept in the root prefix. All roots that collide at point X are kept on a one-way or two-way chain that starts at record X and is kept in ascending order (on the root sequence key) as described above. The advantage of having pointers over, say, the HISAM approach is that subordinate segment inserts can be accommodated easily without having to shuffle existing segments along.

HIERARCHICAL INDEXED DIRECT ACCESS METHOD (HIDAM)

As in HISAM, the indexing is on the root key sequencing field, but the difference is that the index is controlled by IMS and not by the access method. An HIDAM database actually consists of two databases: one for the actual data and one for the index. As with HDAM, the database for the data consist of a single OSAM data set or a single VSAM entry sequenced data set, either being divided into fixed length records.

A root segment is created followed by its subordinate segments in hierarchical sequence as with HSAM databases. Any later insertions of root segments will be placed as near as possible to their root predecessors, whereas any deletions are handled just as with HDAM (i.e. the space is released for re-use).

The pointers linking segments in the HIDAM database are as described in the HDAM section with the difference that the pointers for sequencing the PDBR occurrences can have the following:

(1) One-way pointers (down the hierarchy), in which case the root segments within a single stored record are chained in reverse chronological order such that the newest will be at the beginning. However, it is the HIDAM index that defines the sequence of PDBR occurrences, and the user cannot use the chain mechanism explicitly.
(2) Two-way pointers, in which case the root segments are maintained in proper root sequence. This allows sequential access of the root segments without the need to reference the index.

SECONDARY DATA SET GROUPS

We have assumed up to this point that a database consists only of a single data set group, but this is not the case. With HISAM, HDAM or HIDAM databases (but not HSAM) the database may be split into a primary data set group, which must contain the root segments, and up to nine secondary data set groups. In this instance all occurrences of one segment type must be stored within a single data set group. For example, we might wish to store the CUSTOMER, INVESTMENT and transaction segments in a different data set group to the MORTGAGE segments.

With HISAM, in particular, the advantage of splitting the database in this way is that each secondary group will provide indexed access via the ISAM index and, clearly, this would improve access times for segment types buried deep down in the hierarchy. Alternatively, it may be used for spreading the data across several physical devices (see the discussion in Chapter 2).

With HDAM and HIDAM databases, the advantage lies in saving storage space after a deletion. Suppose that the storage record contains two segment types of size 30 bytes (A) and 20 bytes (B). If a type A is deleted and type B inserted then 10 bytes are wasted. If, however, the two types are stored in two different data set groups, the problem will not arise. In the HDAM case, only the primary data set group contains a root segment addressable area; all other areas are overflow only. However, it must be noted that segments stored in different data set groups cannot be connected by hierarchical pointers (type A in Figure 14.9), but only by child pointers (type B).

PHYSICAL TO STORAGE MAPPING

As mentioned previously, the mapping of the physical database (PDB) to the storage database is specified in the database definition (DBD).

Briefly, the additional specifications are as follows:

(1) The first line of Figure 14.4 would be

ACCESS = HSAM/HISAM/HDAM/HIDAM/INDEX

The INDEX option refers to the index database for the HIDAM access method. For the latter case, two DBD entries therefore will be required. Other options concerning the underlying access method (e.g. ISAM or VSAM) are too detailed for this book (see the Bibliography).

(2) If ACCESS = HDAM is specified then the DBA can also specify the name of the hashing routine and the number of

records to be stored in the root segment addressable area. This is done by using

RMNAME =

(3) If the access method is HDAM or HIDAM, the various pointer options can be specified within the SEGM clause by adding

POINTER = HIER/HIERBWD/TWIN/TWINBWD

The term HIER is used to specify that each segment occurrence will contain a pointer to the next segment on the hierarchical sequence (the last segment thus defined in the hierarchy does not contain a pointer to the next root occurrence). If the segment being defined is the root then that segment will also contain a pointer to the next root occurrence. HIERBWD is the same except that there are also backward pointers. TWIN specifies that each occurrence of the segment in whose definition it occurs will contain several pointers: one to the next occurrence of the same segment type under the same parent (if one exists) and one for the first occurrence of each of its children. If the segment being defined is the root then the pointer of the first kind will point to the next root occurrence. TWINBWD is the same as TWIN except that each type also includes backward pointers.

(4) If the options TWIN or TWINBWD are used as above, it also may be desirable to have a pointer from the parent to the last occurrence of a particular child type. For that child-type SEGM description we would use

PARENT = ((parent,DBLE))

(5) In the HIDAM method we can consider 'the database of data' segment as being a logical child of its associated index database segment. The description for the index database will contain one SEGM statement and one FIELD statement (for the key).

```
SEGM NAME = INDXSEG, BYTES + 6
FIELD NAME =(CUST-NO, SEQ), BYTES = 6,
START = 1
```

In addition, there must exist a LCHILD statement to specify the data segment and the field within it which will be used as the index key. For example:

LCHILD NAME = (CUSTOMER, ACCOUNTS), INDEX = CUST-NO

The corresponding entry in the data database must also have a LCHILD statement:

LCHILD NAME = (INDXSEG, INDXDB), POINTER = INDX

(INDXDB being the name of the index database).
(6) The final DBD statement to be mentioned here is the DATASET statement which is used

(a) to specify which data set groups the various segments are to be assigned to
(b) to specify the job control language statements that will be required when the database is to be invoked by an application program.

SECONDARY INDEXING

All indexings (in HISAM or HIDAM databases) thus far mentioned, have related to root segments, and are therefore termed *primary indexes* since the root segment sequence field is the primary key of the hierarchical occurrence. However, in IMS it is possible to have secondary indexes on:

(1) other data items within the root segments
(2) any data items in any segments
(3) any data items in segments subordinate to those which are desirable to be indexed.

The index is implemented just as the INDEX database of HIDAM except that the underlying access method must be VSAM and not ISAM/OSAM. The database to be indexed can be of any of the access method types except HSAM.

For the same reasons as mentioned in the last section, we must also have a LCHILD entry in the data database description, with the secondary indexing field being described by a XDFLD statement.

Thus, if we wanted a secondary index on the root segment customer field C-NAME, we would use (in the segment description for customer):

LCHILD NAME = (NAMEX, MNXDB), POINTER = INDX
XDFLD NAME = XNAME, SRCH = C-NAME

Here NAMEX is the name of the index segment in the

INDEX database which is called NMXDB. POINTER = INDX states that we are using an index rather than a logical child/logical parent connection. The item C-NAME must be renamed (XNAME) because a segment search argument (SSA) such as

GU CUSTOMER (C-NAME = 'SHAKESPEARE')

will not force IMS to use the indexing facilities. However,

GU CUSTOMER (XNAME = 'SHAKESPEARE')

will inform IMS that an index exists for C-NAME.

If we have the above example defined in the data database description, then the index database description should appear similar to:

```
DBD NAME = NMXDB, ACCESS = INDEX
SEGM NAME = NAMEX, BYTES = 20
FIELD NAME = (C-NAME, SEQ), BYTES = 20,
START = 1
LCHILD NAME = (CUSTOMER, ACCOUNTS),
INDEX = XNAME
```

Having defined a secondary index in this way, the user can either process sequentially the database in the usual way (i.e. via ascending values of CUST-NO) or via the new index (i.e. via ascending values of C-NAME).

It is beyond the scope of this book to give all the possibilities for secondary indexing on subordinate segments, and if interested the reader is invited at look to the Bibliography for further reading (and, in particular, *An Introduction to Database Systems* by C.J.Date). However, there is one more important point to note.

If the segment pointed to by an index is not the root of the hierarchy, then in effect it becomes the root by restructuring the hierarchy as seen by the user. Thus, if in the example as shown in Figure 14.2, there existed a secondary index on IACC-NO in investments, and if this index was then used by an application program then the user would see the hierarchy as shown in Figure 14.10.

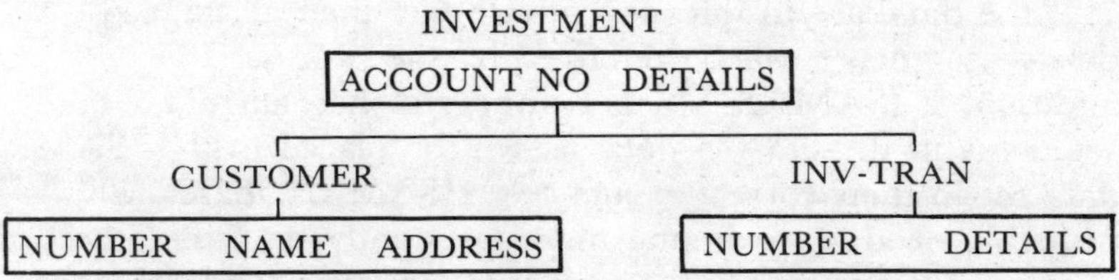

Figure 14.10 *Hierarchy as seen by user with secondary indexing*

Such a hierarchy must be reflected in a PCB definition such that:

(1) parents of the new root segment become the leftmost dependents of the new root segment
(2) parents of the old root segment become children of those dependents (i.e. if customer had a parent it would here become a child of customer)
(3) segments which were on the same hierarchical level as the new root cannot be included in the new hierarchy (i.e. mortgages could not be included), nor their dependents (MTG-TRANS).

The results of secondary indexing are that the user is no longer forced to process only in primary key sequence. Also the user can be afforded a view which is far more conceptual (i.e. true to life). For example, to the customer department, the CUSTOMER segment should be at the top of the hierarchy, but to the investment department the INVESTMENT segment would naturally appear at the top with the customer subordinate.

The main problem with secondary indexing is that, as shown, the application program is forced to use it rather than letting IMS take control. This in turn means that the program is concerned directly with how the data are stored and accessed with the corresponding loss of physical data independence (as defined in Chapter 2).

Restructuring/reorganization

In IMS the process of reorganization of the database (as defined in Chapter 9) means that the existing data must be unloaded and then reloaded to the newly structured database in the desired sequence (but minus any deleted records where they still exist). In practice, the reorganization is carried out by an IMS utility program which basically will retrieve all existing segments in hierarchical sequence and load them in the same sequence to the new structure.

If the database in question is HISAM then all flagged deleted segments will be removed by the process. In addition, if ISAM/OSAM is being used then all root segments in the OSAM data set will be placed in the ISAM data set in their correct sequence. HISAM databases will probably need reorganizing more frequently than the other access types because of the way that insertions and deletions are dealt with.

For HDAM databases reorganization will move root segments from the overflow area into the root segment addressable area. For HIDAM databases all segments will be reloaded in hierarchical sequence.

These processes apply also when the database is being restructured (i.e. the database can be reloaded in a different format). These format differences can be:

(1) new segment types can be added on a level with, or subordinate to, existing segment types, but not in between existing hierarchical levels
(2) the stored record size can change
(3) the HDAM hashing function may be changed
(4) the division of the database into groups can be changed
(5) the pointer options in HIDAM or HDAM can be changed
(6) within a particular access type the access method can be changed (e.g. under HDAM we could change OSAM for VSAM or vice versa).

Integrity

The mere existence of a hierarchy ensures that certain possible losses of integrity are avoided. For example, as in the real world, we cannot have an investment without a customer because the parent must exist before the child.

At first glance there might appear to be a real problem that an investment (in the example) cannot belong to two (or more) customers as we would wish, because IMS will not allow multiple parents for one child, with the result that data stored under one customer root will also have to be stored under another, and hence data duplication creeps in. In fact this is not the case because IMS uses what is known as *virtual pairing* by which the data are stored only once in a single hierarchy occurrence. This can now be chained to a separate hierarchy occurrence by using child pointers with each subordinate segment occurrence having a parent pointer back to the parent. This can be shown diagrammatically as in Figure 14.11.

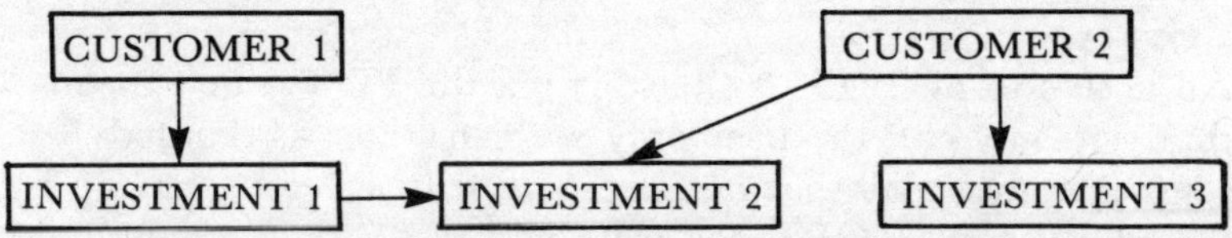

Figure 14.11 *Pointers associated with virtual pairing*

The data communications feature of IMS allows concurrency such that IMS will not initiate a program if the PROCOPT entries in its PCBs conflict in any way with the PROCOPT entries in the PCBs of the currently running program(s): in particular, if a segment type has a PROCOPT = E (Exclusive) in either case.

Otherwise, any program using a GET HOLD operation will be given a shared lock on the accessed segment occurrence. Other users will be able to retrieve the same occurrence concurrently, but not for a GET HOLD operation. If the occurrence is then updated by the first user, the lock becomes EXCLUSIVE and no other user may access it except by an express read (see following). In general, as soon as the segment ceases to be current it is unlocked (except EXCLUSIVE usage; see following section). However, if further updates are interdependent and the DBA wishes to maintain consistency, then the shared lock may be retained for as long as necessary via the Q command code (not described here). When all is consistent and the related updates are finished, all such segment occurrences can be released.

Segments that are locked EXCLUSIVE are released when either a synchronization point is reached or a checkpoint operation occurs (as described in Chapter 7). At these points, any shared locks are also released.

Note: the 'express read' is a special PROCOPT (GO or GOP) in the PCB statement (only) and allows any segments to be retrieved (but not for update) whether they are locked or not, but with the consideration that the data may be inconsistent.

Recovery is effected through the use of journal files with before and after images and by checkpointing (all as described previously in Chapter 8). However, in the event of any failure, the whole of the database must be recovered and not just the affected part.

Privacy

All access to an IMS database is via the PCB which means that not only can the user only see sensitive (as defined) segments, but also that he is restricted in what he can do by the PCB's PROCOPT declarations.

If the data communications facilities are used then it can be enforced that only certain terminals can run certain programs or that passwords must be given to invoke programs or to call certain IMS commands.

CHAPTER 15

DMSII: A Mixture

Background

I have included a chapter on Burroughs' DMSII not because it is a different database system, it is not, but rather because it shows many of the useful features highlighted in Chapters 7 – 10 which in turn display many of the tools often available to the DBA.

Announced in 1974, DMSII was a radical departure from Burroughs' original database system, DM6700, with perhaps the most important difference being that various DBMS routines were incorporated into the operating system (master control program, MCP). It has been noted already elsewhere in this book (see the Problems with operating system section in Chapter 5) that most database management systems interface with the device model through the operating system with inherent problems. Burroughs attempted to alleviate these inefficiencies by making the DBMS a part of the MCP.

By interfacing also DMSII with the network definition language (NDL) via the general message control system (GEMCOS), the database can be used either for batch work or, interactively, on-line.

Architecture

DMSII essentially is a CODASYL product in its concepts of relationships and pointers, but the pointer system (though possible) is not an essential part of the system and, in fact, if used negates many of the advantages of recovery and reorganization highlighted later in this chapter. By and large it is a flat file approach with many disjoint files which are termed *data sets*. However, hierarchies of files can be represented and record types can be said to own member records, but those member records can be accessed only via the owners (see the example). In addition, there are certain features, particularly the key data, that are reminiscent of the inverted file approach to file storage (see Appendix B).

The generalized architecture is as shown in Figure 15.1.

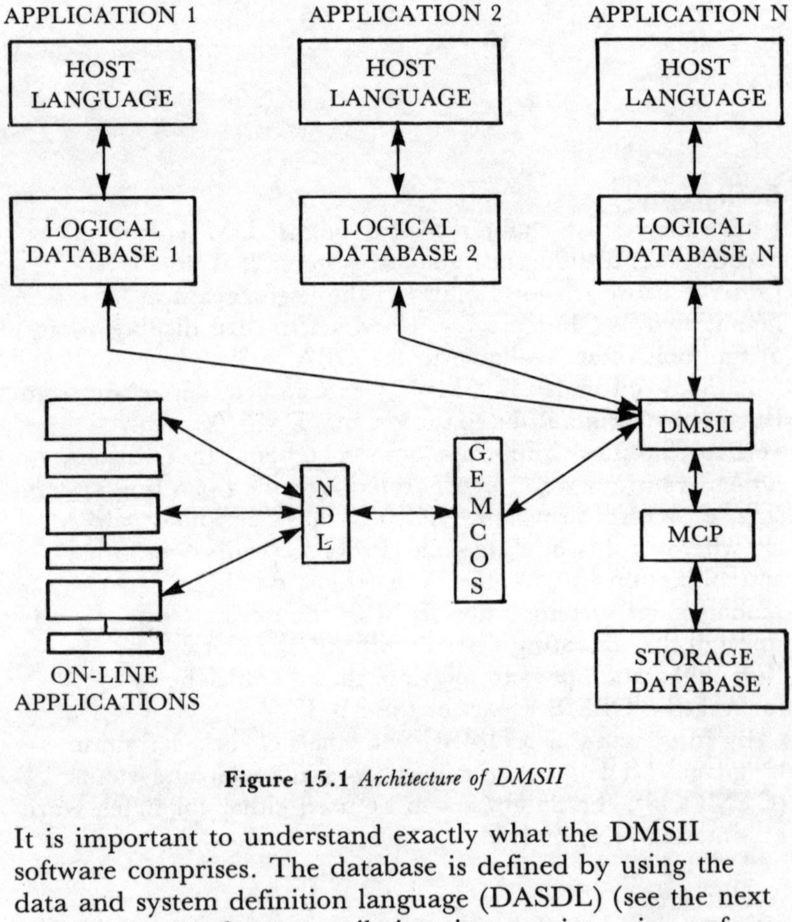

Figure 15.1 *Architecture of DMSII*

It is important to understand exactly what the DMSII software comprises. The database is defined by using the data and system definition language (DASDL) (see the next section). At database compilation time, various pieces of software are generated.

(1) A *description file* that contains all the static information about the database's structure and content, including both storage and device models. This is used subsequently to produce the remaining software, but is not used on the day-to-day running of the database.
(2) A *control file* that contains the dynamic information about the

database such as current audit file numbers, file sizes and locations, populations, a variety of timestamp information, etc. Clearly, this file is updated by the day-to-day running.

(3) *Accessroutines*. This is the software which controls the normal running routines of the database including, as the name suggests, how to access the data (but not where: this is only kept on the control and description files).

(4) A *utility* program that is used to perform dumping and loading of the database mainly, but is used also to initiate manual forms of recovery.

(5) A *recovery* file that is used for rolling back the database. It is fired up immediately by automatic forms of recovery and 'zipped' in by utility with manual recovery.

(6) *Datarecovery* and *reconstruct*. Both of these are used in the rollforward and rebuild recovery options.

The compilation process is in two parts. The first creating the description and control files and the second producing the remaining software. The importance of this division is seen following.

The logical and physical models are thus defined by using the same language in the same source. However, because all of the device model is contained within the control file (in terms of the day-to-day running), it is relatively easy to change packnames, maximum populations and other dynamic data without having to recompile the entire software. Such changes would be invisible to the application program and can be effected within minutes. Thus, a certain degree of physical data independence is afforded, but only at the device model level.

The submodels are termed *logical databases* which provide as good a degree of logical data independence as the standard CODASYL subschemae. However, they are rather awkward to define and involve remapping the logical data model components into the logical model submodel piecemeal, and all within the original database (DASDL) source. In addition, the DBA must also provide their own privacy handling routines, which can only be applied at the logical database level and not at the data item level.

Data manipulation is carried out by means of a host language approach but instead of CALL routines or preprocessors, the extra verbs are catered for by means of special versions of the normal system compilers (e.g. BDMSCOBOL).

Data definition language

As mentioned previously, the database is described by using DASDL. An example is shown in Figure 15.2 though it must be stressed that the example given only shows a small portion of the options available.

```
MTG-RATE              NUMBER(5,3);
MTG-STAFF-RATE        NUMBER(5,3);
MTG-SPECIAL-RATE      NUMBER(5,3);
CUST-COUNT POPULATION(9999999) OF CUSTOMER;
MTG-COUNT POPULATION(999999) OF MORTGAGE;

CUSTOMER DIRECT DATA SET
PACK = CUSTPACK
POPULATION = 1000000
BLOCKSIZE = 14
REBLOCK
REBLOCKFACTOR = 6
BUFFERS = 1 + 1 PER RANDOM USER OR 2 PER
SERIAL USER
AREAS = 900
(CUST-NO              NUMBER(6);
CUST-NAME             ALPHA(20);
CUST-ADD-1            ALPHA(20);
CUST-ADD-2            ALPHA(20);
CUST-SEX              NUMBER(1);
FILLER       2);
CUST-BY-NUMBER ACCESS TO CUSTOMER KEY IS
CUST-NO;
CUST-BY-NAME SET OF CUSTOMER KEY IS CUST-
NAME I-S
DUPLICATES TABLESIZE = 47 ENTRIES
LOADFACTOR = 66%
BUFFERS = 3 + 1 PER USER PACK = MTGPACK;
MORTGAGE DATA SET
POPULATION = 120000
PACK = MTGPACK
BLOCKSIZE = 17
REBLOCK
REBLOCKFACTOR = 10
BUFFERS = 1 + 1 PER RANDOM USER OR 2 PER
SERIAL USER
(MTG-ACC-NO                NUMBER(10);
MTG-TYPE                   NUMBER(2);
AMT-BORROWED               NUMBER(5);
DUE-DATE                   NUMBER(2);
AMT-OUTSTANDING            NUMBER(7,2);
FILLER                     2;
MTG-TRANS ORDERED DATA SET
```

(continued)

```
39   POPULATION = 14
40   PACK = MTGTRANPACK
41   BLOCKSIZE = 224 RECORDS
42   SUBBLOCKSIZE = 14 RECORDS
43   AREASIZE = 200 BLOCKS
44   BUFFERS = 1 + 1 PER RANDOM USER OR 2 PER
     SERIAL USER
45   (MTRAN-NO          NUMBER(2);
46   MTRAN-DATE         NUMBER(6);
47   MTRAN-AMOUNT       NUMBER(6,2);
48   MTRAN-SOURCE       NUMBER(2);
49   FILLER     1);
50   MTRAN-ACCESS ACCESS TO MTG-TRANS KEY IS
     MTRAN-NO);
51   MTG-INDEX SET OF MORTGAGES I-S NO
     DUPLICATES
52   KEY IS MTG-ACC-NO PACK = CUSTPACK
     LOADFACTOR = 85%
53   KEY DATA IS DUE-DATE TABLESIZE = 97 ENTRIES
54   BUFFERS = 3 + 1 PER USER
```

Figure 15.2 *An example of DASDL source listing*

Notes: the database is a cross between flat (standalone) files and hierarchies, each of which is delineated by parentheses. The example shown is equivalent to:

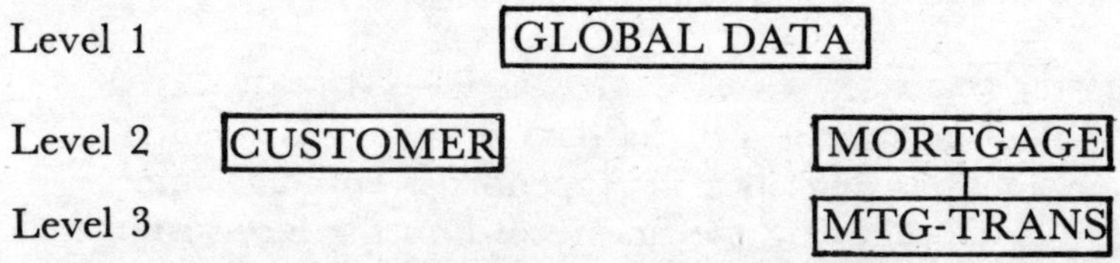

Thus a hierarchical structure exists but there are no links between the global data and customer or mortgage, but mortgage is linked to Mtg-trans. The latter is said to be *embedded* in the mortgage data set and is the DMSII method of maintaining 1:n relationships. The (parent) mortgage will have a pointer to its first Mtg-trans record which will point to the second and so on. However, the last will not point back to the mortgage so we have a linked chain but not a linked loop.

Numeric items are described by their size and (6,2) means six digits of storage including two decimal places. All numeric data are stored in a packed format (see the Preface). For each item described, a value can be specified which will become the initial value when the record is created. In similar fashion it is possible to define check values for each item such that a record cannot be stored with invalid data values.

The database itself is not named within the DASDL listing, but is named explicitly within the compilation process.

GLOBAL DATA

The items defined before the first opening parenthesis (lines 1 – 5) are said to be global data. They form what is essentially a single record file which contains constants or control data accessible to the user program, but which is handled just as a normal file (i.e. it is read and written to). The items on lines 4 and 5 are system-maintained counts of the populations of the customer and mortgage files respectively. They can only be accessed on a Readonly basis.

The name given to the global data record is identical with that of the database itself. Thus if the example were to be compiled as ACCOUNTDB then the user would use:

```
FIND ACCOUNTDB.
```

to access the global data.

DIRECT DATA SETS

The file customer is a direct data set which is essentially maintained as described in Appendix B with customer number 1 occupying the first record on the file, customer 2 the second and so on. For this type of data set an access key must be specified (line 21). However, there is nothing to prevent secondary accessing, in this instance on the customer name via a standard index method (see the Sets subsection following).

DATA SETS (STANDARD DATA SETS)

The file mortgage is defined to be a simple data set (line 25). This is the default data set type, and implies that the file itself will be constructed in chronological sequence (though it can be reordered via a reorganize), but will be accessed generally by an index.

ORDERED DATA SET

The mortgage transactions are accessible only through their parent mortgage record (i.e. they have no direct access of their own). That they be kept in some kind of order beneficial to processing, the data set type is defined to be ordered (line 38) with an access key defined (line 50). This means that if a record of key 9 is added to the file containing numbers 8 and 10 already, then record 10 is shuffled physically down one slot to accommodate 9 (compare this with other database systems where a set of pointers would be used without physically moving the data).

OTHER DATA SET TYPES

There are several other data set types supported by DMSII. These are briefly:

(1) *unordered*, the records are stored as created with no access mechanisms available
(2) *random*, the records are stored in standard random fashion (see Appendix B) with hashing functions producing physical addresses (no index methods are allowed)
(3) *compact*, a variable-length record type useful for storing large quantities of text, etc.

PHYSICAL STORAGE COMPONENTS

Within the example, most of these are self-evident such as PACK =, BLOCKSIZE =, AREAS =. The latter refers to a physical unit of storage but which varies in size from file to file. A file cannot contain more than 1000 areas. If no AREAS clause is specified then DMS can calculate its own number of areas needed from the population specified together with the blocksize. The population specified is not an absolute maximum after which the system will crash, but more a guide to DMS when calculating area sizes, hashing functions, etc.

A more interesting concept lies at line 42 with the clause SUBBLOCKSIZE. Since most mortgages will have a maximum of 14 transactions per year, by specifying this amount DMS will preallocate storage space for all 14 within the same block. Thus at the creation of the first transaction, the appropriate block for MTG-TRANS will contain a single transaction followed by 13 blank records. This does produce a high disk overhead at the beginning of the year, but it does mean that all the related transactions are stored consecutively and can be accessed with a single I/O. Moreover, if a mortgage created a fifteenth then an overflow block would be created to take not only the fifteenth but the previous 14 as well (together with 13 blanks to make the total up to a multiple of 14). Clearly, this will leave space on the original block, but DMS does employ very efficient available space tables and so the space will be used soon. In this occurrence the pointer from the mortgage to its first transaction would be fixed automatically.

A representation of the physical structuring of embedded records is shown in Figure 15.3.

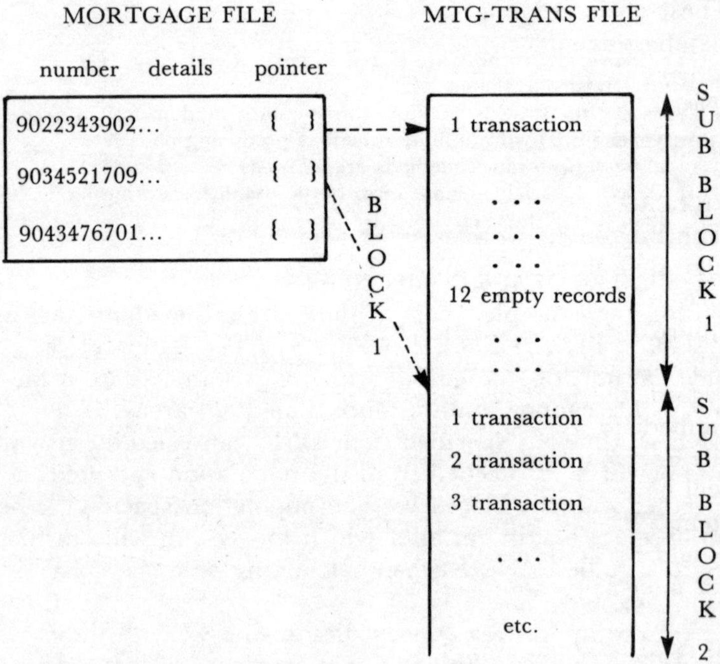

Figure 15.3 *Physical layout of an embedded data set with sub-blocks*

DYNAMIC COMPONENTS

Much of Chapter 10 on tuning the database refers to the ability to alter dynamically the run-time characteristics of the database. Such features are available readily within DMSII.

The clause REBLOCK (line 11) signals to the system that the file in question may be read sequentially and that as such may be I/O bound. It is therefore desirable to read in more than one block at a time to allow the I/Os to keep up with the processing. Exactly how many blocks are read in this mode is specified within the REBLOCKFACTOR clause. The extra memory needed is allocated automatically.

In similar fashion the number of buffers needed can be specified (line 13). Here the first one would be a system buffer usable to read a block in at the same time as another was being written (in other words there must be at least two). The second gives an extra buffer to every random user or two if the user is processing serially (to facilitate Readahead). Other options are specified within Chapter 10.

All of the above can be altered dynamically while the database is open without having to recompile anything. Current options and values are stored in the control file. Thus the database can be tailored dynamically to meet the requirements of a particular application.

FILLERS

The Burroughs word is six-bytes long and each record is allocated an exact number of words. Thus if the defined size in bytes is not divisible by six, a *filler* can be added (line 20) to make the total up to a whole number of words. The advantage of this is that if items later need adding to a record, the filler can be converted into new data items for immediate use. Since the record length is not changed, the file does not need to be restructured and no user programs will be affected (other than those wishing to use the new item). Thus if a file was being developed continually it would be quite reasonable to assign a large filler at the end for later conversion.

SETS

If the data set is of type standard or compact an index must be specified. If the type is direct an index may be specified but is not compulsory. If the type is random, ordered or unordered then no index may be specified.

The index is defined as being a *set* and is the fully indexed variety as described in Appendix B with every record having an index entry. This means a high overhead in tables, but does mean that the useful feature of *key data* can be employed. Items specified as key data are stored together physically with the key in the index. In the example (line 53) if only the due date for a particular mortgage account is needed the information can be obtained without having to access the record itself. Thus DMSII supplies a feature associated with the inverted file approach (Appendix B).

As many sets as are required can be defined. For each a table size (line 53) generally is specified to determine how many entries are to be stored within each table (though this would be calculated by the DMS if not specified). Clearly, such a value has a bearing on how many levels of tables will exist, and must therefore be chosen carefully.

A useful feature is the *loadfactor* which specifies how full each table should be when the index is created. By filling each table only partially there will be plenty of room for future insertions without the need for overflow tables (the curse of all indexing systems). Clearly, how large this loadfactor will be depends on how static the file is and/or whether insertions generally will have key values greater than the last stored record. In the latter case a loadfactor of 98 per cent plus would be appropriate. In the example each branch would probably have its own range of new account numbers and so insertions would be relatively random (hence a loadfactor of only 85 per cent).

The number of buffers allocated to the indexes is also important (see Chapter 10). If there are four levels of tables then it is essential that the highest levels of table (i.e. those in most constant use) are in memory permanently. Hence the buffer allocation of line 54. Again these buffers are changeable dynamically.

It is possible also to define *subsets* based on certain key values. Thus we could define a subset of mortgages where (for example) the amount borrowed is more than £30 000 and DMSII would maintain a mini-index of the physical addresses of all those records satisfying the condition. Again as many subsets as are required can be defined.

Submodels

As has been stated previously, the submodels are derived from the full database by defining *remaps* within the source

DASDL listing. Each dataset may be remapped into a user version with the ability to:

(1) omit data items
(2) omit sets
(3) omit embedded sets
(4) add virtual items
(5) change data-item types.

Each user is then assigned a *logical database* which includes the appropriate remaps. Such logical databases are declared at the end of the DASDL listing, such as:

LDB1 (ACCOUNTDB, CUSTOMER-REMAP1, MORTGAGE-REMAP2)
LDB2 (ACCOUNTDB, MORTGAGE-REMAP3, MTG-TRANS-REMAP1)
etc.

For each of the logical databases, an access-control mechanism can be defined, but it is the responsibility of the DBA to create and maintain these privacy locks.

Data manipulation language

Data manipulation is through the host language approach which includes interfaces with COBOL, ALGOL and PL/1. For each, a special compiler is provided (e.g. BDMSCOBOL).

The COBOL verbs which can be used follow similar principles to the standard CODASYL verbs (Chapter 13) but, again, the actual terminology is different. The verbs briefly are as follows.

(1) FIND is used for record location. On successful completion of a FIND the record is returned to the user work area (i.e. no Get is required). A special extension is the

FIND {set name} WHERE {condition}

which only returns the index key value plus any key data to the user, thus saving an access to the record itself if that is not required.

(2) LOCK which is essentially the same as a FIND except that the record is locked and cannot be accessed for update by any other user. A record can be locked anywhere within an application program but will only be unlocked on successful completion of an END-TRANSACTION (see below) or after a specific RELEASE statement.
(3) CREATE is used to initialize the user work area for a particular

record type.

CREATE MORTGAGE

The numeric items will be zeroized and alpha items space filled unless default values are specified within the DASDL.

(4) STORE is used to write new or updated records back to disk and must be performed within transaction state (see below).
(5) DELETE is used to delete records either directly or after a successful Lock. Again it must be performed within transaction state.
(6) BEGIN-TRANSACTION must be specified if the program is updating the database. It signals to the DMS that an update is about to occur and causes a special record to be written to the audit file (see the next section).
(7) END-TRANSACTION signals that an update or set of updates is complete. An end-transaction causes a special record to be written to the audit file. One or many updates can be performed within transaction state. A program is said to be in transaction state immediately a begin-transaction is performed and remains so until an end-transaction is accomplished successfully.

As can be seen, the DML verbs are fairly simple and straightforward. This is as a direct result of the database being flat because no special navigational verbs are required, unlike the standard CODASYL products (Chapter 13).

Recovery mechanisms

The Burroughs terminology for journal files is audit trails (files) but the principles are identical with those highlighted in the Journals files section in Chapter 8. The maximum file size possible, pack and duplication options for the audit trails are declared within the DASDL source (not shown in example). When an audit trail becomes full, DMS zips in a COPYAUDIT utility automatically which copies the audit trail (or trails if they are duplicated) to the specified destination (again defined in the DASDL source and usually to tape). A new audit trail is created with a number one greater than the previous one and, similarly, with the block numbers. Thus all audit files form one very long continuous trail allowing rollback or rebuild to span as many days as the dumped cycle of audit files allows.

Instead of the checkpoint approach to integrity maintenance (see the Transactions and checkpoints section in Chapter 8), DMSII uses *syncpoints* and *controlpoints*. The former is defined as being n transactions where a single transaction is defined to be an update or set of updates performed by a single program within transaction state. At a syncpoint, DMS will ensure that no other programs enter transaction state until all current transactions are complete. A controlpoint is defined to be m syncpoints and works in the same way as a syncpoint except that at the time of a controlpoint, half of the user buffers are written back to disk. A full description of these mechanisms is given in Chapter 8. Suffice it here to say that a halt/load (restart) recovery involves rolling back the database by two clear controlpoints to ensure that the integrity of the disk-based data is maintained.

An initial failure causing a restart recovery condition (such as a program or system software crash) causes an ABORT/DBname program to run which will tidy up the database and, when complete, will signal that manual forms of recovery (e.g. rollback) may be initiated.

DMSII allows true concurrency of updating programs (see the Concurrency section in Chapter 7) which means that a single program failure will result in all programs being terminated pending recovery and the whole database will need to be rolled back.

The rollback mechanism is as specified in Chapter 8 with provision to rollback to either a specific time or a BOJ. Printouts of what has occurred are supplied, as described in the Recovery listings section in Chapter 8, which aid the DBA/operations to check that integrity has been maintained. Rollforward is termed *rebuild* in Burroughs' terminology and, again, can be performed until a specific time or EOJ. An interesting feature is the ability to reconstruct certain areas of the database without affecting other users. The mechanism for this is as follows:

(1) The DBA is informed that certain database areas (or sometimes simply records) have been corrupted. This will either occur when a user tries to access the record(s) or will be reported when the database is dumped (see the Integrity section at the end of this chapter).
(2) DMS will then lock out the affected areas to prevent future access until recovery is complete.
(3) The DBA can now specify a recovery option which will request the loading of the last dump tapes.
(4) While the relevant areas are being loaded from the dump, recovery scans the audit trails used since that dump and builds a

file of the after images of any records within the affected area updated in that time. Once the dumped areas are reloaded, these after images can be reapplied quickly up to present and users can then again use them. Thus quite a serious hardware error can be recovered quickly, often within minutes, with minimum disruption to the user.

DMSII also allows on-line dumping to take place. While the files are being dumped, any updates are written to the audit trail. DMSII flags the dump as being on-line and only allows it to be re-used in conjunction with a rebuild operation. This will guarantee integrity with the huge bonus that normal processing need not be disrupted while the database is being dumped.

Reorganization

All changes to the database, be they structural or cosmetic, are performed by a reorganize (there is no term restructure).

The DBA has two options: either to allow the reorganize to be performed *in situ* or to dump all the data to tape, delete the file, add a new file in the new format and then reload the data. DMSII will help with both options.

With the first, the proposed changes are written into the DASDL source and an UPDATE clause added to the front. The compilation process then produces a special description file, but no new control file. Once checked, this description file is fed into another compiler which generates software to perform the reorganize. At the appropriate time the reorganization program is run. Since it is an exclusive function no application programs must be running at this time. A file of the new format is created and the old file is mapped across record by record until completion. Usually, this creates a file of identical ordering with the old, though there are options to reorder on, say, the prime key.

If the file has been reformatted in any way (i.e. a CODASYL restructure as opposed to a CODASYL reorganize) then a new control file will be produced also with a new update level and file format timestamps, and the database software as outlined in the Architecture section in this chapter must all be recompiled. If the reorganize has been performed merely to consolidate space or reorder files then this will not be necessary.

In the example, if MTG-TRANS were reorganized then, clearly, all pointers to that file from the mortgage records will need to be changed. This is carried out automatically by the reorganization program.

If the database has been constructed with all the cross-file pointers usually associated with CODASYL products, which is possible on DMSII, then fixing these pointers at reorganization time is a large overhead in processor and I/O time, which is why the flat file approach is used more often.

If the DBA decides to create a new file by dumping and reloading the old one in a new format, by specifying the file name to DMS, a dump program source listing will be generated together with a similar one for reloading. The DBA now has the opportunity to tailor these programs to their own requirements if necessary (e.g. perhaps to reload in a certain order or not to reload out-of-date records) before compiling them into object code.

Both of these options mean that changing the database is relatively straightforward and, whereas it is never a pleasure, it is much less time consuming than many other database systems.

Integrity

DMSII has several mechanisms for checking the integrity of the database at a given point in time and for ensuring that there is minimal risk of the loss of integrity at all other times.

Each block of each file of the database has an associated *checksum* which is the total number of 'on' bits in that block. Whenever that block is read, the checksum is checked and any errors displayed. If any errors are found then that area of the database can then be reconstructed immediately (see the Recovery mechanisms section in this chapter). A similar check is performed when the database is dumped. This does have quite a processor overhead, but the checksum facility (which is optional anyway) does allow any errors on stored data to be detected very quickly.

Another useful device for integrity checking is by means of various *timestamps*. I have covered the mechanism of these in the Database versions and timestamps section in Chapter 7 and the Timestamps revisited section in Chapter 8 and so it will not be repeated here, but by keeping a set of timestamps within the control file, DMSII can ensure that:

(1) old versions of database software are not run against new database files (the UPDATE levels would be different)
(2) an old version of either the full database or parts of that database cannot be loaded accidentally (the FORMAT timestamps or VERSION timestamps would be different)
(3) an old version of a program cannot be run against a different version of a file and can thus prevent corruption (again the FORMAT timestamp compiled into the program would be wrong)
(4) an on-line dump cannot be reloaded except in conjunction with a rebuild (the VERSION timestamps of the files would not match those on the control files)
(5) the normal running of the database cannot proceed if a particular recovery mechanism was not completed successfully (again the VERSION timestamps would not match).

Burroughs provides a piece of software called DBANALYZER which will read through specified data structures (including indexes). If a quickscan option is used then all checksum errors will be reported. A more leisurely full scan will analyse the structure completely, for example, in terms of its:

(1) population
(2) block usage
(3) unused record wastage (i.e. space per block)
(4) overflow block usage (if applicable)
(5) numbers of tables
(6) levels of tables
(7) loading of each table
(8) an indication of the efficiency of the file ordering (for an index sequential file clearly it is beneficial for sequential accessing if the file is in the same order as the index).

Armed with this information, the DBA can determine whether each data structure is used efficiently and can decide whether a reorganization might improve that efficiency.

CHAPTER 16
Relational Databases

Background

Of all the work currently being carried out on new database systems, nearly three-quarters of the effort is in the field of relational databases (though this is a digression from the remainder of this book in that it includes database systems purpose-built for micros. All that has gone before has been solely for use on mainframes.) With that said, there is no current relational system which could possibly cope with the requirements of our bank example (the reasons for this will become apparent in this chapter). Nevertheless, relational databases provide an excellent service for small businesses at present and so their theory is discussed here to compare it with the CODASYL and hierarchical models.

Basic concepts

Relational databases involve data being stored in tables, subject to the following rules and definitions.
Rules:

(1) Each position in the table contains a single value.
(2) All positions in the same column are of the same kind.
(3) Each column is distinct (i.e. has a distinct name).
(4) Every row in the table is unique (i.e. there are no two rows which contain identical values).
(5) The ordering of the rows and columns is not significant.

Definitions:

(1) The set of all tables is the *data model* (equivalent to the database in CODASYL).
(2) A single table is called a *relation*.
(3) A single row in the table is called a *tuple* (equivalent to a record).

(4) The number of tuples in a relation is termed the *cardinality of the relation*.
(5) The columns of the relation are termed *attributes*.
(6) An individual item of data is called a *component*.
(7) The number of components in a tuple (and hence attributes in a relation) is termed the *degree of the relation*.
(8) The set of all possible attribute values compose a *domain*.

An example (Figure 16.1) is now included to illustrate these definitions. In this instance alone I shall change the example from the accounts system of the bank to a student/course administration system. The reason for this is that the latter could be implemented by using a relational database; the former could not.

In this example we have a single *data model* comprising three relations: student, subject and student-subject. Studying the student relation in particular, we have:

(1) a cardinality of six tuples
(2) four attributes
(3) the degree of student is thus four
(4) the domain of reg-date is all the possible values of the year in which the student enrolled (if the maximum length of the course is two years then, in a given year, the domain would contain only two values).

It must be noted that there is a distinct element of data redundancy here, the student number appears in two separate places as does the subject code. The reason for this is that relational databases have no physical pointers acting as links such as those that appear in network models. Associations between different relations are shown by there being common attributes and all tuple accessing and data manipulation are based on this commonality, as will be seen.

It is of interest to note that an involuted relationship (an entity related to itself) can be expressed within the relational model. For example, if some level II subjects required certain prerequisites, as shown in Figure 16.2.

Normalization

At this stage we must return to normalization (though perhaps return is the wrong word, as the process of normalization was developed by E.F. Codd for work on relations and only later adapted for other database systems).

A

STUDENT-NUMBER	NAME	GRANT-PAYER	REG DATE
0001	WEST	LANCS	85
0003	NASH	LINCS	86
0004	INGLESON	YORKS	85
0007	WHITELEY	LANCS	86
0008	BIRCH	HERTS	86
0010	MADILL	LANCS	85

B

SUBJECT CODE	DESCRIPTION	COURSE LENGTH	LEVEL
C01	ENGLISH	2	I
C02	MATHS	1	I
C03	GENERAL SCIENCE	1	I
C04	MATHS	2	II
C05	PHYSICS	2	II
C06	CHEMISTRY	1	II
C07	ENGLISH	1	II

C

STUDENT NUMBER	SUBJECT CODE	FULL/PART TIME
0001	C02	FT
0001	C03	FT
0003	C03	PT
0004	C01	PT
0004	C02	PT
0004	C03	PT
0007	C04	FT
0010	C05	FT
0010	C06	FT

Figure 16.1 *Three examples of relations forming a data model. A, student relation; B, subject relation; C, student-subject relation*

SUBJECT CODE	PRE-SUBJECT CODE
C04	C02
C05	C02
C05	C03
C06	C03
C07	C01

Figure 16.2 *An involuted relationship (the prerequisite relation) as a single relation*

The only rule for relations is that:

EVERY ATTRIBUTE VALUE IN EACH TUPLE IS ATOMIC (i.e. cannot be broken down further).

What this means basically is that each attribute within a tuple must consist of a single item and not a group of items. Thus our student/subject relation in unnormalized form would be as shown in Figure 16.3 (i.e. would contain repeating groups).

STUDENT NUMBER	SUBJECT CODE AND STUDY MODE
0001	C02 FT, C03 FT
0003	C03 PT
0004	C01 PT, C02 PT, C03 PT
0007	C04 FT
0010	C05 FT, C06 FT

Figure 16.3 *An unnormalized relation*

Keys

A *candidate key* is defined as being an attribute or set of attributes which identify uniquely tuples in a relation. Thus student-number is a candidate key for the student relation as is (student-number, name) or (student-number, grant-payer). Clearly, in this example, student-number is common to all candidate keys and itself identifies uniquely a tuple. This is therefore termed the *prime key*.

The attribute student-number would not identify uniquely a student–subject tuple. For this we would need (student-number, subject-code). Similarly, for the prerequisite relation we would need (subject-code, pre-subject-code) as the primary key.

That there must be at least one key is shown by rule (4) of the Basic concepts section which states that each tuple must be unique. Therefore we are guaranteed a primary key even if it consists of every attribute in the tuple (as with the prerequisite relation).

In such cases as there are two candidate keys, each containing no superfluous attributes (such as would be the case if each course existed only at the single level and thus DESCRIPTION would be a unique identifier), we would choose arbitrarily one to be the primary key; in this case we might choose the SUBJECT-CODE because it is shorter although description has the advantage of being more meaningful and 'easier to remember in the outside world'.

An attribute, or group of attributes, of a relation A is termed a *foreign key* if it is not the primary key of A but its values are the values of the primary key of some other relation B. An example exists in the student-subject relation. The attribute subject-code would be a foreign key because its values correspond with those of the primary key of the relation subject.

Data definition language

Suppose that we wished to implement the data model as shown in Figure 16.1 as a relational database. An example of the data definition language might be as shown in Figure 16.4.

It is noteworthy that by declaring domains we can include check value controls. This is similar to CODASYL, except that the declarations are not specific to any record type but are specific to certain attributes which may be common across several relations.

```
DOMAIN    STUD-NO         NUMERIC(4)
DOMAIN    NAME            ALPHA(20)
DOMAIN    GRANT-PAYER     ALPHA(6)
DOMAIN    REG-DATE        NUMBER(2) VALUE 85, 86
DOMAIN    SUBJECT-CODE    ALPHA(3)
DOMAIN    DESCRPTN        ALPHA(15)
DOMAIN    LEVEL           ALPHA(1) VALUE 'I', 'II'
DOMAIN    DURATION        NUMBER(1) VALUE 1,2
DOMAIN    MODE            ALPHA(2) VALUE 'FT', 'PT'

RELATION STUDENT(
   STUD-NO               DOMAIN STUD-NO
   NAME                  DOMAIN NAME
   GRANT-PAYER           DOMAIN GRANT-PAYER
   REG-DATE              DOMAIN REG-DATE)
RELATION SUBJECT(
   SUBJECT-CODE          DOMAIN SUBJECT-CODE
   DESC                  DOMAIN DESCRIPTION
   LEVEL                 DOMAIN LEVEL
   DURATION              DOMAIN DURATION)
RELATION STUDENT-SUBJECT(
   ST-NO                 DOMAIN STUD-NO
   SUB-CODE              DOMAIN SUBJECT-CODE
   FULL-PART             DOMAIN MODE)
```

Figure 16.4 *An example relational database definition language*

Also of note is the fact that within the relation declaration, attribute names can be changed. This is a consequence of being able to have many different attributes belonging to the same domain. For example, if we were to have a domain called simply DATE which was subject to the restriction that the day and the month were valid, then we could have within various relations:

```
DATE-OF-BIRTH      DOMAIN DATE
ENROLLED-DATE      DOMAIN DATE
END-OF-TERM        DOMAIN DATE.
```

The syntax of the above example is not standard simply because there is no standard syntax for relational databases.

There is no mention of key items in this example (although some relational languages do allow for their definition). This is not of great consequence because keys represent neither physical database keys nor separate structures (such as indexes) and, as will be seen in the next two sections, the user can navigate the relations without using keys at all.

Relational algebra as a data sublanguage

The relational algebra approach to data manipulation is based on two parts. The first is traditional set theory involving unions, intersections, differences and Cartesian products, and the second is special relational operators such as select, project and join. Both components are described below.

(1) Traditional set theory can be extended to cover relations if the relations are *union compatible* for at least the first three definitions below. This means that the relations must be of the same degree and that the corresponding attributes must be from the same domain (i.e. one relation cannot have a date whose domain is 83, 84 and another have a date whose domain is 85, 86).

(a) The *union* of two relations X and Y, written as $X \cup Y$ or X UNION Y in relational algebra, is the set of tuples belonging to either X or Y or both. This set of tuples itself forms a relation.
(b) The *intersection* of two relations X and Y, written $X \cap Y$ or X INTERSECTION Y, is the set of tuples belonging to both X and Y.
(c) The *difference* between two relations X and Y, written $X - Y$ or X MINUS Y, is the set of tuples belonging to X which do not belong to Y.
(d) The *Cartesian product* (or simply *product*) of two relations X and Y, written as $X \times Y$ or X TIMES Y, is the set of tuples such that each tuple is the concatenation of a tuple belonging to X with a tuple belonging to Y, and such that the set contains all such tuples. For example, if X = {X1, X2} and Y = {Y1, Y2} then the Cartesian product would be:

$$\begin{pmatrix} X1,Y1 \\ X1,Y2 \\ X2,Y1 \\ X2,Y2 \end{pmatrix}$$

(2) To illustrate the special operators needed, the relations student and student-subject as shown in Figure 16.1 will be used.

(a) *Select* is an operator used for constructing a subset of tuples for which a given condition is true. For example, (1) SELECT STUDENT WHERE GRANT-PAYER = 'LANCS' would give

STUD-NO	NAME	GRANT PAYER	REG DATE
0001	WEST	LANCS	85
0007	WHITELEY	LANCS	86
0010	MADILL	LANCS	85

and (2) SELECT STUDENT-SUBJECT WHERE SUBJECT-CODE < C03 would give

ST-NO	SUB-CODE	FULL-PART
0001	C02	FT
0004	C01	PT
0004	C02	PT

(b) The *project* operator is used for construction of a subset of attributes. Any duplicates are not shown. For example, (1) PROJECT STUDENT OVER GRANT-PAYER would give

GRANT-PAYER
LANCS
LINCS
YORKS
HERTS

and (2) PROJECT STUDENT OVER REG-DATE, NAME would give

REG-DATE	NAME
85	WEST
86	NASH
85	INGLESON
86	WHITELEY
86	BIRCH
85	MADILL

In this example, project has reordered the attributes.

(c) The *join* operation can be used to combine two relations as, for example, JOIN STUDENT AND STUDENT- SUBJECT OVER STUD-NO to give

STUD-NO	NAME	GRANT PAYER	REG DATE	ST-NO	SUB	FULL-PART
0001	WEST	LANCS	85	0001	C02	FT
0001	WEST	LANCS	85	0001	C03	FT
0003	NASH	LINCS	86	0003	C03	PT
0004	INGLESON	YORKS	85	0004	C01	PT
0004	INGLESON	YORKS	85	0004	C02	PT
0004	INGLESON	YORKS	85	0004	C03	PT
0007	WHITELEY	LANCS	86	0007	C04	FT
0010	MADILL	LANCS	85	0010	C05	FT
0010	MADILL	LANCS	85	0010	C06	FT

Note that student 0008 does not appear in the result because he does not appear in any STUDENT-SUBJECT tuples. Note also that there is a degree of redundancy here, the student number appearing twice. In some implementations of relational databases redundant items would not appear in the result.

The OVER STUD-NO refers to the attribute common to both relations on which the system can make a comparison (although the attribute names are different, STUD-NO, ST-NO, they belong to the same domain). Alternatively, we could have used:

JOIN STUDENT AND STUDENT-SUBJECT
WHERE STUD-NO = ST-NO

(d) The only way to illustrate the *divide* operation is to give an example and then explain what has taken place.

PROJECT STUDENT-SUBJECT OVER ST-NO
SUB-CODE GIVING SS
DIVIDE SS BY C03 OVER SUB-CODE

The result would be:

ST-NO
0001
0003
0004

Note the use of naming the intermediate result (SS here), which is itself a relation, so that it can be used in subsequent operations.

Explanation: in its simplest form we are dividing a relation of degree 2 by a relation of degree 1 to give a result of degree 1. Both dividend and divisor must have an attribute belonging to a common domain. If we were to generalize and define the dividend as (X,Y) and the divisor (Z) where Y and Z are of a common domain, then the result would be those X values whose corresponding Y values include every component of the divisor (Z).

What would be the result, then, if we were to:

DIVIDE STUDENT-SUBJECT BY (C05, C06)
OVER SUB-CODE

Here, the result would be all occurrences of ST-NO where the SUB-CODE is C05 and C06, i.e. 0010.

Retrieval by using relational algebra

From the definitions of the previous section and the relational database as described in Figure 16.1, the next stage is to look at some examples of data retrieval.

(1) Obtain the numbers of all students taking subject C02

SELECT STUDENT-SUBJECT WHERE SUB-CODE = 'C02' GIVING R1

R1 =

ST-NO	SUB-CODE	FULL-PART
0001	C02	FT
0004	C02	PT

PROJECT R1 OVER ST-NO GIVING RESULT

RESULT =

ST-NO
0001
0004

Note: it is possible to combine the two statements above. Thus:

PROJECT (SELECT STUDENT-SUBJECT WHERE SUB-CODE = 'C02') OVER ST-NO GIVING RESULT.

(2) What are the names of the students taking maths at level II?

SELECT SUBJECT WHERE DESC = 'MATHS' AND LEVEL = 'II' GIVING R1
PROJECT R1 OVER SUBJECT-CODE GIVING R2
R2 = (C04)
JOIN R2 AND STUDENT-SUBJECT OVER SUBJECT-CODE GIVING R3
JOIN STUDENT AND R3 OVER ST-NO GIVING R4
PROJECT R4 OVER NAME GIVING RESULT
RESULT = (WHITELEY)

Note that the first statement includes an implicit join by the use of the word AND which is equivalent to:

SELECT SUBJECT WHERE DESC = 'MATHS' GIVING S1
SELECT SUBJECT WHERE LEVEL = 'II' GIVING S2
JOIN S1 AND S2 GIVING S3

As with example (1), these five statements could be combined into one by the use of parentheses, but the result would be less understandable to the human eye despite producing a faster turnaround of results.

In general, the more complicated the required process, the more ways there are of actually achieving the goal by combining different statements in different orders. Clearly, some will be less efficient than others.

Storage by using relational algebra

Insertion and deletion as operations on a relation are performed relatively easily by use of the union and minus operations. For example:

(1) Add a new STUDENT tuple where STUD-NO = 0012, NAME = GORMAN, GRANT-PAYER = 'DEVON' REG-DATE = 85.
STUDENT U (0012, 'GORMAN', 'DEVON', 85) GIVING STUDENT

(2) Delete a STUDENT tuple where STUD-NO = 0008
STUDENT – (0008, 'BIRCH', 'HERTS', 86) GIVING STUDENT

(3) Delete all STUDENT-SUBJECT tuples for student 0004
STUDENT-SUBJECT – (0004, '*', '*') GIVING STUDENT-SUBJECT

In the last example, the '*' act as wild cards and imply that the second and third attributes of the specified relation can contain any values. In theory, updates could be performed by removing the old version tuple and then adding the new, but in practice a special update operator would be supplied.

Relational calculus as a data sublanguage

The basic differences between relational algebra and relational calculus are that:

(1) calculus combines the SELECT and PROJECT commands into a single statement, GET or RETRIEVE or similar, by using a selection-criteria WHERE statement
(2) whereas the JOIN command of relational algebra can only apply to two tables, in relational calculus the GET can JOIN many tables.

The attribute names within each relation must be qualified by a relational name prefix if they are the same in two or more relations. In general, they are always prefixed in this way. Thus in the examples given I have used prefixes on each attribute name even though the actual names as described in Figure 16.4 are all different. Again there is no standard for syntax and so the following are in a fairly generalized form relating to no particular system (Appendix A).

SIMPLE RETRIEVAL
What are the names of all the grant payers?

GET (STUDENT.GRANT-PAYER) INTO RESULT

The result here would only show Lancs, Lincs, Yorks and Herts (i.e. there would be no duplication).

QUALIFIED RETRIEVAL
What are the names of all students taking subjects currently?

GET (STUDENT.NAME) INTO RESULT WHERE STUDENT.STUDENT-NUMBER = STUDENT-COURSE.STUD-NO

Loosely translated this means: find the names of all students whose student number appears in the STUDENT-SUBJECT relation, and put them into a relation called RESULT.

RETRIEVAL WITH ORDERING
What are the names and numbers of all registered students from Yorkshire in alphabetical order?

GET(STUDENT.STUDENT-NUMBER, STUDENT.NAME) INTO RESULT WHERE STUDENT.GRANT-PAYER = 'YORKS' ORDER BY STUDENT.NAME

LIMITED RETRIEVAL Give the names of any two subjects which are level II.

GET (2) (SUBJECT.DESC) INTO RESULT WHERE SUBJECT.LEVEL = 'II'

Note that this would not necessarily produce maths and physics; there is no guarantee to the order of processing.

COMPLEX RETRIEVAL

The selection criteria specified after the WHERE can be quite complex. For example: what are the names of the students who are part time on a level I subject.

```
   GET (STUDENT.NAME) INTO RESULT
  WHERE STUDENT.STUDENT-NUMBER =
STUDENT-SUBJECT.STUD-NO
     AND STUDENT-SUBJECT.FULL-PART = 'PT'
AND STUDENT-SUBJECT.SUB-CODE =
SUBJECT.SUBJECT-CODE
AND SUBJECT LEVEL = 'I'
```

As can be imagined, what started out as meaningful attribute and relational names now involve an onerous chore in keying in all prefixes and identifiers. For this reason, many implementations allow abbreviations to be declared. This is often by means of the RANGE command, for example:

```
   RANGE STUDENT-SUBJECT SC
GET (SC.STUD-NO) INTO RESULT WHERE
SC.FULL-PART ='FT'
```

Other common features of relational calculus implementations not used in the examples here include:

(1) OR and NOT operators as well as the AND
(2) key words such as COUNT, MAX, SUM, AVG can be used within the GET clause instead of an attribute name, for example:

```
   GET (COUNT) INTO RESULT WHERE
SUBJECT.LEVEL = 'II'
```

This would produce the number of level II subjects.

Storage by using relational calculus

UPDATING

Some implemented relational calculus database systems allow for a tuple locking system in which the user can HOLD a tuple or tuples (the update equivalent of GET), modify his user work area and then use the UPDATE command to write the modified tuple(s). For example:

Change the course length of subject C06 to be 2 years.

```
RANGE SUBJECT S
HOLD (S.SUBJECT-CODE, S.DURATION) INTO
RESULT WHERE S.SUBJECT-CODE = 'C06'
RESULT.DURATION = 2
UPDATE RESULT
```

The last line would write the user's temporary relation RESULT back to the relation SUBJECT.
Note: the primary key of the required relation (in this case S.SUBJECT-CODE) must also be held, but cannot be updated. If these were needed, the tuple would have to be DELETEd and then INSERTed.
Following a HOLD, the system will not allow any other user to access that tuple until the update is completed.
Whereas GET can be used to access many relations, HOLD is restricted to only one and if more are required then more HOLDs will also be needed.

INSERTION
The general function name for this is INSERT, though on some systems it is PUT. For this we must assume that an implementation allows for the setting up of a blank user work area of a specified tuple format (R). An example should show its usage:
Add a new student tuple.

```
R.STUDENT-NUMBER =0012
 R.NAME = 'OHARE'
 R.GRANT-PAYER = 'KENT'
 R.REG-DATE = 86
 INSERT R(STUDENT)
```

An alternative approach might require:

```
INSERT INTO STUDENT VALUES (0012,
'OHARE', 'KENT', 86)
```

Note: it is a rule of relational models that the ordering is immaterial, and therefore there is no concept of placement as there might be with a CODASYL model (see Chapter 13).

DELETION
The complex selection expressions possible with relational databases allow for the creation of a set of tuples within the

user work area as a result of any one request. It is therefore not surprising that all such tuples can be deleted with a single statement. Thus:
Delete all STUDENT-SUBJECT tuples where the subject is C03.

```
RANGE STUDENT-SUBJECT SS
HOLD (SS) INTO RESULT WHERE SS.SUB-CODE
='C03'
DELETE RESULT
```

Note: although the tuples are deleted from the relation, they stay in memory until the next request is performed. This means that it is relatively easy to change the primary key value. Thus, in the above example, if the problem was to change all references to C03 into C07 it would be feasible to follow up the above statements with:

```
RESULT.SUB-CODE = 'C07'
UPDATE RESULT
```

An example of relational calculus: SQL
An example of relational calculus is included to demonstrate some of the features generally available, and to show how the actual syntax varies from system to system.

SQL is the IBM relational system running on the DOS/VSE operating system. It allows host language interfaces to COBOL, PL/1 and IBM assembler (see next section). Modification of data is basically that shown in the last section, ie it involves the use of INSERT, UPDATE and DELETE. However, the retrieval statements are slightly different to what has gone before. Retrieval is accomplished by means of the SELECT, FROM and WHERE statements.

The select statements can be complex with the use of NOT, OR and AND, and can themselves be embedded in other select statements. For example, to find the names of all part-time students:

```
SELECT STUDENT-NAME FROM STUDENT
  WHERE STUDENT-NUMBER =
  (SELECT ST-NO FROM STUDENT-SUBJECT WHERE
     FULL-PART = 'PT')
```

Perhaps the most interesting features of SQL lie in its data definition capabilities. The most useful commands are described below.

CREATE TABLE
This defines a new table (relation) and its attributes. For example:

```
CREATE TABLE STUDENT-SUBJECT
  (ST-NO          INTEGER NOT NULL,
  SUB-CODE        CHAR (3) NOT NULL,
  FULL-PART       CHAR (2))
```

In similar fashion we could define all three relations of Figure 16.1 and thus create the data model.

NOTE:

1. There are various data storage types possible — only two, INTEGER and CHAR, are shown here.
2. By specifying NOT NULL, the DBMS will not allow a tuple to be stored without a value in the declared item.

A table can be deleted by using DROP TABLE.

ALTER TABLE
This caters for the 'restructuring' of a table by allowing the addition of new columns.

CREATE INDEX
In SQL, physical indexes are maintainable for each relation to allow both fast random access and efficient sequential access. This feature removes one of the problems normally inherent in relational databases, ie slow speed when dealing with large numbers of tuples.

An example of index creation might be:

```
CREATE INDEX GRANTS ON STUDENT (GRANT-
PAYER)
```

Each table can have as many indexes as required. In addition, each 'key' need not be a single attribute but could be a concatenation of several. Not surprisingly, the indexes can also be removed by using DROP INDEX.

CREATE VIEW
A very interesting feature of SQL is its ability to permit application views of the data. These are very easy to define, allow certain levels of access control to be specified (via

GRANT or REVOKE statements), and generally provide all the features of logical data independence as outlined in Chapter 2. Such a view is virtual and is only constructed when invoked by the user, and could therefore contain derived (virtual) attributes.

An example of a view might be:

```
CREATE VIEW FIRST-YEARS AS
  SELECT (STUDENT-NAME, STUDENT-NUMBER, ST-NO,
      SUB-CODE,
    SUBJECT-CODE, FULL-PART) FROM STUDENT,
      STUDENT-SUBJECT,
    SUBJECT WHERE STUDENT-NUMBER = ST-NO AND
      SUB-CODE = SUBJECT-CODE.
```

Tuple-based languages

The two approaches to relational database data manipulation described to date are a marked variation from all data manipulation approaches which have gone before in this book. They are essentially (relation) file-at-a-time approaches as opposed to the previous record-at-a-time. However, this is not to say that the host language approach is not possible with the relational database.

By referring again to the tables shown in Figure 16.1, it is noticeable that the relations are very similar to conventional files containing six, seven and nine records, respectively, with each record containing a number of fields. Thus the STUDENT relation could be expressed as that shown in Figure 16.5.

```
01    STUDENT-REC.
      03 ST-NO                     PIC 9999.
      03 ST-NAME                   PIC X(12).
      03 ST-GRANT-PAYER            PIC X(5).
      03 ST-REG-DATE               PIC 99.
```

Figure 16.5 *Student relation as a COBOL record*

With it defined in such a way there is no reason why a particular record cannot be found using a COBOL search.

```
LOOP.
  READ STUDENT AT END GO END-FILE.
```

```
IF ST-GRANT-PAYER NOT = 'HERTS' GO LOOP.
...ETC....
```

Similarly, COBOL facilities could be used to create, delete or update records.

In this way many essentially non-procedural language-based relational databases have been extended to cater for procedural languages (e.g. COBOL and FORTRAN). Contrast this with Chapter 11 in which it was highlighted as to how procedural language-based databases (CODASYL, IMS, etc.) have been extended to allow a non-procedural interface in the shape of a Query language (which is very similar to relational algebra or relational calculus as described in this chapter).

Comparison of the three approaches

It must be said that to any reader familiar with COBOL but not with relational algebra or calculus, the tuple-based approach might seem easier to understand, but a moment's thought will show that the latter two require far less training and time for the casual user to use, and within a matter of hours a user could grasp most of the necessary syntax and semantics.

It must be borne in mind also that relational databases are constructed of relations whose relationships are shown only by the commonality of attributes between them. Thus many of COBOL's advantages in allowing complex navigational aids are inappropriate.

Both the relational algebra and calculus approaches are more complete than the tuple approach in as much as no looping or branching requirements are needed to extract all desired data.

As has been mentioned many times in this book, nearly all non-relational database philosophies incorporate the 'how and where' of record storage within the schema definition. As a result of this physical data dependence, the COBOL program needs to know how the record is to be accessed (e.g. whether it has a Calc key) and very often where it is to be accessed from (ACCESS IS VIA SET). These combine to make the host language approach very procedural. The algebra approach is partially procedural because the user has to specify how to get the result (though never from where) by using JOIN and PROJECT. The calculus approach, however, is entirely non-procedural.

Any non-standard extensions required within the tuple-based approach must be dealt with programmatically. Thus if a count of records satisfying a particular condition is required then extra code must be written. Relational calculus, in particular, allows the usage of many library functions to perform these tasks and, with the algebra approach, the creation and storage of user-defined functions and procedures (and abbreviations) is possible usually.

Integrity

It has been stated already that data duplication is not only a part of relational systems but it is an essential part without which relational associations could not be used. E.F Codd defines two classes of data redundancy. A group of relations is defined as *strongly redundant* if it contains at least one relation itself containing a projection which could be derived from another relation in the group. For example, if there existed another relation to those as shown in Figure 16.1 called SUBJECT-LECTURER which contained three attributes: SUBJECT-CODE, SUBJECT-NAME and LECTURER-NAME. In this instance the projection of the first two could also be obtained from a projection of SUBJECT. Hence the two relations SUBJECT and SUBJECT-LECTURER would form a strongly redundant group.

Such redundancies could be detected and the offending attribute(s) removed from one of the relations. Clearly, this would only involve SUBJECT-NAME because the SUBJECT-CODE is the primary key in both relations.

A group of relations is defined to be *weakly redundant* if it contains a relation, a projection of which could be derived from a projection of some joins of other relations of the group. For example, if there existed a relation STUDENT-ATTENDANCE containing STUDENT-NUMBER, REG-DATE and FULL-PART then the whole relation could have been derived from a join of STUDENT and STUDENT-SUBJECT. Thus the group of relations STUDENT, STUDENT-ATTENDANCE and STUDENT-SUBJECT are said to be weakly redundant.

As weak redundancy is difficult to detect, usually it forms a part of any given data model and little can be done to prevent it. Procedures to check for such redundancies could be defined within the DBMS but, since they would involve scanning the whole of the data model, the processing overheads would be high.

Privacy

There are no specific proposals for the provision of data submodels within relational systems, but allowing for a data definition language such as described in the Data definition language section in this chapter, the renaming of attributes is possible (a common submodel feature) and it should be possible for the user to invoke only those relations which he wants or is allowed to see. Therefore there is no reason why access-control locks could not be applied at the data model, relation and attribute levels. Such mechanisms would be of particular use in a database approach which allows the user to roam all stored data with a single command.

Restructure/reorganization

By bearing in mind possible strong redundancies of data, it is very easy for a DBA to create and maintain a relational database. Moreover, he need never worry about that nightmare of most DBAs, that the database keys or embedded pointers will be corrupted and will point to the wrong records, simply because there are no hidden data. All the data stored is user data as opposed to system required and maintained data.

As relations can be broken down and built up easily, restructuring exercises should present few difficulties. The DBA can simply define a new relation similar to an existing one, but containing the required change, and then use relational algebra or calculus to join the two relations. Again with no hidden pointers, he would know that no other relations could be affected.

The term reorganize has no real meaning for relational systems. Because linear searching is the only available option and relations can be reordered by the SORT command (or similar) to improve search hit rates, there is very little point in reorganization of a relation to improve efficiency or to consolidate space (the DBMS automatically will cater for this by using available space tables or by performing its own 'reorganize' as soon as a tuple is deleted).

APPENDIX A

DBMS/Machine Reference Guide

Type	*Product*	*Originator*	*Machine*
Network			
	IDMS	Cullinet	IBM/ICL
	PRIME DBMS	PRIME	PRIME
	DMS 170	CDC	VARIOUS (under NOS)
	DBMS 10	DEC	DEC (under TOPS)
	IDS II	Honeywell	Honeywell
	SEED	International Database Systems	PDP minis and CP/M micros
	DMS 1100	Univac	Univac (under EXEC 8)
	TOTAL	CINCOM	IBM 360/370 Harris, NCR, CDC Honeywell
Limited network			
	IMAGE	Hewlett-Packard	HP3000
Complex network			
	DMS II	Burroughs	Burroughs (under MCP)
	MDBS II	Micro Data Base Systems	CP/M & MS-DOS micros
Hierarchical			
	IMS	IBM	IBM
	SYSTEM 2000	INTEL	INTEL

Type	*Product*	*Originator*	*Machine*
Relational algebra			
	RIM	Boeing	PRIME 750
	dBASE II/III	Ashton-Tate	CP/M & MS-DOS micros
Relational calculus			
	SQL/DS	IBM	S/370; 3033 (under DOS/VSE)
	INGRES	Relational Technology	DEC VAX-11 (under VMS & UNIX)
	ORACLE	Relational Software	DEC PDP-11 VAX & IBM S/370
Relational like			
	ADABAS	Software AG	IBM 370+ others
	NOMAD	National CCS	IBM 370+ others

APPENDIX B

Data Storage and Access Methods

Introduction

Much of this book refers to standard computer-based access and storage mechanisms, and perhaps not all readers will be overly familiar with them. This appendix therefore sets out to redress that deficiency, but also can be used to refresh the memory of other readers.

At the most basic level, files consist of groups of related records which each consist of a set of data items. The records can be stored physically in blocks (=pages on some machines) such that several records can be read into memory (or written from memory) with a single physical I/O. The remainder of this appendix will look at each of the different methods of physically storing those records (in a non-database sense) on backup storage and how to access them. All of the following are possible on disk-based storage, but only serial and sequential accessing are possible on tape storage.

The actual syntax for each method varies from manufacturer to manufacturer and for that reason none is given here. Readers who wish to follow this book in a practical sense are recommended to refer to their own user manuals.

Serial access

This is the simplest form of file organization. Records are written to the file purely in the order in which they are created, the physical address of the next available record being kept usually in a 'header block' at the start of the file. The advantages lie in its simplicity. The disadvantages are that a specific record cannot be located without a serial (linear) search through the file and that any deletions (if permitted) will leave holes in the file. The general usage for such files is for workfiles where the ordering is unimportant.

Sequential access

Similar to serial files except that the records are presorted into some defined sequence based on one of the constituent data items. Clearly, this sorting means high processor overheads which must be repeated every time new records are added. The result of this is that sequential files are used usually in practice for fixed files with little record creation. Advantages over serial files are that, for the latter, to establish whether or not a record exists will take n reads if the record does not exist whereas, with sequential files, the average number of reads necessary will be n/2.

Indexed files

The essential ingredients of indexed files are that the records themselves are kept in arbitrary order, but an index of the records' keys is maintained separately in key order with each index owning a pointer (a physical disk address) to the associated record/block. The index can be one of three forms.

IMPLICIT

All possible keys are maintained in sequence. As a result a dichotomizing (binary) search can be used to locate the required entry (whereby the index is split in two, the file management system decides whether the required record's key is greater or less than the mid-index value, the other half is discarded and the remaining half is split again and the process continues until the relevant entry is found).

The advantage of this method is that target records can be found quickly without block searching (see the next two sections following). The disadvantages are several.

First, if there are a great many entries in the index, the binary search may be slow. The answer to this would be to have levels of indexes as shown in Figure A.1.

Here the index is split into a number of tables, each having a fixed maximum number of entries. To find the record whose key is 73, the file system first looks to the coarse table (sub-subindex) and ascertains that the required subtable is 2. This is then read into memory and from it the file system determines that the fine table required is 10. This is in turn read into memory, the key for record 73 is found and hence the physical address of record 73.

INDEX

KEY			
1	address	1	TABLE 1
2	"	2	
4	"	4	
7	"	7	
9	"	9	TABLE 2
10	"	10	
15	"	15	
17	"	17	TABLE 3
20	"	20	
21	"	21	
23	"	23	
24	"	24	

ETC.

SUBINDEX

TABLE NO	HIGHEST VALUE	
1	7	SUB TABLE 1
2	15	
3	24	
"	"	
"	"	
8	63	
9	72	SUB TABLE 2
"	"	
"	"	
16	128	

ETC.

SUB-SUBINDEX

SUB TABLE NO	HIGHEST VALUE
1	63
2	128
"	"

ETC.

Figure A.1 *Levels of tables within an implicit index*

In practice, the number of entries in a table is far greater than eight, which lessens the number of I/Os, but in general if m is the number of entries in a table, then if m is exceeded a new subindex will be required, if the number of records exceeds m × m then a sub-subindex will be required and so on. Thus in general the number of levels of tables required will be k where:

$$m^{k-1} > n > m^{k} \quad (n = \text{population of the file})$$

This in turn implies k + 1 reads are required to access a particular record, a high overhead.

Another disadvantage is that, in reality, the keys are rarely numbered 1, 2, 3, ...8, etc., so that the tables have to be maintained with any m discreet (but not contiguous) values. Thus, if a table contained the following values, with m = 8:

10386
10402
10407
10413
10483
10489
10491
10523

if we now wished to create an entry for value 10437, then it will not fit into the above table. Rather than shuffle all existing entries around from table to table to create room for the new value, the file system would create an overflow table (here containing the entry 10523) with a physical pointer to it from the above table, and a physical pointer from it to the next logical table. Since the overflow table is likely to be situated elsewhere on disk, a large number of overflow tables will give expensive I/O costs and a loss of efficiency.

BASIC

These tables are used to support index-random files. An index might appear as shown in Figure A.2.

In this methodology, the ordering of the index is random but, should sequential reading be required, a set of chain pointers allows access to the next highest key value. Thus for entry 1, key 1 the chain points to entry 3 as containing the next highest key value. Entry 5 has a chain value of zero because the next highest value also is the next physical entry. This method has the advantage of never needing overflow tables (becausc new entries are simply added at the end with the relevant pointers being 'fixed up'). Also multi-levels of indexing are not required, but the disadvantage is that for large files a sequential read will involve many head movements in following the chains.

This type of file organization is not supported by COBOL but is found in certain database systems.

ENTRY NO	KEY	PHYSICAL ADDRESS	CHAIN
1	1	0	3
2	3	12	5
3	2	42	2
4	6	79	0
5	4	84	0
6	5	29	4

Figure A.2 *Example index of basic type*

LIMIT

This type of file organization is a compromise between the above two types. The records are grouped in blocks, each block having an exclusive range of keys, the highest of which is stored in an index (similar in principle to the subindex of Figure A.1). The file management system can thus find out from the index which block to search for a given record. Because not every record has a key entry, the number of tables is reduced. Within each block the records are chained as in the basic index filing described above, to cut down on linear searching.

Note: the definitions of index random and index sequential here are generalized definitions. Some manufacturers have evolved their own forms of indexing which are idiosyncratically labelled index random or index sequential. For the purposes of this book, the general definitions will suffice.

Direct files

Again the definitions vary from manufacturer to manufacturer. In particular, the following are two fairly common forms.

(1) The records are grouped into blocks with no indexes. Instead, the user provides a hashing or address-generating algorithm to calculate the block address from the key, and once the block is found a serial search locates the desired record. The user must also provide means for dealing with overflow records. Unfortunately, it is difficult to design an algorithm which allows for future insertions and overflow situations. In addition, sequential processing is not possible, and so direct files (of this definition) are limited to on-line files for which fast random accessing is required. In many ways they are similar to random files (see following), but not as fast.

(2) Perhaps the more common definition of direct files is where the records are ordered (beginning at 1) with the record key corresponding to the position on the file. Thus a record with key 236 will be the 236th record on the file. Knowing the size of each record, the system quickly can calculate the offset down the file and locate the record. Thus it is extremely quick and sequential processing is possible. The disadvantage is that the file may have no natural keys of 1, 2, 3, etc., and if, for example, it actually contains four records whose values are 1, 236, 467 and 1045 then space is allocated for all of the missing records with the resulting file being 1045 physical records long.

Random files

These are a special case of (1) in the previous section where the hashing function is supplied by the manufacturer (as are the means to overcome overflow problems). The user (file manager) must usually state how many records will exist in the file and the system will calculate a suitable block size and generate a hashing function which will minimize overflow problems. This probably will mean that, at initial creation time, each block may only be half-filled leaving room for further creations at a later date although the user can often specify the volatility of the file which, clearly, has some bearing on this. Given a key value, the system will use the hashing function to calculate the disk address at which the record is to be stored. Retrieval involves exactly the same procedure. Clearly, the hashing function must be 'clever enough' to fill the blocks roughly equally though as they are 'randomly' stored, there is always the chance that some blocks will be more full than others. To this end there are several types of hashing function, but all are beyond the scope of this book.

The advantages of random files are therefore that very quick accessing is afforded (a single I/O unless there is overflow), but the disadvantage is that sequential reading is impossible.

Inverted files

The files mentioned to date have been simple in terms of them all having (at most) a single key. Accessing a record by multiple keys involves the inverted file approach. This can take three forms.

FULLY INVERTED

Every data item is a key and an index is maintained for all their values. As all the data items of each record are stored within the index table, there is no need to store the data record in the usual way.

PARTIALLY INVERTED

Records are stored in the usual way, as well as in the index table, and therefore not all the data items need be keys.

SECONDARY FILE INDEXING

This frequently is seen in normal file management systems whereby one key is designated as a *primary* key and any others are *secondary* keys (the number of secondary keys permissible varies from system to system). Each key type is maintained within its own index. In general, the prime key must be unique, but the secondary keys need not be necessarily so.

List, chain and ring files

These all refer to similar types of file. Related records are connected by pointers, either in a forward direction, a backward direction, or both. If the last record in a chain has a pointer back to the first then we have a chain or ring.

In the conventional filing system sense, these are used for available space tables. Suppose that we have a file from which several records have been deleted, leaving holes. If we now wish to create new records it would be more space-efficient to be able to reuse these holes. Good file management systems will therefore keep a linked list of pointers to the various holes such that new records can be directed to the next available gap. If a record is deleted then its address is added to the end of the chain. Usually, but not always, the oldest space is filled first. This is shown diagrammatically in Figure A.3.

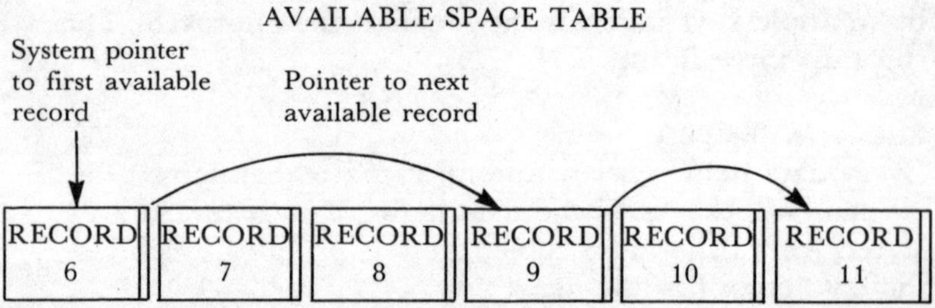

Figure A.3 *A linked list*

Other uses of these structure types are common within database management systems (as in index random files; see previously, and throughout the CODASYL database philosophy).

APPENDIX C

Dictionary of DBMS Terms

Introduction

Owing to the fact that all the various database systems have their own special terms of reference with respect to names and definitions which can cause great confusion if chapters are read consecutively within a short space of time, I have summarized the names used within Chapters 13 – 16 here. Where possible I have used the standard database terminology (see Chapter 3) within each subdefinition.

CODASYL (network model)

Access-control lock
See Privacy Lock.

Alias
The renaming of an area, set or record within a subschema.

Area
A physical collection of records usually, though not always, corresponding to a file, e.g. investments and investment transactions could be stored in the same area.

Calc
A random access method.

Checkpoint
A time when no programs are allowed to enter transaction state until all updates are complete at which time the buffers are written to disk.

Currency
A concept referring to the most recently accessed realm (/ area), set or record. Currency indicators are maintained by the DBMS for each program (run unit).

Data aggregate
A collection of data items within a record (usually a repeating group).

Data base key
A unique identifier for a record, corresponding to a storage location (see Chapter 13 for a fuller explanation).

Data item
A piece of data.

DBCS
Database control system, the piece of software within the DBMS which supports access to the database.

DMCL
The device media control language which is used to map data onto the physical storage addresses.

DML
The data manipulation language used to describe the schema.

DSDL
The data storage definition language used to describe how the data is to be stored (CODASYL 78).

Empty set
A set occurrence with an owner but no members.

Member
A record related to an owner record on an n:1 basis and connected physically via a set.

Network
A structure composed of owner and member records (which can either be simple or more complicated).

Owner
A record related to other records (members) on a 1:n basis.

Privacy lock
A value or procedure used to check user passwords for specific database operations. Current CODASYL terminology has renamed this ACCESS-CONTROL LOCK.

Privacy key (access-control key)
A password applied to a privacy lock.

Realm
The subschema name for an area (the latter being a reserved word in COBOL).

Run unit
The CODASYL term for a program.

Schema
The description and content of the database in its entirety.

Set
An association between different record types.

Singular set
A set type defined to have the DBMS as its owner such that only one set occurrence is possible.

Subschema
The application's view of the database, i.e. a submodel.

Via
Storage of records of a given type so as to minimize access times when reading through a set.

Virtual
A data item which is not physically stored but is derivable from other data items.

IMS (hierarchical) model

BSAM
The OS/VS sequential access method.

Child
A member record.

Collisions
If two record keys are passed through a hashing function and produce the same physical location, then they are said to collide.

DBD
Database description, also specifying the physical to storage structure mapping.

DL/1
The data manipulation language invoked by subroutine call from the host language.

HDAM
The hierarchical direct access method.

HIDAM
The hierarchical indexed direct access method.

HISAM
The hierarchical indexed sequential access method.

HSAM
The hierarchical sequential access method which basically is a sequential file type (no indexes).

ISAM
The OS/VS indexed sequential access method.

Logical database record (LDBR)
The user's view of the physical database.

OSAM
The overflow sequential access method.

Parent
An owner record.

PCB
Program communication block.

Physical database (PDB)
A collection of all hierarchical occurrences.

Physical database record (PDBR)
A single hierarchical occurrence, i.e. a single 'master record' and all its related children plus their children, etc.

Procopt
A processing option used to specify the access rights of a particular user.

PSB
Program specification block.

QSAM
The OS/VS sequential access method.

Root segment
The record on which all other record types are dependent.

Secondary indexing
Any indexes on any items in the root segment other than the root segment sequence field (which is the primary key) or, indeed, on any items in any other segments are said to be secondary indexes.

Segment
A record.

Sensitive
Those records 'visible' to a user are defined to be sensitive.

Senseg
A sensitive segment, used within the logical database definition to define which records are available to a user.

SSA
Segment search arguments used when the host language calls DL/1.

Twins
Two or more children of the same parent.

Virtual pairing
An IMS method of linking associated segments on which data would 'normally' be duplicated such that the data only need storing once.

VS
Virtual storage.

VSAM
The virtual storage access method.

DMSII

Access
Used within the database source to specify an access path to, or an ordering on, a data set.

Accessroutines
That part of the database management system used for the day-to-day running of the database.

Areas
A physical storage area, but which varies in size from file to file.

Audit file (trail)
The journal file.

Compact
A data set type involving variable length records.

Control file
The file containing the dynamic (i.e. changeable) parameters associated with the database.

Controlpoint
A predefined time when half of the system buffers are flushed out to disk.

DASDL
The data definition language.

Data set
A file.

Datarecovery
A piece of software used in rolling forward the database.

Description file
The file created initially in the compilation process, containing static data about the database, and used to generate the rest of the software.

Direct
A type of data set using relative positioning of records as its access method.

Embedded
A file is embedded if its access paths depend entirely on another file (i.e. a file of member records is embedded within the file of owners, but only at the logical level and not physically).

GEMCOS
The on-line message control system.

Global data
The 'single record file' of data having the same name as the database and containing constants and/or control data.

Key data
Items of data physically stored within the index.

Logical database
The user's view of the database (i.e. a submodel).

MCP
The master control program or operating system.

NDL
The network definition language used to define lines and terminals, etc.

Ordered
A data set type in which the records are ordered on some defined key.

Random
A data set type involving hashing functions.

Rebuild
A rollforward.

Reconstruct
A piece of software used in the rebuild process.

Recovery
A piece of software used to rollback the database.

Remaps
A method of mapping the schema components into the user's view and defined within the database source.

Reorganization
The name given to both restructures and reorganizes as defined in Chapter 9.

Set
An index method of access.

Standard
The default data set type in which records will be stored randomly, but will be accessed by an index.

Subset
A mini-index containing the physical addresses only of those records satisfying some predefined condition.

Syncpoint
Roughly equivalent to a checkpoint.

Unordered
A data set type in which records are only stored chronologically.

Utility
A piece of software used to dump or reload the database, but also performing other useful functions.

Relational model

Attributes
The differing data items within a relation (file).

Candidate key
Any data item or group of data items which identify uniquely tuples (records) in a relation.

Cardinality
The number of tuples in a relation.

Component
A data item within a tuple.

Data model
The set of all relations (i.e. the database).

Data sublanguage
A language for interrogating and updating a relational database.

Data submodel
Those relations available to a given user.

Degree
The number of data items in a tuple.

Determinant
An attribute or set of attributes on which the value of one or more other attributes depend.

Domain
The set of all possible values for a given data item.

Flat file
A relation in normalized form, i.e. a single-level record array with only one record type.

Foreign key
One or more data item types in a relation whose values correspond to those of a candidate key in another relation.

Normalization
The process of altering the format of relations to improve their overall performance and efficiency when used.

Primary key
The attribute or set of attributes which identifies uniquely a tuple.

Relation
The set of all tuples of a given type.

Tuple
An ordered group of two or more data items (i.e. a record).

Bibliography

Chapter 1

McFadden, F.R.; Hoffer, J.A. (1985) *Data Base Management* Benjamin Cummings.
Robinson, H. (1981) *Database Analysis and Design* Chartwell-Bratt.

Chapter 2

ANSI/X3/SPARC Study Group an Data Base Management Systems: Interim Report 1975.

CODASYL data description language committee. (1978) *Journal of Development*.

Date, C.J. (1981) *An Introduction to Database Systems* 3rd edn, Addison-Wesley.

The ANSI/X3/SPARC DBMS Framework (1977) (D. Tsichritizis and A. Klug, eds) AFIPS Press.

Chapter 3

McFadden, F.R.; Hoffer, J.A. (1985) *Data Base Management* Benjamin-Cummings.
Robinson, H. (1981) *Database Analysis and Design* Chartwell-Bratt.

Waters, S.J. (1974) *Introduction to Computer Systems Design* NCC.

Chapter 4

Codd, E.F. (1970) *A Relational Model of Data for Large Shared Databanks* Comm. ACM, **13**, June.

Codd, E.F. (1971) *Further Normalization of the Data Base Relational Model* IBM Research RJ909, Aug.

Codd, E.F. (1971) *Normalized Data Base Structure: A Brief Tutorial* IBM Research RJ935, Nov.

Codd, E.F. (1972) Further normalisation of the relational model. In *Data Base Systems* (R. Rustin, ed.), Courant Computer Science Symposium 6, Prentice-Hall.

McFadden, F.R.; Hoffer, J.A. (1985) *Data Base Management* Benjamin-Cummings.

Robinson, H. (1981) *Database Analysis and Design* Chartwell-Bratt.

Chapter 5

Robinson, H. (1981) *Database Analysis and Design* Chartwell-Bratt.

Waters, S.J. (1973) *Introduction to Computer Systems Design* NCC.

Chapter 6

CODASYL Data Base Task Group Report April 1971.

Lefkovitz, D. (1969) *File Structures for On-Line Systems* Spartan Books.

McFadden, F.R.; Hoffer, J.A. (1985) *Data Base Management* Benjamin-Cummings.

Stacey, G.M. (1978) *The Data Storage Description Language* Database Developments CODASYL 1978 Conference, South Bank Polytechnic, London.

Chapter 7

BCS/CODASYL DDLC Data Base Administration Working Group Report British Computer Society.

Conway, R.W.; Maxwell, W.L.; Morgan, H.L. (1972) *On the Implementation of Security Measures in Information Systems* Comm. ACM, **15**, April.

Curtice, R.M. (1977) *Integrity in Database Systems* Datamation, May.

Chapter 8

BCS/CODASYL DDLC Data Base Administration Working Group Report British Computer Society, 1975.
Verhofstad, J.S.M. (1978) *Recovery Techniques for Database Systems* ACM Computing Surveys, **10**, June.

Chapter 9

BCS/CODASYL DDLC Data Base Administration Working Group Report British Computer Society, 1975.

Chapter 11

BCS Data Dictionary Systems Working Party Report, March 1977.

Bibby, M.E. (1977) *The Role of a Data Dictionary* Online Database Conference, London.

Lefkovitz, C. (1978) *Data Dictionary Systems* Q.E.D.

Robinson, H. (1981) *Database Analysis and Design* Chartwell-Bratt.

Chapter 12

BCS/CODASYL DDLC Data Base Administration Working Group Report British Computer Society, 1975.

McFadden, F.R.; Hoffer, J.A. (1985) *Data Base Management* Benjamin-Cummings.

Chapter 13

BCS/CODASYL Data Base Administration Working Group Report 1975.

Brown, A.P.G. (1977) *Progress of the CODASYL Data Base Specifications* Online Conferences.

CODASYL COBOL Data Base Facility Proposal 1973.

CODASYL COBOL Journal of Development, 1975.

CODASYL COBOL Journal of Development, 1978.

CODASYL DDLC Journal of Development, 1973.

CODASYL Data Base Task Group Report, April 1971.

CODASYL DDLC Journal of Development, 1978.

Manhood, R.W. *Storage Level Control of a CODASYL Data Base Part I* Computer Bulletin, September.
Olle, T.W. (1978) *The CODASYL Approach to Database Management* Wiley.

Chapter 14

Date, C.J. (1981) *An Introduction to Database Systems* 3rd edn, Addison-Wesley.

McFadden, F.R.; Hoffer, J.A. (1985) *Data Base Management* Benjamin-Cummings.

Tsichritzis, D.C.; Lochovsky, F.H. (1977) *Data Base Management Systems* Academic Press.

Chapter 15

Burroughs' DMSII User Manuals

Chapter 16

Codd, E.F. *A Relational Model of Data for Large Shared Data Banks* Comm. ACM, **13**, 6 June 1970.

Codd, E.F. A data base sublanguage founded on the relational calculus. *Proceedings of the 1971 ACM SIGFIDET Workshop on Data Description, Access and Control*.

Date, C.J. (1976) *Relational Database Concepts* Datamation, **22**, April.
Date C.J. (1981) *An Introduction to Data Base Systems* 3rd edn, Addison-Wesley.

Dee, E.; Hilder, W.; King, P.; Taylor, E. (1973) *Syntax for a COBOL Based Data Manipulation Language* Report of BCS Advanced Programming Group Database Working Party, BCS, October.

Index

Page references in italic indicate the page on which a term is defined.